Multiple City

Multiple City

Writings on Bangalore

Edited by Aditi De

PENGUIN BOOKS

An imprint of Penguin Random House

PENGUIN BOOKS

USA | Canada | UK | Ireland | Australia
New Zealand | India | South Africa | China

Penguin Books is part of the Penguin Random House group of companies
whose addresses can be found at global.penguinrandomhouse.com

Published by Penguin Random House India Pvt. Ltd
4th Floor, Capital Tower 1, MG Road,
Gurugram 122 002, Haryana, India

Penguin
Random House
India

First published by Penguin Books India 2008

ISBN 9780143100256

Typeset in Venetian by Mantra Virtual Services, New Delhi
Printed at Repro India Limited

www.penguin.co.in

MIX
Paper from
responsible sources
FSC® C047271

For Ayan shona,
With unconditional love from Pish,
and a city you came to love as a 'working man' of 18!

Contents

PART VII: THE 24/7 CITY

Acknowledgements

I owe a huge debt to Vivek Shanbhag, Bageshree S., Deepa Ganesh, S.R. Ramakrishna and Prathibha Nandakumar, who helped me to find Bengaluru within Bangalore, and to Suchitra and Mohan Kutty, who offered me a unique angle on our city from way up above! My thanks to all of you!

Introduction
First Person Singular:
In Search of a City

Aditi De

IT'S A windy May morning in the year 2007. About 7.15 a.m. I'm helmeted, strapped into the passenger seat of a motorized hang-glider. At the helm is a veteran naval officer with a passion for the air sport. The glider, 1000 feet above the city that I've called home since May 1992, soars skywards from Jakkur, then banks, glides and, as I seem to suspend my breath for an incredible fifteen minutes, offers me an alternative lens through which to view Bangalore or Bengaluru. Or is that a mythical landscape that unfolds below us?

I'm conscious that I have no parachute on board, nor the shell of a cabin to cushion me from the breeze that had the windsock at the airfield jigging furiously since dawn. The chill morning air nips at my ear lobes, teases my bare toes. Wonder surges through me as I consciously shift gears mentally—and jettison inherited or collective notions about the city we hover over.

I gaze upon sheets of pristine water. Is that Hebbal lake? Verdant stretches, seemingly unpopulated, cross, twist and zigzag on terra firma. Is that the Life Insurance Corporation building on arterial Mahatma Gandhi Road, and the new United Breweries tower on Vittal Mallya Road? Impeccable toy-sized houses swing into sight, as if conjured up from a Lego kit, with dinky red, yellow and blue cars arrayed in open garages. The scene unfolding below has the unlived-in openness of a Google Earth exploration.

I mull over the past years of searching for our city through writings on it. My journey has unfolded through stop–start scenes where I've stumbled upon facts and features, characters and cartoons, even alternate or divisive perspectives, in lieu of a grand, linear narrative. I've sensed unidentified shadows through multiple conversations, had chance encounters both literary and political, gauged readings over steaming by-two cups at the India Coffee House, even entered high-voltage debates about the interior landscapes of gays and *hijras*. I've listened to the narratives of Generation Next and tuned in to their grandparents' *ajja-ajji* stories over set dosas at stand-and-eat *darshinis*, often buoyed by excursions into the Kannada literary landscape with practitioners and interpreters.

What layered identities exist, or once flourished, within this emerging global city? What schismatic tugs of war rage between Bengaluru and Bangalore, between the western *pete* that can be traced back at least five centuries and the eastern Cantonment, at least three centuries younger, between the City and the Civil and Military Station, the native and the colonial, as the Mysore *peta* and the silk *roomal* from northern Karnataka come to terms with the Gandhi cap? Did the traditions of stately Mysore vanish when the City and the Cantonment were united under a single municipal administration in 1949? Is the cosmopolitan nature of Bangalore, then, a stumbling block to defining its identity? Has the IT-propelled new city taken the shine off its established public sector undertakings, its famed silk looms? Will the city on fast-forward mode towards the future spell its doom, especially since its population has boomed from 1.5 to nearly seven million in barely three decades?

As I fly over these warring entities, deep-seated flickers of unknowing flutter within me, along with unrequited curiosity, and yet a sense of belonging. This is a city, or multiple cities within, that has enfolded me and drawn me in, oddball that I am, Bengali by birth and south Indian by choice. Is this the terrain of the four boundary *mantapas* or towers that the Yelahanka *nadaprabhu* or chieftain Kempe Gowda is said to have founded around 1537, celebrated in folk ballad and contemporary narratives alike? Why did he choose the village of Sivanasamudram, ten miles to the south of Yelahanka, to build his mud fort in? Did the city derive its name from the meal of boiled beans or *bendakalu* that an old woman shared with him?

Every city dweller I interact with seems to espouse a private vision of Bangalore. I stumble upon hidden stories retold in whispers, threadbare yet convergent narratives. Of a memorial to a ninth century hero commemorated during an ancient Battle of Bengaluru. Of megalithic tombs and iron tools dating back to 1000 BC, besides records of Roman silver coins that hark back to the emperor Augustus. Of a tutelary deity named Annamma, whose temple borders the Dharmambudhi tank. Of a Jewish settlement that gave rise to Asia's biggest shoe store of the early twentieth century. Of a city that had access to electricity before the rest of Asia. Of the base where India's first indigenous helicopter was developed, and where the Bangalore torpedo was devised by British Captain McClintock of the Bengal, Bombay and Madras Sappers in 1912.

When the British defeated Tipu Sultan of Mysore in the Battle of Bangalore in 1791, the rural aspect of the location was its defining feature. It was a location defined by its *keres* or tanks. That's besides its large temple complexes, its *agraharas* or Brahmin settlements. In the twenty-first century, the technopole represents the city as much as the annual Karaga rites at the Dharmaraya temple in the old city.

'Jeans pants on the outside and *madi panche* on the inside,' wrote Bargur Ramachandrappa, former chairman of the Kannada Development Authority, describing the reluctant metropolis. Is the Mysore state emblem of the two-headed Gandaberunda bird, then, an apt representation of the city's state of mind, straddling the *puranas* and technological advances with equal felicity?

Even as I juggle these notions, I carry memories of other cities, other homes, within me. Of the quintessential Tamil culture that enriches Chennai/Madras, where silk-draped *mamis* in Hakoba blouses and rubber slippers critique a Carnatic music concert with as much panache as they weigh up Thiruvalluvar against Shakespeare. Of the jostling mass of Mumbai/Bombay, with its folk-rich Ganesh Chaturthi and equally fervent Bollywood worship, its capacity to make outsiders feel at home despite the ebb and flow of a city constantly on the move to wherever. Of eating rich *shahi tukra* and *biryani* that the palate still lusts for at intimate *chowkis* at the Qutb Shahi tombs, or bargaining for mirror-studded Ladla Bazaar bangles in the bustling Charminar at Hyderabad. Of the beat of the *dhaak* and the sensuous, swirling aroma of *dhuno* as the priest calls the deity into public consciousness at the annual conclave that is Durga Puja in quintessential Kolkata/ Calcutta.

How does Bangalore fit into this framework that defines a city for me? It seems to engage with its past with insouciance, within a continuum where the past, the present and the future collide every milli-moment. Its streets voice their cosmopolitan culture and urban angst as much in Kannada as in Hindi, Telugu, Tamil, Malayalam or English. Bangalore does not offer outsiders a pageant of archaeological monuments; instead, in the words of a wag, it has just 'two rambling gardens and a crumbling palace'. It is as much at ease with the masala dosa of Vidyarthi Bhavan as with the stiff upper lip colonial traditions of the Bangalore Club, or the shining new towers and gated communities of IT-based international commerce.

I try to touch base with the essential Bangalore/Bengaluru. But for every home truth that stands its ground, I chance upon a contradiction that seems equally valid. Questions jostle with answers in uneasy combat. What makes Bangalore pulse with life? Could it be the yoking of the local and the global, the contradictory aspirations of a 'wannabe Singapore', as media debates would have us believe?

Fifteen years ago, my friends from Chennai, New Delhi or Jaipur and I would often lie back on the grass in a secluded patch of Cubbon Park and ask the lazy, wandering weekend clouds in the blue sky overhead: What defines this city? Where is it going? Where is the Garden City? The Pub City? What makes this a resurgent hub of contemporary Indian art and dance today? What heaves through the underbelly of Brand Bangalore? Will it explode when the past and present collide with the future? Or will the laid-back nature of its citizens soothe ruffled feelings so that life flows on?

From the hang-glider, the numbing crush of traffic on roads gone berserk seems like science fiction. Even the erasure of the pensioner's paradise by realtors and mall maniacs appears unreal, however temporarily. For the city I spy below is green, calm, an eminently desirable location, even a space of infinite promise. Of what?

Of a home truth that I acknowledge as we ease into a gentle touchdown at Jakkur. An essence that is celebrated in Bangalore or Bengaluru daily, through its myriad tongues, its multiple origins, the cacophony of soundtracks within curvilinear recountings.

It is a truth that this anthology seeks to represent. Not within an encyclopaedic sweep or a comprehensive, defining narrative. The multi-pronged gaze of the contributors trace the city, its culture of confluences both real and surreal, whether viewed from terra firma or while airborne. As flexi-cities within the single location tumble into view, it would be impossible not to celebrate their underlying spirit. A spirit that, to me, is best summed up in two words: *Multiple City*.

PART I

ONCE UPON A CITY

The Ballad of Kempe Gowda

A Helava folk narrative

Translator's Note: This excerpt is from an oral Helava narrative on Magadi Kempe Gowda. The Helavas, an itinerant community dedicated to preserving the narratives of powerful families, are described as 'custodians of village histories' by E. Thurston in The Castes and Tribes of Southern India, *Volume II. Their narratives are not 'historical' in the modern sense, but instead a curious mix of myths and verifiable events.*

The ballad depicts Magadi Kempe Gowda as a man from a poor agricultural family, who rose to be a chieftain and the founder of Bengaluru. Fame and fortune came his way as a result of his widowed sister-in-law's devotion towards Lord Magadi Rangadhama. His downfall is brought about by his arrogance towards the beneficent deity.

In the manner of folk narratives, the ballad incorporates miracles and collapses two different personalities into a single entity—Kempe Gowda of Yelahanka, believed to be the founder of the city, and Kempe Gowda of Magadi, who lived much later.

The first excerpt below describes how a miracle revealed the special powers of Kempe Gowda to a Brahmin in whose fields he worked as a labourer, while the second recalls the apocryphal story of the old woman who gave Kempe Gowda 'bendakalu' or boiled beans. This incident is said to have occurred when, after acquiring a fortune and building a fort in Magadi, he was on a journey to visit his mother. Popular stories say that is how the location came to be named 'Bendakaluru', and eventually 'Bengaluru'. After briefly describing events at his mother's home, the narrative returns to the story of Bengaluru, when Kempe Gowda revisits the old woman out of gratitude.

'Hey you, Kempa, where are you?'
Shouted the Brahmin and

From folklorist H.L. Nage Gowda's compilation *Helavaru Mathu Avara Kavyagalu* ('Helavas and their literature'), Akhila Karnataka Janangada Sangha, 2004.

Looked for him in every corner.
He then saw Kempe Gowda
Sleeping under a banana tree.
The shade of the tree had receded.
In the form of a mighty serpent;
Magadi Rangadhama was
Sheltering him under his seven hoods.
Garuda hovered high in the sky,
Protecting both from the scorching sun.
Annoji the Brahmin stood, shocked.
What miracle was this, he thought,
Taking out the *panchanga* from his pocket.
The boy is destined to hold court
In Magadi, he exclaimed!
Magadi Rangadhama will
Watch over him all the time.
The Brahmin threw the stale ragi balls
He had brought for the boy
Into a well and shook him awake.
'Wake up, Kempe Gowda, wake up now.'
The boy woke up, shivering and sweating.
Why was the man, who always called
Him Kempa, now calling him Gowda?
Folding his hands, the boy begged,
'Master, I was hungry and tired.
Forgive me, I fell asleep.
I will work harder tomorrow.'
'Forget about work,' the Brahmin said.
He bathed him and gave him new clothes.
He served him hot rice and milk.
'You are Kempe Gowda,' he said.
'I don't deserve that name, master,'
Said the boy. 'Call me by my old name.'
'You will be king,' said the Brahmin.
'When you get wealthy, what will
You give me?' asked the Brahmin.
'If I am the king,' said Kempe Gowda,

'You will be my teacher and guide.'
The Brahmin then sent him away
Without paying him for the work.

*

As he travelled, he felt very hungry,
But found not a morsel to eat.
He walked on and on and came upon
The house of an old woman.
'Dear Ajji, give me a
Mouthful of rice,' he asked.
'I have neither rice nor *rotti*,
I only have some boiled beans.
Will you eat it, my child?'
Asked the old woman,
And gave him a handful.
Kempe Gowda ate the boiled beans,
Drank some water and moved on.

*

A thought struck Kempe Gowda as
He stood at the threshold of the
Home of the boiled beans-woman.
Lord Shiva, may this place grow into
A big town some day, he prayed.
He built three *gopuras* at three corners.
He saw Lord Gangadhara in a cave,
And built a temple for him at Gavipura.
He built the tank of Kempambundhi,
And then a temple for the big bull.
Kempe Gowda stood at a height
And gazed at the land all round.
He built a strong fort around the
Town of the boiled beans-woman.

Translated from the Kannada by Bageshree S.

A City Yet Unborn

Suryanath Kamath

BANGALORE CAME into existence as a town surrounded by a fort when the Yelahanka nadaprabhu or chieftain Kempe Gowda made it his capital, around 1537. However, a wide village called 'Bengaluru' pre-dated this, as testified to by a ninth-century inscription, a memorial to a hero who died in the Battle of Bengaluru. This inscribed stone is found in the premises of the Parvathi Nageshwara temple at Begur on the outskirts of the present city, dating back to the Ganga dynasty, which ruled as a sovereign power from AD 350 to AD 550. As a result, the legend that Hoysala king Ballala named the location Bendakaluru in the eleventh century when his hunger was satiated by the boiled beans offered to him by an old woman, tends to lose credibility. The city more likely owes its name to *benga*, the Indian kino (*Pterocarpus mersupium*) tree that grew here abundantly.

The region where the city stands today appears to have been inhabited during the Stone Age. Microliths dating back to 600 BC have been unearthed at the site of the present-day Race Course and near Hindustan Aeronautics in the vicinity of the Konena *agrahara* (or settlement of scholarly Brahmins). Jalahalli, Bairasandra, Bellandur and Begur have megalithic tombs with iron tools dating back to 1000 BC. Roman silver coins from the time of the emperors Augustus, Tiberius and Caligula have been unearthed at both Yeshwantpur and Jalahalli. These finds indicate that the region was then commercially alive, with overseas connections.

We have few clues about what happened over the next five or six centuries. However, the Ganga dynasty ruled from Kolar and later Talakadu as a sovereign power from about AD 350 AD 550, then as a feudatory power under the imperial Chalukyas of Badami, followed by the Rashtrakutas, till the tenth century. It left behind lithic records of the deaths of two eighth-century soldiers within the present Bangalore Corporation limits. One is at the Dasarahalli agrahara area, the other at Krishnarajapura. The area they ruled over was then called Gangavadi.

At Begur, we know that a Ganga officer named Nagattara, who administered a unit of twelve villages, built the beautiful Begur Nageshwara temple there around AD 860. He died in battle, and is immortalized by a hero stone in the Bangalore Museum, which shows him being lifted by an elephant, and perhaps crushed to death! Even at Agara, we know of the existence of two tanks and an agrahara.

. Around AD 1004, during the reign of Rajaraja Chola, the Cholas of Tanjore defeated the Gangas, thus bringing about a shift in the fortunes of Bangalore. The Chokkanatha temple at Domlur, the Aigandapura complex near Hessaraghatta, the Mukteshwara at Binnamangala, the Choleshwara at Begur and the Someshwara at Madivala are all Chola temples. During their reign, a temple was a centre for both religious and scholarly activities, where the Puranas were recited, and musicians and dancing girls performed during religious rituals. It provided employment to many local people, besides sheltering pilgrims. The agrahara at Madivala, and the Bellandur and Pattandur tanks, are relics of their rule. Domlur was then a separate town, named Desimanikapattanam, while Yelahanka was the headquarters of their *nadu* or district.

When the Hoysalas overthrew the Cholas in AD 1117 at the battle of Talakad in south Karnataka, Bangalore came under their rule. The new rulers built a *prakara* or compound in the Begur temple complex and granted land near the Begur tank to the Nageshwara temple. They founded an agrahara near the Devanahalli Road, and constructed the Champakadhama temple to Lord Damodara at Bannerghatta, in addition to donating money to it for services and festivities. The Hoysala ruler Vishnuvardhana built the beautiful Chennakeshava temple at Chikkajala on the Devanahalli Road.

By the close of the thirteenth century, the Bangalore region became the battleground for two warring cousins—the Hoysala ruler Ballala III (1291–1343) from Halebid and his cousin Ramanatha, who ruled from Kannanur Kuppam in Tamil Nadu. Ramanatha had made generous grants to all the temples in the region while the area was under his control. His successor Vishwanatha, who ruled for a short while, died in 1300. Ballala had no rivals to fear after this.

What were Ballala III's notable achievements? He established a weekly fair or shandy at Chikkahundi, now Hudi, and appointed a pattanashetty or civic head there in 1332, thus promoting the village to the status of a *pattana* or town. (Hudi is now within the Bangalore Corporation limits). Under Ballala III, an ancestor of Kempe Gowda worked as nadagowda, the head of a *nadu* or cluster of villages, at Yelahanka. A *kattukodige* or land grant was made to a peasant to enable him to take care of the tank at Hudi. Tanks or *kere* were of great help in irrigating fields. So, a Hoysala officer named Allaranatha built a tank at Allalasamudra, beside the now-extinct Varadaraja temple at Jakkur.

But the Hoysala empire was on the decline because of attacks from the Delhi Sultans. Their commanders, who later founded the Vijayanagar empire, were beginning to assert their power. Ballappa, Ballala's sister's son, reigned over Bangalore, *circa* 1340. He had married the daughter of Harihara I, the founder of the Vijayanagar kingdom. Ballala III passed away in 1343 and his son Virupaksha in 1346, so Harihara I and his brother Bukka I consolidated their power.

Since Harihara I had no son, Ballappa tried to strengthen his own position. But Bukka appears to have resented this. He dismissed Ballappa, while appointing his own son Kampana as the *mandaleswara* or viceroy, with his headquarters at Mulbagal. The area thus saw a peaceful transition to the Vijayanagar empire. The nadaprabhus of Yelahanka also transferred their loyalties to it.

There is evidence that, in 1365 and 1366, Kampana made donations to the Madivala Someshwara temple. When the surrounding villages began to hold weekly fairs, indicating greater local economic activity, they acquired the status of towns.

At Bannerghatta, a prince of the imperial Vijayanagar family extended the Champakadhama temple. One of its pillars has the imperial insignia of Varaha or the divine boar engraved on it, while its sculptures include two life-size elephants. The Chokkanatha temple at Domlur also received a royal grant in 1440. During the nearly three centuries of its existence, the Vijayanagar kingdom saw the rule of four dynasties—the Sangamas (1336–1485), the Saluvas (1485–1491), the Tuluvas (1491–1565) and the Aravidu (1565–1646).

As the hold of the Sangama dynasty grew weaker, the time seemed ripe for change. Saluva Narasimha, a powerful commander who owed allegiance to the Sangamas, was stationed at Chandragiri. In 1485, he conquered Bangalore and its surrounding areas, and finally usurped power at Vijayanagar. On his death, a commander of his, Tuluva Narasa Nayaka, claimed the throne. The latter's sons—Tuluva Narasimha, Krishnadeva Raya, and Achuta Raya—ruled as emperors in succession.

During his reign, Achuta Raya, raised the Shivasamudra dam across the Arkavati at Hesaraghatta, founded an agrahara, and built a temple there the same year. This reservoir, widened in 1896, is the present city's supply of regular piped water. In 1532, Achuta Raya conferred the superior title of Nayakatana on the Yelahanka nadaprabhu or chieftain, Kempe Gowda.

Five years later, Kempe Gowda raised the Bangalore fort on the orders of Achuta Raya. He established his headquarters there, extending the reach of the Vijayanagar empire. And there hangs the story of the city and its origins.

The Town of Boiled Beans

R.K. Narayan

This piece, from a book commissioned by the Government of Karnataka, was first published by the Director of Information and Publicity in 1977.

A HUNTER was separated from his companions. Night came on suddenly. He sighted a small hut, and knocked at the door; an old woman came out.

'I've lost my way, mother, give me some food.'

'You look a noble man, sir, and what should I have fit for you to eat?'

'Anything. I am hungry.'

'I have a bean-field behind my house and it has yielded me a good crop this year. If your taste permits it . . .' Presently she placed a plateful of beans before the visitor, and he ate it with great relish, found grass for his horse too, and was on his way again.

It was later learnt that this visitor was none other than the king himself, and the village came to be known as the Town of Boiled Beans (*Bendakaluru*, later abbreviated to 'Bengaluru').

*

WHEN WE emerge from the mists of tradition we learn that Kempe Gowda I built the town in AD 1537 and constructed a mud fort around it. Sensing that this town was bound to grow beyond the walls of his mud fort, he built watch-towers at four points to indicate its future boundaries. On the north at Bellary Road, south at Lalbagh,

From *The Emerald Route*, Penguin Books India, 1977, and Indian Thought Publications.

the eastern one on a rock near Ulsoor, the western overlooking Kempambudi tank.

An astrologer studied the conjunction of stars and fixed an auspicious day on which Kempe Gowda marked off, with the sharp end of a plough, two streets, one running east to west (between Ulsoor Gate and Railway Goods shed) and the other running north to south (from Yelahanka Gate to the fort). Thereafter he built temples for Vinayaka who brings luck, and Anjaneya, the God of Power. He also built the famous Bull Temple (Basavangudi) and many others.

The astrologer had displayed great astuteness and foresight. The area within the markings of the plough now throbs with life and activity (even too much of it as it may seem), and if one watches the flow of traffic and the jam of pedestrians in the street running east to west, and north to south, intersecting, cutting, weaving themselves into a bewildering maze of main streets, proliferating into side streets, lanes, bylanes and blind alleys, without a square inch of space being left unused.

The octogenarian one notices on a *pyol*, spiritedly arguing with a circle of cronies, must have learnt or taught the alphabet in that children's school under a faded signboard, those pawnbrokers seated cross-legged in their narrow parlours, amidst a heap of used clothes and metalware, probably have been philosophers and guides to desperate souls seeking ready cash. And ranged along further, yarn-brokers, cycle-repairers and grain merchants; vendors of sweets displaying seductively a hundred delicacies on trays, all these must have come of a long line of octogenarians, sweet-vendors, pawnbrokers, and the rest, forming the warp and weft of the social fabric hereabout.

Passing down, one may also have a sudden glimpse of the face of a god, shining in the soft light of a wick-lamp inside a shrine, of devotees kneeling in silent prayer inside a mosque, and a church too, where I step in to read the inscription under a portrait in the foyer: 'Rev. Benjamin Rice (1814–1887)—an unwearisome labourer in various departments. An excellent Kanarese Preacher, who delivered his sermons in Kannada for over fifty years.' That was in 1830 or thereabouts. The loungers, one notices, reclining on the rusty shutters of a closed shop, also have a look of permanence about them. Everything and everyone here bears an institutional touch, giving one a feeling that they have gone on living here generation after generation, never stepping beyond their teeming orbit, and they may not have even noticed the development of Bangalore in other directions. Sadashivnagar, Jayanagar and Raj Mahal Extension may sound alien to their ears, accustomed as they are to 'Nagarathpet', 'Tharagupet', 'Chickpet', and 'Doddapet'.

This hoary nucleus of the city retains an indescribable charm, although the architecture may look outdated, and one's passage at first may appear hazardous through its traffic, but actually the wheels steer off within a hair's breadth and spare the pedestrian's toes, who must survive by lightly leaping aside, and recovering his balance from the very edge of the granite pavement, and may not suffer more than an occasional jab from a cycle handle or a bump from its mudguard as crack-riders dash past, weaving their way through. Here the shops may look unsophisticated, being mostly without glossy counters, glazed windows, or furniture, except a desk for the proprietor at the entrance, but you could get anything and everything you may desire within this ancient perimeter (crowned by the magnificent Krishnarajendra Market), if you stand on the threshold, catch someone's eye and make your demands clearly heard over other people's demands and general conversation. Anything and everything including a full regalia with sparkling crown and robes for an emperor in a court scene for a theatrical production, and also false hair, beards, lace caps and masks. A whole row of them I had seen some years ago, as they seemed to have got hemmed between watch-repairs and automobile spares and tinkers.

*

FOUNDER KEMPE Gowda's vision has been fulfilled and exceeded. One has only to go up the Corporation multi-storey twenty-fourth floor to appreciate the vastness of Bangalore spreading out in every direction for 130 square kilometres. I was overwhelmed with its extent again during a drive through the city with the Corporation Administrator, Mr Laxman Rao (who leaves home at the dawn of each day to inspect this vast city methodically inch by inch and pass orders on the spot to the staff accompanying him, dedicated as he is

to the task of maintaining Bangalore as a city of beauty and comfort—
'It is like house-keeping, you have to be at it continuously,' he
remarked), from Jayanagar shopping complex (the biggest of its kind
in Asia, with its 225 shops, super bazaars, fruit and vegetable market,
offices and a cinema theatre) at one end, to Ulsoor Tank at the other.
Parks and mini forests that are being created and cherished all along
the way seemed countless. Eliminating congestion by demolition and
widening of roads, construction of pavements, garbage removal through
slow-moving trolleys into which people are encouraged to throw all
waste and rubbish, and building of a wholesale market at Kalaspalayam
to draw away the concentration of lorries and men at Krishnarajendra
Market, are major plans that are being executed without respite or
pause.

A section of the city where you can hear statements such as:
'Winston Churchill lived here' or 'We were suppliers of cigars to
Churchill', or 'Duke of Wellington's descendants have always ordered
their shoes from us. They are still sending us Christmas greetings.'
One can still hear such claims in and around Commercial Street or
Brigade Road or Russell Market, which prospered in the days when
this part of the city was very much anglicized, being occupied by
British or Anglo-Indian officers and military personnel.

This part of the city enjoyed a topographical caste superiority at
one time, being a 'Cantonment' area distinct from the 'City,' which
was Native. Even today certain streets and areas retain their British
association, such as Richmond Road, Cox Town, Lavelle Road, Frazer
Town, St Mark's, Kensington, Johnson Market and so forth. I fervently
hope that some zealot will not think of changing them but appreciate
their historical flavour—at least to honour the memory of men and
women who set forth from far-off Britain in those days with dreams
of a flourishing career in the 'Orient' and sadly enough, laid their
bones in Bangalore soil.

I visited an old cemetery in the Cantonment in order to look for
the grave of a soldier, who was court-martialled and shot for
indiscipline, the said act of indiscipline being nothing more than
quaffing a glass of water, while the commandant had ordered the
company to drink only beer. The soldier had no taste for beer (or any
alcohol) and had to face the death penalty for it. In that forest of

tombstones, overgrown with weeds and thicket, I could not find this
particular grave of one who was forbidden to drink water, perhaps as
a protection against cholera, but could not escape death anyway. The
inscriptions over the tombs have a harrowing tale to tell of men,
women and children who could not survive the Indian climate or
conditions of those days, and seemed to have come thousands of
miles only to die. In addition to Smiths and Ogilvys, captains,
lieutenants or corporals, dead in their thirties, their wives passed
away mostly in their twenties or even less and the children never lived
beyond ten, and infants aged a few days. In the early eighteenth century,
before the discovery of inoculations and antibiotics, when pneumonia,
dysentery and malaria struck, there could be no hope of survival. I
noticed in a whole row, an entire family wiped out by cholera.

The Battle for Bangalore

M. Fazlul Hasan

Bangalore Through the Centuries, published in 1970, is one of the most popular history books on the city, though it is now out of print.

THE YEAR 1791 is the most disastrous one in the annals of Bangalore. None of the sieges laid and battles fought previously at Bangalore were of such magnitude as the fierce combat which raged for fifteen days from 7 March 1791.

On that day a tremendous cannonade shook Bangalore! The relentless barrage of 18-pounders, newly got from Europe, practically darkened the sky. And, as the assailants worked their way up to effect an opening in the formidable Halasoor Gate of the Pettah Fort, the gallant defenders poured a destructive musketry and rocket fire on the enemy from the turrets of the gateway. As the tempo of resistance reached its peak, the bombardment continued in all its fury. For long, the battle raged. Finally, the enemy forced its way into the fort through an opening made in the gate. The loss of life on the side of the assailants was considerable. Notwithstanding their loss they pressed forward and met the defenders face to face. Then began a heroic struggle in which every locality, every street and every corner of the Pettah was hotly fought over.

The boom of cannon which shook Bangalore, early in 1791, was a distant echo of the American War of Independence! The same English general who had surrendered to the 'Old Fox', at York Town on 14 October 1781, had now come to grapple with the 'Tiger of Mysore'. Washington's dramatic crossing of the Delaware to beat the English

From *Bangalore Through the Centuries*, Historical Publications, 1970.

armies at Trenton and Princeton, the surrender of General Burgoyne
at Saratoga, and finally the capitulation of Lord Cornwallis, the
English commander-in-chief, at York Town, in that memorable
struggle which is known in history as the American War of
Independence (1775–83) was of most disastrous consequence to
England. The English reverses in this war not only entailed loss of
vast colonies in America but struck a great blow to English prestige.
They were, therefore, determined to make good their losses in America
by fresh conquests in 'Hindoostan'. Now established firmly in Bombay,
Calcutta and Madras, they were not slow in extending their sphere of
activity in different parts of the country. But Mysore, one of the
most powerful kingdoms in India at that time, was a thorn in their
way. If the East India Company's forward march in India was to
continue unimpeded, the company's servants felt the kingdom of
Mysore must be crushed.

After the signing of the Treaty of Mangalore, eight years of uneasy
peace prevailed between the East India Company and Mysore. For
Mysore, however, those years were as turbulent as the previous years.
The belligerency of the Marathas and the Nizam, and the insurrections
in Coorg and Malabar had given little respite to Tipu Sultan, son and
successor of Hyder Ali Khan, to reorganize the Mysore army and
improve its striking power. The intelligence corps of the army lacked
initiative and there was a lacuna in vigilance. Although Tipu Sultan
was a powerful sovereign, a great innovator and a man of tremendous
patriotic fervour, he kept little pace with the improvements made in
Europe in the destructive power of siege arms and siege warfare.
While the East India Company utilized the eight years following the
Treaty of Mangalore in strengthening its armed forces by deriving
the benefits accrued from the great strides made in military science
in Europe, the Sultan spent much of his time in strengthening the
defences of the forts of his kingdom in a conventional way. As a
result Mysore had to reconcile with the consequences of its
complacency, however unpleasant they were to its interests.

In all fairness to the English, it must be said that the East India
Company had reasons to be vigilant. Not without reason, the
company's servants, both in India and England, were closely watching
the hostility that was developing towards them from the Mysore

side. The alleged bad treatment by Tipu Sultan of the English prisoners captured during the Second Mysore War, his dispatch of emissaries to Turkey and France to obtain military aid in order to rid the country of alien domination and his avowed hostility to the English greatly strained good relations between the two powers. In particular, the odds imposed by the Mysore ruler in invoking aid from foreign powers which were hostile to England was viewed with great alarm by the English. And when, by these means, the Sultan rendered the success of the arms of the East India Company in this country more difficult, the long-fomenting bitterness of the East India Company's servants broke out into the open in 1790, when he led his army into Travancore, whose Raja was an ally of the English. The war that now erupted between the two powers was the third in the series of four Mysore wars, and in this struggle Bangalore was to bear a heavy brunt.

*

THE GOVERNOR General knew well the consequences that would ensue if the English met with reverses in their war against the Sultan. He, therefore, decided to take command of the English army himself. A picture of the progress made by the English in the Third Mysore War, prior to the siege of Bangalore, can be obtained from the letter that Lord Cornwallis wrote to his brother, the bishop of Lichfield, from Calcutta, on 16 November 1790. The Governor General, who was then making preparations to embark for Madras, wrote:

> Our war on the coast has not succeeded so well as we had a right to expect. Our army, the finest best appointed that ever took the field in India, is worn down with unprofitable fatigue, and much discontented with their leaders ... I have in this war everything to lose and nothing to gain. I shall derive no credit for beating Tipu, and shall be for ever disgraced if he beats me.

Indeed, it was 'the finest best' English army that ever took the field in India. In discipline, in the use of destructive power and in the possession of good equipment it was far superior to any of the armies of the Indian potentates of the time. In number it was no less inferior to the hordes of Timur, Babar and Ahmed Shah Abdali. There were 22,300 combatants, with 130,000 camp followers in this army which also consisted of 80,000 bullock transport and 100 elephants. There were cavalrymen with horses and camels carrying light arms. A park of finest artillery, a large equipage of camp materials and ordnance carriages rolled behind the army in its march from Vellore, where it was regrouped before proceeding to Bangalore, the major target of the English in this war.

Courier, a Calcutta periodical of the time, gave a fine description of this grand army. One of its field dispatches stated:

> The sun rose to display the scene in all its extent and splendour and certainly it would be difficult to imagine one more sublime. And when the vastness of the multitude is considered, the train of cannon and the quantity of baggage with all the draught and carriage cattle requisite, and the servants and followers of every denomination, multiplying perhaps tenfold the actual number of 17,000 or 18,000 fighting men in their various and emulous departments of infantry and cavalry, European and native artillery volunteers, pioneers and all, it will be impossible to contemplate with too much admiration the effect of military discipline, and the experience aided by a spirit of a cause so great and good as the present.

Manoeuvring skilfully and feigning demonstrations of force in order to conceal the real movements of his army, Cornwallis succeeded in bringing it to the gates of Bangalore. The first encounters of the forward elements of the English army with the Mysore armed forces in the vicinity of Bangalore were typical of initial skirmishes which precede a general flare-up. Before the English cannonade of 7 March 1791, Colonel Floyd's English cavalry which impetuously penetrated into the Mysore lines was beaten back with heavy losses.

*

THE RETREAT of the English cavalry convinced Lord Cornwallis that for a quick decision the general attack should be mounted without any further delay. In pursuance of this decision on 7 March 1791, he ordered General Medows, who was second in command, to direct heavy fire on the fort. Field artillery of the latest 18-pounders, which was under Lieutenant Colonel Moorehouse, was commissioned into service supported by a regiment of Europeans and one of native infantry and with equal reserve under Colonel Cockeral. The English attack was concentrated on the Halasoor Gate and the area around it, so as to force open a passage. In the meantime, however, the defenders were equally active. Under cover of the protective projections of the ramparts, they hit back spiritedly as the battle raged. It was a grim struggle.

*

A GRAPHIC description of the storming of the Halasoor Gate of the Pettah Fort and the hand-to-hand fighting that followed after the assailants forced their way in, has been recorded by Colonel Wilks (the first English historian of Mysore):

> The application of field piece was expected to force the gate, but it was built behind with masonry. Iron 18-pounders, prepared for the purpose, were then brought up, and during a very considerable period of resistance, the turrets of the gateway, lined with musketry and rockets, poured a destructive fire on the column of troops. Two ladders would probably have saved many lives, but there was not one in the camp, and after a long delay in making a practicable opening (General Medows, whose presence on such occasions always dispelled gloom, watched with anxiety for a sufficient opening, the fragments of the gate were torn open with each discharge until a small man, Lt. Ayre of the 36th, made his way through. 'Well done,' said the general, 'now, whiskers, try if you can follow and support the little gentleman,' addressing the grenadiers of the same regiment, a winding sallyport was found from within by the first who entered; a respect for the 18-pounders kept clear the direct line of the gate; but neither pike or any troops had been placed on the flanks of the terreplein to provide against a passage being forced) in the

gate which the troops bore with the greatest steadiness and patience, the place was at length carried; but its great extent, and the difficulty of acquiring sufficient knowledge of all the localities, protracted the occupation of the whole.

The Sultan, astonished and indignant at this event, moved from Kengeri with his whole force for the recovery of the Pettah; a long but thin column with numerous guns, moved in sight of the English army, in a direction to turn to its right, the cavalry made a concealed detour, to a position where it was well-placed to take advantage of any forward movement. But the main strength of the infantry under Kummer-u-deen moved by a route concealed from view into the Pettah, with positive orders to recover its possession at all risks; Tipu himself being on the western glacis to inspect and animate their exertions.

Lord Cornwallis was not deceived by the demonstrations which he saw but distinctly anticipating what he did not see, strongly reinforced the Pettah, and changed his disposition on the right: a distant cannonade was not returned, but in the meanwhile efforts for the recovery of the Pettah were made on a great scale, and for some time with considerable spirit. So long as English troops continued to fire, the Sultan's were not inferior. It may perhaps be stated without exaggeration that the fire was superior, the musket balls were cast in moulds intersected by two divisions, at right angles with each other and the shank was left, by which the bullet was fastened to the cartridge; the bullet accordingly separated into five parts, or if very close, a large spreading wound was inflicted, in either case the wounds were difficult to cure but particularly the latter but this mode was soon abandoned by the Europeans for the never-failing bayonet. In a contest for the possession of the streets and roads, this mode could neither be evaded nor withstood, and after a prolonged contest, in which the Mysoreans were sufficiently driven from every quarter of the town in which they took part, and even pursued across a part of the esplanade, with a loss in killed and wounded upwards of two thousand men, they ultimately evacuated the Pettah.

The casualties on both sides were heavy. But no loss made so deep an impression on the English as the fall of Lieutenant Colonel Moorehouse, who was killed at the Halasoor Gate while directing the fire. The victors found within the Pettah considerable quantities of much-needed foodgrains for the army and forage for its cattle. That this portion of Bangalore, during this time, was a great industrial and commercial centre is discernible from the narrative of Colonel Wilks. 'The most valuable property had been removed on the approach of the English army,' he writes, 'but bales of cotton and cloth in every direction indicated a great manufacturing town; and the private hoards of grain of the opulent merchants and inhabitants could alone have prolonged the existence of the public followers till the termination of the siege.'

*

DURING THE last part of the military operations the Sultan, who was encamped at Jigni with the bulk of his army, frequently sent detachments of troops to the succour of the hard-pressed garrison. But he was not successful in his efforts in dislodging the enemy mainly due to his deplorable indecisiveness in attacking the assailants at moments most suitable. Commenting on the indecision of the Sultan to strike at the right hour, Mir Hussain Ali Khan Kirmani (the author of *Nishan-i-Haidari*) remarks:

> Although at the time of the assault the Sultan mounted his horse, and with his troops stood ready to engage the enemy; still he restrained his hand from shedding the blood of God's people and although Khammar-ud-din and Syed Sahib often requested orders to charge the English troops, the Sultan replied that the time would come by and by, for that favourable opportunity had passed, and that they were on no account to allow their men to fall into disorder.

But the favourable opportunity never arrived. And Lord Cornwallis was swept to victory on the high tide of Bangalore.

From Garden City to *Tota*?

Anuradha Mathur and Dilip da Cunha

THE CHANGE from Bangalore to Bengaluru is not just an alteration in the name of a city, it is also a change in what is named. If Bangalore corresponded to the 'Garden City', Bengaluru relates to a place that has more in common with the *tota*. Often translated from its Kannada heritage as garden, the tota actually defies the central idea of the English word garden, namely, an enclosure that is different from its surroundings.[1] This etymological reading of garden dovetailed very well with the European desire to see settlements of significance as definitive objects called cities that were further identified as urbane worlds distinct from their rustic rural surroundings. Bangalore to the British, and to the administrators and planners who followed them in dividing urban from rural areas, was in this sense a double garden: it was a place that in the early twentieth century had become famous for its horticultural exploits in parks, bungalows, traffic islands, institutional compounds and flower shows, all of which contributed to the title Garden City; and it was an urbane entity amidst a rough and lesser controlled hinterland.

Its urbanity was called out early on by William Arthur, a Wesleyan minister who reached Bangalore with relief after crossing a wild terrain from Madras in the 1830s: 'About an hour after night, hedgerows skirting the broad, regular roads, English-looking gates, lights shining from between clumps of trees, the white fronts of houses glistening in the brilliant moonlight and the stir of buggies hurrying hither and thither, told us that the merciful care of our heavenly Father had conducted us to the English capital of Mysore.'[2] After decades of the difference between urban and rural being enforced and exemplified by administrators, writers and indeed the everyday conversations of ordinary people, Bangalore would become an entity for 'master planning' in the 1960s. The future city would henceforth be articulated with clear and distinct land uses and separated from the world around it by a 'green belt'. Bangalore, in short, was not just a Garden City because it was a city of gardens; it was a Garden City because it was itself considered and presented in terms of a garden.

But the garden has never quite worked. Bangalore has leaked into and across the green belt. People's uses defy planners' land uses. And there is a certain wildness within the city that eludes the control requisite for maintaining a garden—in, for example, the streets, markets, maidans, besides, of course, the 'slums' generated by people coming from across the green belt. Despite the rhetoric of the Garden City, Bangalore has long defied enclosure and difference.

The tota offers a new landscape metaphor, released from the measures of the English garden and the city. Far from an enclosure that thrives on difference, the tota is an open field of relations. It is peculiarly Bengaluru in an era witnessing the simultaneity of global village and local freeway. It is also perhaps what Bengaluru always has been, but was never seen as such by English eyes because the tota eluded translation.

The tota was introduced to the English language by Francis Buchanan in 1800, the year after Tipu Sultan fell in the Fourth Mysore War. Buchanan was called upon by Richard Wellesley, Governor General of the East India Company's possessions in India, to investigate 'the state of agriculture, arts, and commerce; the religion, manners, and customs; the history natural and civil, and antiquities' of the lands of the Sultan. He travelled from Madras to Mangalore identifying, among numerous other things, three cultivated grounds: the tota, the wet land and the dry field. The wet land and dry field he describes as 'open' and planted with crops and grains. The first was irrigated with water collected in tanks, the second was dependent on rains alone. The tota, which he translates as garden, was by contrast enclosed and of four kinds: the kitchen garden (*tarkari tota*) for growing vegetables, the coconut garden (*tayngana tota*) which included other fruit trees, the betel-leaf garden (*yellay tota*) producing the leaf chewed with betelnut (*supari*) and the flower garden (*buvina tota*) cultivated by those who made garlands.[3]

At Bangalore in the second week of May 1800, Buchanan records a visit to the 'gardens made by the late Mussulman princes, Hyder and Tipoo'. Although he refers to them as gardens, they do not appear to fit any of his categories of the tota. The gardens, Buchanan notes, '...are extensive, and divided into square plots separated by walks, the sides of which are ornamented with fine cypress trees. The plots are filled with fruit trees, and pot-herbs. The "Mussalman fashion" is to have a separate piece of ground allotted for each kind of plant. Thus one plot is entirely filled with rose trees, another with pomegranates, and so forth.'⁴ He observes a working aspect to the gardens, an experimental side directed to improving economies, such as the introduction and acclimatizing of mulberry from China via Bengal for generating a silk industry.⁵ There were also custard apples, apples, peaches, varieties of rice, wheat, sorghum, beans, roses and other plants in the works. This was apparently the case with all the Sultan's gardens across the state, of which there were at least six. Lieutenant Roderick Mackenzie describes the one at Seringapatam, which he visited in 1792. It was, he writes,

> A princely nursery for the produce of Mysore; trees bearing apples, oranges, guavas, grapes, plantains, cocoanuts, beetlenuts [sic]; as also sandal-wood, sugar-cane, with cotton and indigo plants, rose from out the several inclosures; and paddy, raggy. Choulum, chewaree, nachine, coultie, with various other species of pease, grains and pulses, might be seen in different directions. Plants of mulberry too, from the extraordinary attention with which they were treated, discovered that the Sultaun had set his mind on the manufacture of silk.⁶

These gardens did not just elude Buchanan's categories of the tota; they eluded his scheme of cultivated grounds. The British took over the Sultan's gardens in Bangalore in 1800 with the object of extending their working and generative nature. Here, they cultivated plants (many of them new to the area) for the English troops and settlers of the camp that would become Bangalore Cantonment in 1807, while also anchoring these gardens in flows of useful and exotic plants across the world. The gardens would pass through many hands in the nineteenth century: the East India Company, the Mysore Raja, Major

Gilbert Waugh, the Agri-Horticultural Society, the British administration.[7] All of them operated these gardens as an open surface inscribed simultaneously by global trajectories of plant movements, botanical knowledge, and horticultural enterprises and local trajectories of education and cultivation of lands in and around Bangalore. Sir Mark Cubbon, who was appointed to administer Mysore in 1831, speaks of the gardens benefiting the community 'not only in objects merely Horticultural and the extension of Botanical knowledge, but in the promotion of the agricultural interests of the country by the introduction of new and valuable productions . . . and by affording the people the means of obtaining gratuitous instruction in improved modes of cultivation'.[8] It is difficult to draw boundaries around this operation that worked to transform lands and economies far beyond the 41 acres that it was said to measure at the time of Buchanan's visit.

This open, dynamic and working landscape, however, would be subdued in the public imagination, overwhelmed by measures of enclosure and difference, particularly a difference that presented the Sultan's gardens as a place of leisure, an escape from surroundings associated with work. Already in 1827 Sir Walter Scott in a novel, *The Surgeon's Daughter*, set in the time of Hyder Ali and Tipu Sultan, would describe the Sultan's gardens in Bangalore not in terms of the working environment that Buchanan found but in terms of a 'royal retreat'. Lewin Bowring in the 1860s describes it as a 'retreat' for the public. The visitor, he writes, 'might at first imagine himself transported to a purely European pleasure-ground, till advancing he sees the gorgeous creepers, the wide-spreading mango and the graceful betel-nut trees which characterize the East. The garden is a beautiful retreat . . .'[9] It was not long before this otherworldly experience of Lalbagh, as the gardens came to be called in the 1820s, would become a nurtured difference. And it was not long before this difference would be used analogously to articulate Bangalore as an urban retreat in a rural hinterland. The exclusiveness of Bangalore would be furthered in many ways, not least by a green belt and by public parks that replicated on a smaller scale and within walking distance of homes and workplaces, the otherworldly nature of Lalbagh. These *charbaghs*, which helped to make the neighbourhoods 'self-sufficient' units with regard to 'open space' and 'recreation', underscore the firmness with

which the English garden and its notion of difference had taken root
in the public imagination of Bangalore.

The change from Bangalore to Bengaluru is an opportunity to
recover the working nature of the Sultan's gardens in the public
imagination. With their defiance of boundaries and diversity of plants,
these gardens could not be held to the premise of enclosure any more
than they could be held to a category of plants or to a clear and
distinct difference from dry fields and wet lands. Yet this is the tota,
a landscape that takes much more than the gaze and measuring devices
of a surveyor like Buchanan to accommodate. The enclosures that he
called totas, in a classification scheme still used by the State Gazetteer
to describe the rural world around Bangalore, are merely points in a
web of activity. It is this open web rather than enclosure that is the
tota.

In this context, the *huvina tota* is as present in the plantations of
flower-producing plants sighted by Buchanan, as it is in City Market
or Krishna Rajendra Market. Here, the tota is in the threading of
flowers and in their sale by string or weight. It extends from this
market through buyers to other markets but also to homes, temples
and places where flowers are used in worship, felicitations and
ceremonies. Many of these flowers remain in movement in women's
hair and on deities in vehicles. This landscape is only momentarily
contiguous; it extends not by growing but by seeding a multiplicity
of spaces that are ephemeral, rather than permanent. It is perhaps
more conveniently described in temporal terms as operating by a
diverse and emergent calendar of events, by walks in a market that
are dictated by the immediacies and adjacencies of the daily settlement
of vendors, by acts of bargaining, and by the contingencies of a largely
unpredictable terrain and infrastructure. The huvina tota draws other
trajectories as well. Many of the flower-producing plants come through
acclimatizing or bioengineering efforts of nurseries like the Sultan's
gardens. These nurseries are openings on to a world wide web of
plant movements and knowledge that extends by ship-holds, 'plant-
boxes', schemes and ambitions to distant lands and peoples. This tota
is evidently a landscape that cannot be confined to the space of maps;
it is rather tracked through the plotting of links and events, some
momentary, some momentous.

It is not long ago that the tanks of Bengaluru were on this open web. Tanks, which Buchanan called wet lands, were used to gather surface water and deposits eroded off a gneissic terrain with the help of constructed earthen embankments or *bunds*. They were networked through sluices and weirs, forming systems of 'not-flows' as much as overflows. When waters receded in the tanks, plants were accommodated and clay and silt were harvested. There were times when tanks were available for other activities—fairs, camps, festivities, sports. For much of the year and sometimes for more than a year, tanks did not appear anywhere like the tota that Buchanan would expect to see. Yet, they were points of emergence of a tota, a landscape that could not be restricted to a defined use any more than it could be confined to the space of a map.

The tank was much too complex for the controlled environment of the English Garden City; perhaps too agricultural for an urbane world. As such, it was given over to more permanent and definitive uses such as housing, stadiums and bus depots. Most recently this definitive use is the 'lake': a scenic, perennial, and often gated water body that is really just another retreat of the Garden City. Lakes deny tanks, particularly their temporal, systemic and working nature; but, more significantly, they deny the tota, both as a landscape and a metaphor for settlement.

On the ground of the tota, the landscape that Buchanan journeyed across in 1800, is a working continuum divided between urban centres and rural surroundings. In fact, when Kempe Gowda I initiated a settlement apparently by the name Bengaluru on this terrain in 1537, he did not necessarily design it as the walled entity that is ascribed to him by British surveyors who drew it as such for the first time in 1791 when Lord Cornwallis's army captured it. Folklore suggests that this agricultural chieftain may have imagined something quite different. The story goes that at an auspicious moment, at a place where, in a dream, he saw a hare chase a dog he pointed 'four milk white bullocks . . . harnessed to four decorated ploughs' in four directions and let them furrow four streets.[10] The gates that the British troops broke through two and a half centuries later were moments in the unfolding of this significant event which Kempe Gowda very likely did not foresee growing like an organism as much as being another seed in an open field. He himself sowed other seeds in the vicinity of the four streets, constructing tanks, temples and agraharas (in the present Ulsoor and Basavanagudi, for example). These constructions, each of which probably had their own dramatic and propitious beginning, were potent interventions, generating and gathering trajectories of their own on a surface that was evidently active with similar initiatives for centuries before the chieftain. The site of his dream and other initiations undoubtedly hung on trajectories of projects begun in his past, even as they added to future possibilities. In 1807, when William Bentinck, Governor of Madras, decided to consolidate the British troops in the southern peninsula, he sowed yet another seed in this active field of possibilities: a cantonment that he chose to call Bangalore. This terrain at the heart of the south Indian peninsula is evidently one of ongoing movements and moments, opportunities and contingencies more than it is a city that has grown from a walled entity as is popularly believed.

On this emergent terrain the assertion that four historic 'watch towers' in the vicinity of Kempe Gowda's ploughed streets mark the limits of a future city envisioned by his son stands exposed as just another garden myth. Plaques at the site of each of these towers restate a nineteenth-century consensus amongst Bangalore's administrators: 'At each of the cardinal points (of Bangalore),' writes Lewis Rice in the first State Gazetteer in 1877, 'is an old watchtower, which marks, it is said, the limits to which it was predicted [by Kempe Gowda II] the town would extend.'[11] The view marginalized by this consensus is that these towers or *mantapas* were four among many lookouts or shrines that celebrated the rises and rock outcrops in this gently undulating terrain; they marked an expanse, rather than limits. But the idea of the garden, which was evidently taking root in the language of administration and in popular imagination, enforced them as signs of enclosure: a second line of limits after the walls of the 'inner city' came down.

It was a matter of pride when this second line was crossed. The Raja of Mysore, Krishna Raja Wodeyar IV, addressing the Bangalore City Municipality on the occasion of his golden jubilee in 1927, says: 'In your long life you have seen (the city) doubled in its population; you have seen it stretch its bounds till Kempe Gowda's prophecy is more than fulfilled.'[12] Other hypothesized limits have followed, only to be surpassed. More recently these limits have been the aspirations of 'comprehensive development plans'. They are marked not by towers or walls but by 'green belts' in the fashion of twentieth-century English city planning, a regulatory art that professes and enforces the garden at the scale of what is believed to be a city.[13]

It is perhaps time to ask if the garden that enforces enclosure and difference with its surroundings is worth pursuing. Is the change in name from Bangalore to Bengaluru an opportune moment to turn attention to the possibilities of the tota, a landscape and lens that may very well be more appropriate to our time? By the measures of the tota, Bengaluru is not an entity as Bangalore was; much less a controllable entity. It is rather an open surface inscribed with initiations and trajectories. It is certainly more difficult to visualize. But perhaps it is not meant to be visualized particularly through the commonly used methods of picturesque art and maps, both of which were introduced by English surveyors in the 1700s and both of which have worked to undermine the tota while being instrumental in promoting the garden. The map and picture after all provided the English with their first 'capture': a land that was already controlled by the eye before efforts were made to control it on the ground.[14] The tota resisted this eye and, today, it continues to escape it. As such it requires new modes of representation, modes that engage it as a landscape that is inhabited rather than defined, seeded rather than planned, extended rather than limited.

Bengaluru is not alone in declaring an end to the garden. In a world in which relations (material and digital) across boundaries are increasingly more significant than those within them, cities are searching for ways to reinvent themselves. On the one hand this reinvention could begin with a redefinition of the city; on the other hand, it could begin with a new imagining of the land as a field of relations rather than discrete urban objects amidst rural hinterlands. Indeed, the tota is the more operative idea of our time. It signals the end of the Garden City with its master plans, scenic (and increasingly) gated lakes, parks and enclaves and heralds the recognition of the extended surface with its enterprising initiatives, maidan-like tanks, and inscribed trajectories. In this sense, Bengaluru with a present and past re-envisioned in terms of the tota must take the opportunity of the change of its name to not merely inscribe a new future for itself, but to lead in a new articulation of land and landscape.

Notes

1.   John Dixon Hunt, *The Dictionary of Art*, Vol. 12 (1996).

2.   William Arthur, *A Mission to the Mysore* (London: Partridge and Oakey, Aternoster Row, 1847).

3.   Francis Buchanan, *A Journey from Madras through the countries of Mysore, Canara, and Malabar* (Madras: Higginbotham and Co., 1870), Vol. I, 28, 76–79.

4.   Buchanan's categories are repeated by Lewis Rice a century later in *Mysore: A Gazetteer*, compiled for the Government of India, Vol. I (Westminster: Archibald Constable and Company, 1897), 101.

5.   Ibid., 32.

6.   Roderick Mackenzie, *A Sketch of the War with Tipoo Sultan; or A Detail of Military Operations, from the Commencement of Hostilities at the Lines of Travancore in December 1789, until the Peace concluded before Seringapatam in February 1792* (Calcutta, 1793), 215–16.

7.   See Anuradha Mathur and Dilip da Cunha, *Deccan Traverses: The Making of Bangalore's Terrain* (New Delhi: Rupa & Co., 2006).

8.   Suryanath U. Kamath, 'The Early Long History of Lalbagh', *Glass House: The Jewel of Lalbagh* (Bangalore: Mysore Horticultural Society, 1991), 7.

9.   Lewin B. Bowring, *Eastern Experiences* (London: Henry S. King and Co., 1872), 9.

10.   Fazlul Hasan, *Bangalore Through the Centuries* (Bangalore: Historical Publications, 1970), 14.

11.   Lewis Rice, *Mysore and Coorg: A Gazetteer Compiled for the Government of India*, Vol. II (Bangalore: Mysore Government Press, 1877).

12.   Fazlul Hasan, *Bangalore Through the Centuries* (Bangalore: Historical Publications, 1970), 215.

13.   The tradition of planning practised in Bangalore can be traced to Ebenezer Howard's 1898 book, *Tomorrow: A Peaceful Path to*

Real Reform, which was reissued four years later as *Garden Cities of Tomorrow*. Howard's central idea is the Garden City: a town of a size (1000 acres and 32,000 people) that would allow all its residents easy access to a surrounding green belt or country (5000 acres). This town—country marriage was the basis of a 'balanced region'. Howard's Garden City is acknowledged in successive master plans for Bangalore.

14. This point has been made by many scholars of late, in particular, Matthew H. Edney, *Mapping an Empire: The Geographical Construction of British India, 1765–1843* (University of Chicago Press, 1997).

Ramakant in the City

Kerooru Vasudevacharya

Indira, *a Kannada novel first published in 1908, is considered one of the earliest 'social' novels. This work is often cited as an example of the shift that occurred in Kannada prose during the early twentieth century. It centres around the love of Ramakant, a man of radical views, and Indira. Her father is uneasy about Ramakant, so he creates hurdles along the way. Set in Bangalore and Srirangapatna, the novel has a happy ending.*

IT WAS the middle of spring. The spring goddess flaunted her wealth in all four directions. Colourful flowers in the parks and gardens gave Bangalore an unusual charm. The gardens around the palaces and the bungalows of the rich could have astounded even an artist like Ravi Varma. The birds sang in tune as though they were praising the glories of spring. The breeze seemed like a lover, going about wearing a gentle perfume.

One morning of this pleasant season, a young man came walking along the wide roads, gazing at the rows of fine houses on either side, marketplaces brimming with buyers too busy even to chat, temples that touched the skies, the *choultries*, and the hospitals. From his keen interest, it was obvious he was new to Bangalore. He reached a huge, old house near Seshamma's Choultry. It had two storeys. The young man took the stairs outside and went up to the first floor. It had a spacious hall, and two rooms. In the middle was a large table, and around it were several chairs and two shelves filled with books. On the table were scores of books and some writing material. The young man changed, and lowered himself into an easy chair.

Downstairs, in the dining hall, the manager told his servant, 'Gopala,

From *Indira*, Usha Sahitya Male, third edition, 1984.

Ramakant has arrived. Serve him coffee and breakfast.' Ramakant, that is our young man, sat down to eat.

Ramakant was strong, his body firm from bodybuilding. You could say his complexion was fair and his face handsome. His broad forehead, shining eyes and sharp nose gave him the appearance of a good-natured and intelligent man.

After breakfast, Ramakant began to look around. The neglected garden seemed to suggest the house was past its prime. The gilding on the doors had faded but was still visible. On the walls were traces of pictures drawn by expert painters. Ramakant looked up at the ceiling. He saw a picture of Lakshmi done with great artistry, and wondered how anyone could have reached up there. He was admiring the detail when he heard a knock on the door. He said, 'Who is it? Come in.'

A young man pushed open the door and walked in. Ramakant welcomed him, saying, 'Oho Rangarao! What a rare privilege! Come in and make yourself comfortable.' Rangarao sat down and said, 'Yesterday, I was passing by Chamarajpet, and noticed you standing here. This morning, when I was going for a drive to Lalbagh with the Dewan, I saw you. I knew for certain you were here, and came to see you.'

'Rangarao, I'm so happy to see you. One never knows when one meets friends. I'd never have imagined I would see you in Bangalore.'

'Yes, but what brings you here?'

'I was told Bangalore is very beautiful, and its weather cool, so I thought I'd spend some time here.'

'How did you miss the first rank in the civil engineering exams? I read in *Indu Prakash* that you came third.'

'What do you mean how? Do you believe no one in Pune is more intelligent than I am? Besides, my father fell ill and passed away around the time I had to write the exams.'

'Kamalakant passed away? What a tragedy! Thinker, freedom lover, scholar, philanthropist ... he had so many great qualities, I can't praise him enough. Vishwanath Shastri Mandalik of Maharashtra, Pandit Ayodhyanath of North India, and the pride of Karnataka, Kamalakant ... Who will show us the way, now that these pillars of our country have departed?' Rangarao said with real sorrow.

Ramakant wiped his eyes and said, 'Rangarao, it's my misfortune that I lost such a father. What can one do?'

They sat peering at the floor, unable to look at each other.

Finally, Ramakant said, 'Rangarao, you couldn't have had breakfast and coffee. I'll call for some. What do we gain by worrying?'

'I'm sorry. I've already had coffee,' said Rangarao.

'You grow coffee. You wouldn't like the coffee we offer, would you?'

'Who says coffee growers shouldn't accept coffee from others? I'll send across a tin of coffee powder tomorrow. Try out the flavour ... In all this talk, before I forget ... you must come over for dinner to this humble friend's house tonight.'

'Why not? I won't refuse, like you might! But stay awhile, won't you?' said Ramakant.

'No, I have some work with the Dewan. Big shots! Have to go in time and sit with folded hands! I'll come over for coffee tomorrow. *Namaskara*,' Rangarao said, and left.

Ramakant picked up the magazines *Ondu, Bangali, Times, Indu Prakash,* and *Kesari,* and started reading them.

He soon heard someone climbing up the stairs. He had kept the doors open. A man in a silk scarf and dhoti walked in with his chest puffed out, like a proud army officer. He was short, with a ruddy complexion and a well-oiled, turned-up moustache, and carried a silver-capped cane on his shoulder as if it were a rifle. He had lost his job because of his arrogance; he was now planning to open a clinic in Bangalore. His name was Dr Bashkala Pant.

'*Namaskara*. Recognise this humble man? Am I disturbing you?' the doctor said.

'*Namaskara*, come in. No, I was just flipping through some magazines. Dr Bashkala Pant, aren't you? Would you like lunch?' Ramakant said.

'No, thanks. I've had lunch. I'll sit back and see what restaurant food in your Bangalore looks like,' said Bashkala Pant and parked himself daintily, like the God of Love, on a chair.

'Your Bangalore? Doctor, aren't you from these parts?'

'No, I am a Maharashtrian Brahmin from the Raigad province. I have been travelling around for work, and have forgotten my Marathi customs. Ramakant, we from Maharashtra are never ungrateful. That's the truth. I don't exaggerate. You helped me in the fight yesterday. I came here to thank you.'

'Forget it. I didn't do much,' said Ramakant.

'Would gentlemen like you praise themselves? Those four Muslim rowdies ran for their lives the moment they saw you, looking like Bhima. Otherwise they would have finished me off. That's the truth. I don't exaggerate. Gentlemen like you are rare. And these days, everyone claims to be a gentleman. But, please go on, start your meal,' said the doctor.

'If you won't join me, I have no choice but to start,' said Ramakant and began eating.

'Please. Do you mind if I smoke a cigar?'

'No objection at all. You can start your factory,' Ramakant joked.

The doctor scratched a match and lit up a Trichinapally Bahadur. He said, 'Sir, this is a good place. Look at this picture on the ceiling. It's so lovely. Could be Rambha or Rati Devi. What chairs are these? They look like little girls' toys. I would have thrown them out, frankly.'

'Where can you get better ones, doctor?' asked Ramakant.

'I have a friend in Balepet. Now, of course, Balepet is ruined. I can't recognize the old Balepet. What was I saying? Ha, yes. About the furniture. Tell him my name, and he'll give you whatever furniture you need at the right price. Sir, your house is excellent. My sister will feel very happy if she could see it. Don't you know my sister? You must have heard the name of the scholar Radhabai, who runs Saraswati Sadana. She will feel happy to see you. I'll get you to meet her one of these days,' said Bashkala Pant, pulling on his Bahadur and blowing out smoke.

Ramakant sipped some water, put down the tumbler, and said, 'Doctor, you are kind.'

'Ramakant Rao, I don't exaggerate. You will be happy to meet such a scholar. Anyone would feel that way. Great scholars like Lingam Pantulu, Ranade and Krishnaswamy used to treat her like a goddess. The two of us disagree on everything, but we share a lot of affection,' he said.

'Is that so?' Ramakant said, and smiled.

'I subscribe to the philosophy of Kaka Joshi of Pune, but she acts like a puppet of the American missionaries. She even likes the idea of

Hindu women behaving like English women and changing their religion. On the other hand, I am against women's education. But sometimes I go along with Radhabai. We have to keep up with the times, you see! Are you new to these parts?'

'I'd visited the city eight years ago. After that, I arrived here only the day before yesterday.'

'Do you think this is a good city?'

'Oh yes. Malleswaram, Chamarajpet, Basavanagudi … how well they are laid out. Lalbagh is worth visiting. The rich folk live in style. I feel I want to live here. What do you think?'

'Nothing. Let's hear more of your description. You talk about everything so entertainingly. But I don't like this city one bit.'

'But why, doctor?'

'What's left here? Everyone dresses like the foreigners. We have learnt all their bad ways. Do you think the number of drinkers here is small?' the doctor showed his hypocrisy.

'I haven't seen such people. Maybe only you come across them. Since education is widespread, people have fine thoughts. I believe they are on the right path.'

Translated from the Kannada by S.R. Ramakrishna

City for a Song

C.V. Shivashankar

Translator's Note: 'Beledide noda Bengaluru nagara', *from the 1966 Kannada film* Manekatti Nodu *(Try building a house) is unusual. Written with the explicit purpose of showcasing the city of Bangalore, on the lines of a guided tour through lyrics, the film's songs showcase different localities. The film was subtitled* Idu Bengalurina kathe *(This is the story of Bengaluru).*

Starting at the Vidhana Soudha, the state legislature, the song offers glimpses of important city landmarks. These include educational institutions such as National College and S.J. Polytechnic College, public sector undertakings or PSUs such as Hindustan Aeronautics Limited, Indian Telephone Industries and Hindustan Machine Tools, tourist attractions such as Lalbagh, Cubbon Park, Bull Temple and Tipu's palace, and cultural centres such as the Kannada Sahitya Parishat.

C.V. Shivashankar, the lyricist and director of the film, says the song had a cultural intent, 'We wanted people in distant Bidar or Karwar, who could not travel this far, to see their capital on screen and feel proud. We wanted to show how the city, whose limits were marked by the four gopuras built by Kempe Gowda, had grown far beyond them.' The song projects the city as having three identities: as a beautiful city of gardens, as a city with the potential for economic and industrial growth, and as a centre of Kannada culture.

LOOK how the city of Bengaluru has grown ...

Look at the beautiful building there,
That's a masterpiece of art and culture,
Kannada land's pride Vidhana Soudha.
Look how the city of Bengaluru has grown ...

Look at these great centres of knowledge,

And those hubs of industry and commerce.
Listening to melodious Kannada songs,
In the lap of lovely gardens,
Look how the city of Bengaluru has grown ...

Look how tourists flock to the charming city,
The favourite haunt of Kannada writers.
Like a precious gem in the
Crown of Mother India
Look how the city of Bengaluru has grown ...

It holds a mirror to every Kannadiga's soul
Come and see it once to swell with pride
Do come and see it once
Look how the city of Bengaluru has grown ...

Translated from the Kannada by Bageshree S.

PART II

COFFEE BREAK 1

A photographic essay from the turn of the twentieth century
postcard collection of Clare Arni

South Parade, now Mahatma Gandhi Road, where the shaded avenue constituted a fashionable promenade. Lined with salons and shops catering to westernized tastes, the steet was as much for shoppping as for socializing and being seen.

St Mark's Church caught fire in 1923 and was renovated in 1927. Its neo-classicism displays the Scottish congregation's sense of belonging to the grand history of European architecture.

Commercial Street is at the hub of a network of intersecting lanes
with shops that stock everything from hardware to hosiery. This has
been so for a hundred years, though vehicles have replaced horses,
and smart new buildings now assert their presence.

The Pond behind the Museum: In 1864, City Commissioner Richard Sankey had planned four linked ponds through which water would flow, collect in a moat, then water the trees around Cubbon Park. This system worked for over a century. Today, the area is used to dump construction waste.

Hindu car or *ratha*: The ratha procession fascinated tourists in colonial India. Drawn to its size and the zealous devotion offered to the divinity within, the temple car was a central image of exotic religious practices which mark native urban spaces.

Bull Temple: The massive Basava: Shiva's divine bull at Basavangudi is worshipped in the sixteenth-century temple built by the chieftain Kempe Gowda. Located on a hill, it became a picturesque site for colonial tourists, perhaps representative of Bangalore's rural and Hindu history. Today, the temple is famous for the historic Peanut Fair held every December.

PART III

THE CITIES WITHIN

New Shoots and Old Roots:

The Cultural Backdrop of Bangalore

Chiranjiv Singh

'WE WERE simple people; these north Indians have come and spoilt us,' said my friend recently, unaware of the irony of the situation since we were talking in Kannada. Language has become the cultural fault line which divides Bangalore into 'us' and 'them'. Earlier there were other dividing lines: starting with that between the Military Station which was set up by the British in 1809 (later called the Cantonment), and the native City of Tipu Sultan and the Wodeyar kings. This dividing line was, not just linguistic and cultural, it was also physical. The two were separated by a wide strip of land running north to south from the present Indian Institute of Science to the eastern edge of the old city, and comprised parks, orchards, irrigation tanks and open ground, the remnants of which are the truncated Cubbon Park (which has now been turned into Cubbon Grove), Sankey tank, and Sampangi tank, of which a minuscule corner has been retained for ritual purposes, the rest having been converted into stadiums. People from the City did not venture into the Military Station after sunset for fear of the hooliganism of drunken Tommies, as the British soldiers were called. The broad gauge railway line from Madras, which ruled over the Military Station, stopped at Bangalore Cantt. Station. The City and the Cantt. stations were joined in the 1950s, well after the Tommies went home.

The culture of the City was based on the native traditions; that of the Cantonment was colonial and Anglo-Indian. This cultural dividing line has remained to this day. One is Bangalore, the other is Bengaluru, though there is no physical dividing line now. The lakes have been drained and the orchards axed, and all built over. The pensioners' paradise has become the developers' domain and realtors' realm. Property dealers of Bangalore style themselves as realtors; American vocabulary and accents have followed American firms and call centres. The state emblem of Karnataka, the mythical two-headed bird, Gandaberunda, is an apt metaphor for the capital of the state.

Bangalore grew from the mingling of courtly and colonial cultures after the death of Tipu Sultan in 1799. It underwent a change in 1947 when Mysore State became a part of free India. The Congress culture of khadi dress and Gandhi cap replaced the old gold lace Mysore turbans and dark long coats. The seat of power shifted from Mysore to Bangalore. Mysore was reduced to the status of just one more pleasant provincial town, not the power centre that it was under the maharajas. In old Mysore, Bangalore was the seat of government and Mysore was the seat of the maharaja. Power and patronage were in Mysore.

The new, elected rulers of Mysore State made Bangalore the state capital. A new legislature and secretariat building, the Vidhana Soudha which has graced countless calendars, was built in 1954. The chief minister, Kengal Hanumanthaiah, who took the same kind of interest in its design and construction as Shah Jahan in the building of the Taj Mahal, saw himself as a successor of the maharajas of Mysore. Hanumanthaiah was not destined to sit in the building he had so lovingly overseen. He lost power and there were allegations of impropriety in the construction of the Vidhana Soudha. A formal inquiry was held and the file was closed two decades later by the chief minister, Devaraj Urs. Hanumanthaiah was exonerated. He stepped into the Vidhana Soudha after that. When he met Urs in his room, he asked in surprise, 'Why are you sitting here?' to which Mr Urs replied, 'But where else shall I sit?' Hanumanthaiah said, 'No, no, I had the opposite room built for the chief minister.' That room, the most ornate one in the Vidhana Soudha with massive carved sandalwood doors, had become the cabinet room. But one can see what Hanumanthaiah had in mind: the room he had planned for himself had a balcony with a platform for giving an audience to the public in the manner of royalty. Perhaps the chief minister imagined himself waving to the subjects like the Maharajas of Mysore. Hanumanthaiah's statue now stands in front of the west gate of the Vidhana Soudha below that balcony. This incident is mentioned because it sums up the culture of Bangalore of that period: courtly inclinations and democratic practices. Appropriately the Vidhana Soudha stands opposite the nineteenth century neoclassical Attara Kacheri building, which formerly housed eighteen offices of the Maharaja's government and now houses the high court, reminding one of D.V. Gundappa (DVG), one of the venerated poets of Kannada, who is as often quoted in the Karnataka legislature as Iqbal is in the Indian parliament, when he wrote, 'New shoots and old roots together give the tree its beauty.'

After the end of the princely state and its merger with India, the next major development was the reorganization of the state in 1956. Bangalore became the capital of a large state with Kannada-speaking areas from Bombay, Hyderabad and Madras being added to Old Mysore. This was the culmination of an old struggle for the unification of all Kannada-speaking areas. For the people of northern Karnataka, it was an emotional union. They had dreamt of it and they had sung of it. But their ardour was not reciprocated in Old Mysore. The new state was still called Mysore and continued to be called so for the next sixteen years. When Urs changed the name of the state from Mysore to Karnataka, there was jubilation in northern Karnataka but a sense of loss in Old Mysore. I remember the unhappiness which many people expressed to me at this symbolic act; for them it was a break with a cherished past, a loss of the rich cultural legacy of the maharajas of Mysore.

In Bangalore, in a matching symbolic act, K. Balasubramanyam, the respected revenue commissioner of the state, gave up his old Mysore gold lace turban (Mysore *peta*) in favour of the black cap of northern Karnataka. 'When there is no Mysore now, why should I continue to wear the Mysore turban?' he said. The elegant Mysore gold lace turban vanished, along with the culture it represented. It is seen now in Sir M. Visveswaraiah's portraits which hang in schools and offices and in the 'in memoriam' columns of daily papers, where grandparents are occasionally remembered with their photographs. In the Vidhana Soudha, the northern Karnataka turbans (the *roomal*) drew attention amidst the Gandhi caps for a while. The minister of urban development, Mr Upnal, with his outsized turban, was jokingly called the 'minister of turban development'. Now, Bangalore has no time for Gandhi caps or turbans.

The divide between the *zari* peta and the silk roomal remains. A saying current in northern Karnataka, which was quoted to me by Mahalinga Shetty of Hubli, who was married into the Old Mysore family of S. Nijalingappa, the first chief minister of unified Karnataka, meant, 'Don't trust the zari peta-wallas'. The zari peta-wallas thought the roomal-wallas were odd and rough. Rajaji Nagar, which was developed as an industrial suburb of Bangalore, became the colony of migrants from northern Karnataka. The influx of so many persons with strange surnames and alien accents, ranging from the refined Hyderabadi Urdu to down-to-earth Bombay Karnataka tastes, was a cultural upheaval for a city of laid-back ways. The newcomers' music was Hindustani, their staple food was jowar and their idiom was laced with Urdu and Marathi. Across this Old Mysore–northern Karnataka divide stereotypes persist. When I suggested to a film maker who was planning to make a film and a television serial on Shishunal Sharief, the mystic poet saint of northern Karnataka, who is sometimes compared to Kabir—raised a Muslim and becoming the disciple of a Hindu—that he should use the northern dialect which Shishunal Sharief spoke and wrote in, he said, 'No, it won't run. The northern Karnataka dialect in Bangalore is still used only for comic effect.' If jokes are at the expense of the other, then Bangalore has many others besides the northern Karnataka ones: north Indians, Tamils, Telugus, Marwaris, Christians, Muslims, each one laughing at the other, behind their backs. But for all that, Bangalore remains a serious city.

The preponderance of the old Mysore culture with its heavy overlay of courtly and Brahminical mores gave the pre-unification way of life in Bangalore an air of seriousness, a gravitas. There was no place for levity in the Durbar, which set the standard for the subjects. Dr Venkatalakshamma, the great exponent of the Mysore style of Bharatanatyam and the last court dancer of Mysore, explaining the difference between the Tanjore style of Bharatanatyam and the Mysore style, said to me, 'In the Durbar, while performing before the maharaja, one could not leap with abandon or show exaggerated movements.' The traditional culture of Bangalore had no place for abandon; dignified restraint was its characteristic feature. It led to the exquisite refinement of Doreswamy Iyengar's veena, Venkatappa's paintings,

R.K. Srikantan's singing, Masti Venkatesh Iyengar's fiction and DVG's poetry, to give just a few examples.

Speaking of Bangalore and those from northern Karnataka who came to Bangalore and never went back, the Kannada and Marathi writer of Belgaum, Sarju Katkar, said to me, 'For us Bangalore is a Mayaloka, a place of enchantment. Once our people go there, they are bedazzled and bewitched.' This is what Bangalore has been doing to all the outsiders who have flocked to the city over the years. The question is: for how long? Going from a population of 1.5 million to nearly 7 million in three decades has strained not only the resources of the city but also its spirit. Road rage in Bangalore is now as common as in Delhi. The city reflects these changes. When a new building was inaugurated in the campus of Infosys, the cultural programme on the occasion was a performance by a modern dance troupe brought from Bombay, who danced to the recorded film music of A.R. Rahman. The young IT crowd loved it. Formerly, it would have been an inauguration with *nadaswaras* and Bharatanatyam.

To the earlier dividing lines of the City and the Cantonment, the native and the colonial, the courtly and the democratic, the Old Mysore and New Karnataka, has been added the IT people and the non-IT people. IT has impacted Bangalore as nothing else since the merger of princely Mysore with India and the unification of Karnataka. The presence of young IT professionals drawing big salaries has influenced the culture of the city. Many of them are from outside the state. They want to live it up. Youth and available cash and fewer inhibitions have resulted in a proliferation of pubs, fast food joints, cafés and restaurants. A measure of this is the fact that on 31 December 2006, the offtake of rum, whiskey, wine, beer, etc. or what the Excise Department terms as 'Indian made foreign liquor' from their bonded warehouse was to the tune of Rs 15 crore in Bangalore and Rs 10 crore in the rest of the state.

From a culture of simple living to one of conspicuous consumption, Bangalore has been transformed by the arrival of multinationals and IT professionals. High levels of stress, depression and alcoholism are the downside of the IT success story. This was confirmed to me by a staff member of the National Institute of Mental Health and Neurosurgery (NIMHANS), which providentially is also located in

Bangalore. Besides being the IT capital of the country, Bangalore is also said to be its suicide capital. Young professionals, earning unheard-of salaries, have created emotional schisms in many families. One comes across parents of modest means abandoned by their children, who are well paid by IT companies. Some old notions persist: two friends who were looking for matches for their daughters mentioned to me that they did not want IT grooms, for different reasons though. One talked of the unconventional morals of IT boys and girls who are thrown together at all hours of the day and night and get into intimate relationships, so he did not want a son-in-law from amongst them. The other one said that highly paid IT boys were often from family backgrounds that did not match their salary levels. But this snobbery is paradoxical: what is not desirable in a son-in-law is desirable in a son. People tell it with pride when their sons or daughters join IT majors like Infosys or Wipro.

IT companies have also changed the look of the city, its architecture. The glass-chromium-aluminium-cladding look is giving the city a nondescript character. The traditional bungalows with their gardens have been replaced by flats. Architecturally, Bangalore was an interesting mix of East and West. Koenigsberger, the maharaja's town planner, and Krumbiegel, the superintendent of gardens, between them had evolved a style of architecture combining Indo-Saracenic, neo-classical and native traditions which was just right for its time and place. The two Germans had the example of the capitals of various German principalities before them. The refined taste of the dewans (prime ministers of Mysore State) like Sir Mirza Ismail imposed certain elegance on all public spaces and buildings. With the retirement of earlier trained personnel, engineers of the Public Works Department (PWD) and politicians became arbiters of the architectural taste. Chaos replaced harmony. Some representative buildings of the earlier architectural style remain here and there. The Koenigsberger–Krumbiegel–Mirza Ismail Mysore style gave way to diluted art deco, which in turn yielded to the modernism of the Le Corbusier kind, but in a debased form. Then the PWD of the state and central governments set the style, especially in the townships of the public sector undertakings. Now there is an architectural free-for-all. Ironically, all the by-laws were first broken by the government departments or undertakings. Others followed the example. When Charles Correa, who designed the Life Insurance Corporation building, which houses offices of the Government of Karnataka, violated the by-law about the height restriction in the vicinity of the Vidhana Soudha, he justified it by saying that beauty also arose from contrast. His building, the Viswesvaraiah Towers, is a counterpoint to the Attara Kacheri and the Vidhana Soudha. It stands in place of the house of Sir M. Viswesvaraiah, the engineer-statesman and former Dewan of Mysore, an icon of Karnataka. Appeals were made to save the house and convert it into a museum, but it was demolished. Sentimental attachment to the past apparently is not a part of Bangalore's ethos.

The townships and colonies of public sector undertakings in Bangalore have played an important role in its cultural life. Their drama clubs and art circles nurtured talent and gave patronage to performers and artists. The schools of these colonies prepared the skilled manpower which later served the needs of the knowledge-based industries in Bangalore. They made Bangalore a cosmopolitan city since their recruitment of personnel was on an all-India basis. Bangalore originally was not designed to be a metropolis of millions. As one of the two principal cities of the princely state of Mysore, its scale was just right. It did not have to display imperial might like Madras, Calcutta, Bombay or Delhi. Many of Bangalore's intractable problems, like inadequate water supply and sewerage and congested traffic, are the result of that scale being violated. The culture of the city was moulded by its size; people knew each other and they could walk to the venues of talks and performances. Intellectual discourse thrived. With the expanding geographical distances and traffic jams making movement difficult, the city is getting culturally fragmented. The old division of the City and Cantonment has come back in the form of east Bangalore and west Bangalore, the east being home to many outsiders. Curiously, this east–west division follows the natural lay of the land. Bangalore is situated on a ridge which divides the Arkavathi basin on the west from the South Pinakini basin on the east.

As in the case of other cities, the culture of Bangalore is a product of the interplay between its geography, history and climate. Alone among the major cities of India, Bangalore is not on the banks of a river or seashore. Since being founded in the sixteenth century, its residents had constructed reservoirs on small streams taking off from the ridge. These tanks or *keres*, as the reservoirs are called in Kannada, were the lifeline of Bangalore. The absence of a river or seashore, I think, made the people inward-looking. The mild climate, arguably the best of any city in India, made people reluctant to move out. They had all they wanted in Bangalore. Probably this climatic factor has contributed to the culture of tolerance; it certainly has contributed to the laid-back attitude of Bangaloreans. One cannot imagine the passions of Heer Ranjha or Kannagi in a setting with Bangalore's climate. The Bangalore ideal was, in the words of DVG, 'Be a blade of grass at the foot of the mountain and a jasmine flower at home.'

This attitude draws the ire of Kannada activists, who think outsiders take advantage of the mildness of Kannadigas and do not give respect to Kannada. Thus, language becomes a cultural fault line. The issue of language is sensitive because it is linked to the questions of identity, unification of Karnataka, and status of Bangalore as the cultural capital of Karnataka, supplanting Mysore and Dharwad. Kannada was earlier a uniting factor and not a dividing factor. One might speak Telugu at home like DVG or Tamil like Masti Venkatesh Iyengar, T.P. Kailasam, G.P. Rajarathnam and P.T. Narasimhachar, but one wrote in Kannada, expressed oneself in Kannada. Mother tongue was for the home, Kannada for the world. The lure of English and the career opportunities that go with it has made Kannada almost a minority language in the state's capital. The location of Bangalore on the border of Tamil Nadu and Andhra Pradesh does not allow for cultural exclusiveness. Bangalore was destined to be a confluence of cultures. In no other city of India are films shown regularly in as many languages as in Bangalore including Hindi, English, Kannada, Tamil, Telugu and Malayalam. Church services in Bangalore are held, besides English, in all the south Indian languages, including Konkani. Of the two metaphors of cultural assimilation, melting pot and salad bowl, Bangalore has not become a melting pot. The importance of Rajkumar, the most popular actor and singer of Karnataka, lay in articulating the Kannada identity in a city where it is perpetually under pressure. When Rajkumar died in April 2006, the city came to a halt. Prasanna, the theatre activist, had to go on hunger strike in Bangalore to get due recognition for Kannada theatre.

In the 1970s, there was a ferment in theatre, films, music, literature and the arts. In 1974, the chief secretary to the state government, G.V.K. Rao, could say with pride in a television interview; 'Show me another city which has such a gathering of talent!' This gathering of talent includes scientists, sportsmen, managers, entrepreneurs, artists, musicians, designers and technicians. At one point of time, the Indian cricket team included seven players from Bangalore out of eleven (the eighth Kannadiga was from Mysore). Bangalore is a sponge that has been soaking up talent. The great Hindustani singer Gangubai Hangal said to me ruefully in Hubli that she had to get accompanists from Bangalore as nobody was left in Hubli or Dharwad to accompany her. The migration to Bangalore has been impelled by greater opportunities for earning a living. The line between art and commerce has been obliterated. Great artists like Venkatappa, Doreswamy Iyengar and Rama Rao Nayak did not commercialize their art. Venkatappa did not sell his paintings. (They are now housed in the Venkatappa Art Gallery, set up by the state government in his honour.)

But with all the talent in the city, one may still ask, 'What is the Bangalore culture like?' Bangalore is a city of subcultures: the Basavanagudi culture, the Chickpet culture, the Ulsoor culture, the Malleswaram culture, and so on. Then, there are the other broad subcultures: the Muslim and the Christian. These are vital parts of Bangalore's culture. Christians brought Western influence to the city's culture during British rule. English is the Christians' preferred language, but some are now turning to Kannada. Kannada-speaking Christians agitated to get church services performed in Kannada. The Christian subculture had given to Bangalore a certain sophistication and a cosmopolitan air. Thanks to it, one can listen to Handel, Mozart and Beethoven performed in Bangalore. Songs from *No No Nanette, Showboat, Sound of Music* and a host of musicals have not been forgotten here.

The Muslim subculture has played a prominent role in the city since the days of Hyder Ali and Tipu Sultan. Muslims, with their colourful Dakkani and Urdu and distinct cuisine, have enriched both Bangalore's culture and the Kannada language. While so many

Bangaloreans are going the American way, the Muslims of Bangalore have generally remained loyal to the old Bangalore culture. After attending a qawwali programme in September 2006, M. Bhaktavatsala, the former president of the Film Federation of India, observed that nothing had changed in the audience or the atmosphere during the last fifty years. In the Muslim wedding receptions, one may still find separate enclosures for men and women. Muslims of Bangalore are in no hurry to cut themselves off from their roots. But the sad part is that Christians and Muslims, to a lesser and greater extent, remain in their respective parts of the city, which sits ill with the cosmopolitan culture of Bangalore. Qawwalis, ghazals, mushairas and biryani have become a part of the mainstream culture, though.

The role of caste and community in people's lives in Bangalore has increased over the years. All the major *maths* of Karnataka have registered a prominent presence in the city. They run educational institutions, hostels and community centres, reinforcing the community identity of their followers. Maths often organize music and dance events, which can be as spectacular as anything organized by the government. Thus, one sees Lingayat singers singing *vachanas* and Vaishnava singers singing Haridasa *padas*. The problem of communal identity and artistic expression is not new to Bangalore. Masti Venkatesh Iyengar, the first of Karnataka's seven Jnanpith laureates, once said to me, 'I told Kuvempu, "Ayya, be a writer for humanity, not just for Vokkaligas."' Kuvempu was a genius and a great writer; he transcended his community's narrow confines. But lesser mortals are unable to do that even in Bangalore. In a city of whirlwind social and cultural change one's math, one's swami, one's sangha, are reassuring refuges of identity.

Politics in Bangalore, as elsewhere, feeds on caste and communal identities. Karnataka has seen four major political developments since its formation in 1956: consolidation and integration of the new state and laying the foundations of development under S. Nijalingappa; amelioration of the condition of the downtrodden and giving them voice under D. Devaraj Urs; ushering in Panchayati Raj and introducing democratic decentralization under Ramakrishna Hegde; and empowering the gram panchayats under Dharam Singh. The political culture of Bangalore has been influenced by these developments. Politics has exacerbated the divisions in the city. Civil society in Bangalore is active and vocal. There are groups championing every worthy cause under the sun. But owing to the changing complexion of the city's population, Bangaloreans have increasingly tended to be aloof from the rest of the state. Politicians who pander to them are reminded in the elections that Bangalore is not an island; that its development cannot be at the cost of the rest of Karnataka. As the number of American-style gated communities rises, so do the number of slums which provide services to those communities. Increasing economic disparities have brought the city to a low boiling point.

'*Swalpa adjust maadi*' (Please adjust a little), that clichéd phrase often quoted while referring to Bangalore's culture, has become meaningless. Calcutta and Hyderabad could as well claim the phrase and, during floods, Mumbaikars showed more adjustment than Bangaloreans. Perhaps the distinguishing feature of Bangalore's culture is the ability to live within divisions and to rise above them at the same time and accept the new with openness. This flexibility is helpful in times of constant change. Food habits are changing; clothing is changing; houses are changing; ways of life are changing; entertainment is changing; culture is changing. Jasmine sellers are changing over to selling vegetables; demand for jasmine strands is declining because many women now sport short hair and do not decorate their hair with jasmine and *kanakambra* flowers. Looms that weave Bangalore silk saris and dhotis are dwindling because men and women have taken to Western and Punjabi garb.

The north Indianization of Bangalore's culture in the last quarter century has been fast. Chennai was the cultural reference point for Bangalore during the Old Mysore days, though Kannada sensitivities occasionally used to get ruffled by Tamil expansiveness. In the 1950s, cinemas showing the Tamil film *Parthiban Kanavu* were stoned because the film showed the Kannada king Pulikeshi in a negative light. Then, over the years, Delhi as the seat of political power and patronage became the reference point. The Bangalore city corporation has even installed a statue of Kempe Gowda in a churidar pyjama! My friend was right in complaining about the north Indians spoiling the simple Bangaloreans.

The old survives: the annual Kadalekai Parishe, the groundnut festival in Basavanagudi, recalling the agricultural roots of Bangalore's culture, still takes place in December but now has the tawdry look of any Indian market. On Sankranti day sesame, groundnut and jaggery are exchanged, signifying sweetness, smoothness and warmth in relations; and on Ugadi day neem leaves and jaggery are partaken of, signifying the acceptance of the bitter and sweet in life. D. Balakrishna keeps alive Veena Doreswamy Iyengar's tradition of the celestial veena, without contact mike and electronic gimmickry. In the narrow lanes where old Bangalore survives, rangolis adorn home fronts, signifying welcome to the passing gods who might be attracted by the designs to enter the homes. But girls studying to compete for jobs in multinational companies will not have time to learn and make rangolis and attract gods. Do these symbols of the traditional culture of Bengaluru mean anything to modern Bangalore? Perhaps they do; perhaps they do not. Bangalore, like India, defies generalizations and simplifications. As the Talmud says, we do not see things as they are but as we are. Across the dividing lines the old and the new coexist; old roots and new shoots. Coming back to DVG, his verse referred to earlier is:

New shoots and old roots together give the tree its beauty.
New thoughts and old values together form Dharma.
The wisdom of seers joined with art and science
Would bring glory to life, O Manku Thimma

The Sikh tradition records that Guru Nanak halted at Bangalore on his return journey from Sri Lanka. Kempe Gowda, the chieftain, came to see the guru and seek his blessings. Guru Nanak blessed him and told him to develop the place, which also he blessed. Kempe Gowda did that by building his four towers and founding the city. The wisdom of seers is joined with art and science in Kempe Gowda's blessed city.

Directions

Prathibha Nandakumar

'The Hanuman temple street is one way now,
come from the old pond side, it's right opposite
the big banyan tree'

Chandru wanted his mother to close down the old house
and move with him to America,
she wanted to give me
a pair of traditional brass lamps,
'An heirloom piece, so come and take it'

It was not the old familiar place any more
In less than two kilometres I had lost my way
four times. Asking for directions is
a woman's preoccupation, they say

The auto driver was quick:
'Oh, it's right next to the next road hump,
just slow down and you will hit it'

I missed it.

The traffic police was more helpful:
'Just go back and it's at the first signal'

It was the same one I had passed

This English translation was originally published online in
www.poemhunter.com.

The doctor in a fancy car was more specific:
'Take a right. It's right next to the super-speciality
diagnostic centre; you can't miss it'

His right was my left.

Surely they were on a weekend picnic;
the SUV was full of sweatshirts and football:
'It's behind the gym, auntie, just drive on'
What gym?

The postman, I thought, would lead:
'I am going on the other beat, this is the old number,
now all that has changed, 88 comes after 97, ask anyone'

The priest, aha, he will definitely know the banyan tree,
there must be a temple and the old pond near the tree:
'What pond? There is no pond here, all the water has dried up,
I take my holy dip under a tap, it doesn't even wet me whole,
this is the house next to the xerox shop, the old lady rented out a
portion of the garage for my son, he will show you, tell him
his father is going to the market, will come later'

I just stood there, wondering which way to turn
Someone was frantically waving out from a window.
It was grandmother. I looked around.
The asbestos sheet roof: super-speciality diagnostic centre,
next to a corner called gym, behind number 97,
opposite to the signal without lights turning right to the hump,
a small tree sort of a trunk cut into half, an old temple
hiding behind a giant billboard calling out freshness, my old ancestral
home that was going to be pulled down to make way for a mall.

Translated from the Kannada by the author

Ooru and the World

U.R. Ananthamurthy

The Karnataka government officially changed the name of the city from Bangalore to Bengaluru on Rajyotsava Day, 1 November 2006.

GET FAMOUS, no matter through what route, goes a sarcasm-laced saying in Kannada. I had achieved that without building anything, destroying anything or even writing anything when the change of Bangalore's name to Bengaluru was in the news. Those were the days when BBC, the *New York Times*, *USA Today* and a host of Indian newspapers and television channels called me incessantly. My apologies, if that sounds a bit like boasting.

All my interviewers would start with the same question: 'So, was it you who proposed the idea of the change of Bangalore's name to Bengaluru?' I could often predict the next set of questions and answered without waiting to be even asked: 'Yes, of course, change of name alone will not ensure better infrastructure.' Or, 'You say Bangalore has a "brand value" today and it may lose out on all the economic gains that come with it by changing the "brand name". But kind sir, why don't we look at it in a slightly different way? Bangalore became a "brand" because of its great weather. But *because* it is a "brand", the weather went bad. Now we have so many people, so many cars, and so much dust and smoke that we can hardly breathe.'

A couple of Bangaloreans wrote letters to me in bad English, asking who on earth I was to suggest a change of name. Why should we learn Kannada, they asked; had I sought the permission for this name change business from 50 lakh people living in the city? My friends Ashish

The Kannada original of this piece was published in *Udayavani*, Bangalore, in November 2006.

Nandi and H.Y. Sharada Prasad too are asking me questions, without getting so angry, though. 'Bangalore is not one city. It is both Bangalore and Bengaluru. Let them both be,' they say.

I feel inclined to accept their liberal line of argument. But I would still like to offer a counter-argument, though tinged with hesitation:

You see, most people of Bangalore are unaware of even the existence of Bengaluru. They come face to face with it when buses are burnt or stones come crashing at their expensive cars when Rajkumar gets kidnapped or dies. But that's a brief encounter. There was a time when people who didn't speak Kannada in their homes learnt the language. Someone like Masti Venkatesh Iyengar or Pu.Thi. Narasimhachar, who spoke Tamil in their homes, became great writers in Kannada. But these are times when you don't need Kannada to even buy brinjal in the market. There are food malls and food worlds where you can buy 'ladies' finger' and 'banana' without knowing they are called *bende kayi* and *bale hannu* in Kannada. Of course, there is no question of doing a bit of haggling with the seller there on the prices. Small retailers, with whom you could haggle, argue and exchange gossip, have shut shop. If they own the piece of land on which they have their shops, it is more lucrative for them to sell the plot and sit at home. Those who have rented establishments, of course, find themselves in a pathetic situation. The children of those who buy brinjals in food malls also grow up without a touch of the soil. The schools they go to and the school the Kannada children go to might well be on two different planets. By Kannada children, I mean here the children of poor people. The children of rich Kannada-speaking people also, of course, can get on in life without uttering a word of Kannada. They travel one and a half hours every day to go to schools that cost a lakh a year and remain untouched by Kannada children. No, no chance at all of lice from a poor child's head crossing over to a rich child's head!

It was just with the hope that these people would be compelled to learn at least a word of Kannada that I had proposed the name change to Dharam Singh, when he was the chief minister. That's all. No more than that.

Some people ask me if it's not hard for outsiders to get the 'la' sound in the word 'Bengaluru'. That reminds me of how I have spent the better part of my life trying to learn the distinction between the pronunciations of 'e' as in 'ye' sounds in English. Let those who speak English struggle a bit with the world Bengaluru, I would say. Then people warn me, 'Careful, if you start troubling business people like this, they will shut shop and go home. It's not a good idea to provoke the noble souls who have opened call centres here to improve our lot.' Then I extend my stupid argument without any sense of shame: *Tchu, tchu,* don't worry. Business people are a very wise lot. They will learn even Kannada if it will add to their profit. If the 5 million people (50 lakh, as we say in our language) here begin to read and write the language, they will not only have name boards in Kannada, but will also start using it in their transactions. They will speak Kannada like we speak English, I tell them. After all, it's not as if there is 'one' Kannada. Let's add to the already existing variety.

The British, who fancied they ruled an empire over which the sun never sets, did want everyone to speak their kind of English. But see how spectacularly they failed even in their own America, Australia and London! Think of why George Bernard Shaw wrote a play like *Pygmalion.*

I will tell you one of the many stories of my struggle with English. I went to England to study in the early part of the 1960s. When I went to the well-known historian K.M. Panikkar, who was then the vice-chancellor of Mysore University, to seek permission, he asked me what my area of research would be. Lawrence, I said. He asked me what new perspective I could offer on Lawrence without studying writers like Kalidasa, Bhasa, Bhavabhuti and so many more in my own language. There was a lot I could offer, I argued, with respect but not without the arrogance of modernity. He wished me well and granted me leave.

I left for Birmingham with my family. I got a pin-striped woollen suit, a prestige symbol in those days, stitched and worn with pride. But there I met Richard Hoggart, a brilliant scholar who came from a working-class background, wearing a cap typically worn by labourers. The much-respected man would be dressed in a faded coat and never wore a tie. He wore a black gown only when he taught. He would sit and chat with students in pubs. His book, *Uses of Literacy,* had won the praise of even someone like Raymond Williams.

Though I wanted to get close to this circle, they sent me to do English composition classes for six months. I put up with it, though I had already done my MA. After all, English is an alien language and there may be many more things to learn, I thought. I passed the exam. Then I had to discuss my area of research with my tutor. A great deal had already been written about Lawrence. I thought I should work on writers like Orwell, Auden and Isherwood, who wrote in the 1930s when almost all of Europe was in Hitler's clutches. I wanted to especially concentrate on a writer called Edward Upward, who had escaped the attention of critics. I had the support of Malcolm Bradbury of my own age, who was already famous as a novelist, critic and teacher. But the tutor had to agree to my proposal. He was a good man, but an old and old-fashioned man. He had just then returned from a tour of India. His advice to me was along these lines: 'Don't do literary research, do phonetics instead. If you learn the English phonetic system, you could even land a U.N. job. See how high Rajan, who studied in Cambridge, has risen. You know why? Because if you hear him speak in the dark, you would think you are talking to an Englishman. I met a big professor of English in India. I believe his name is Iyengar. But I could hardly make out what he was saying! Anyway, what do you want to do research on?'

I suppressed my embarrassment and said: Edward Upward. The tutor knitted his brows and asked again: Who? I cleared my throat and said in a clearer voice: Edward Upward. Running his fingers through his white goatee beard, my tutor told me in a voice dripping with pity: 'Do you know why I asked someone as intelligent as you to study phonetics instead of literature? Because you don't know the difference between "e" and "ye". Say "Edward", it's "ed" and not "yed".'

That was the limit. I blurted out: 'Sir, you don't know how to say "Iyengar", you say "Eyengar". Then why can't I say "Yedward"? If I speak as you do while teaching students in Mysore, they will call me an ape with silly English pretensions.'

I went straight to Richard Hoggart, after saying bye to him. He was a senior teacher there. I narrated what had happened and told him: 'I would rather surrender my Commonwealth scholarship and go back to Mysore than do phonetics.' Hoggart smiled and said:

'Your tutor is a good man, I will tell him. I will hold an MA exam for you at the end of the year. You take four papers of your favourite Shakespeare and pass the exams. Then you do research on whatever you want. The English I speak in my unselfconscious moments is the English spoken by the labour class. Your tutor could well have told me the same things!'

The same tutor was my examiner in M.A. He liked my paper, and praised me to the point of making me feel embarrassed about what I had told him in those moments of anger. He approved my research proposal.

*

DURING MY meeting with Dharam Singh I had proposed many things, besides the change of Bangalore's name: Karnataka should become a fully literate state; all children should get free and equal education in common schools; English should be taught to all in a way that makes it possible to use it the way we want to without illusions about its superiority; and an engineering and a medical college should be opened with Kannada as its medium of instruction.

Surprising how the high priests of globalization are threatened by the mere issue of a name change! Do our IT companies fear that the Sensex that fluctuates at everything from the tsunami to farmers' suicides, might be affected if Bangalore becomes Bengaluru?

I hope the name change is a symbolic step towards Kannadization. By Kannadization, I mean the ability to belong to the world at large even as one is rooted in one's Kannadaness. I hope it does not become a mere publicity gimmick that doesn't rise beyond symbolism.

I went to England to see daffodils celebrated by Wordsworth 'tossing their heads in sprightly dance'. And I have a dream. I dream of a time when people who visit Karnataka want to smell the fragrant Mysore jasmines, eat the bananas of Nanjangud and read the great *vachanas* of Basaveshwara and Allama Prabhu. I dream of a time when those who admire the wanderings of Joyce's hero Daedalus also open their eyes to the rich Dalit world that Kuvempu's character Nayigutti leads us into.

Translated from the Kannada by Bageshree S.

Mall Miscalculations

Pankaj Mishra

Bangalore in the twenty-first century is a city of mushrooming malls. Yet, at the turn of the century, outsiders did not perceive it as such a 'hip, hep and happening' place, to quote its most popular daily today, as these observations in 1995 make clear.

'SEE, I told you! It's empty!' exclaimed my friend Sanjai, as we walked into one of Bangalore's newest shopping malls. It was my third day in Bangalore. I visited the city almost every other year, and found something new each time. This time, it was the shopping malls on Brigade Road. There were several of them, built in a variety of adventurous architectural styles, and, seeing them from the road, I had first thought them larger, slicker versions of the 'air-conditioned markets' one saw opening up in small and big towns across India.

It was Sanjai who made me look at them differently. Sanjai was an old friend from Allahabad, who worked now for the Income Tax Department. We had gone together one day to Brigade Road for lunch; later, he had taken me to see the malls.

His contention was that, contrary to media images, Bangalore wasn't prepared as yet for the new money pouring into it. And the empty malls did bear him out. They had been built mostly by expatriates seeking to emulate in India what they had been impressed by during their time abroad, and they looked like serious miscalculations. People had either miscalculated the city's spending power or were trying to fast-forward the place into the future through the sheer illusion and panoply of affluence. Whatever it was, it hadn't worked: more than a year after opening, the malls still awaited shoppers.

From *Butter Chicken in Ludhiana: Travels in Small Town India*, Penguin Books India, 1995.

More accurately, they awaited shops. Very few people looked to have bought space in the malls. 'The rents are too high,' explained Sanjai. 'Those who can afford them overprice their stuff, but people aren't willing to come here and pay more just for the escalators and the glass elevator. Anyway, they can just ride them for free,' he said, pointing to a couple of teenage girls in jeans nervously gliding onto the escalator, 'and do their shopping outside.'

The malls, Bangaloreans proudly told me, were modelled on those in Los Angeles. There were other much-remarked similarities between the two cities. The temperate weather, for instance. Although the sun didn't always shine in Bangalore—it rained quite a lot—but when it did, it didn't scorch you as it did in Madras, Calcutta and Bombay.

Then, there was Bangalore's much-trumpeted cosmopolitanism whose greatest achievement, in the few days I spent there, seemed to lie in importing the latest Hollywood films faster than any other Indian city. Another prominent sign of Bangalore's cultural pluralism were the accents on fashionable Mahatma Gandhi Road, a beguiling mix of both Indian and American.

'C'mon, yaar, Demi Moore was *there* in *We're No Angels*,' shrieked a young woman in black nylon tights, waiting outside a cinema hall showing *Indecent Proposal*. 'Wanna have a bet?' her ponytailed boyfriend in flared bellbottoms calmly responded.

The appurtenances of modernity were all very conspicuous: the kids in Reeboks and Nikes, chewing Wrigley chewing gum, clamouring to be taken to Spencer's open-air café. Yuppies, in loosened ties, sipping lager beer, talking stock-market jargon at Rice Bowl, the Chinese restaurant reputedly owned by the Dalai Lama's sister, the muzak on the sound system appropriately by Nirvana.

Bangalore, I soon became tired of being told, had the largest number of pubs in India; it was the only place to have draught beer, the best place to have Thai food. Many of its streets, a token few I was to discover, were lit by solar-powered lamps. Bangaloreans were modern people with sophisticated sensibilities. And the confirmation seemed to come one evening, watching *Indecent Proposal*, when not a squeak came out of the lower stalls as Demi Moore's breasts popped into view on the screen. Up in the uncivilized north, they would have been, I knew from experience, tearing the stuffing out of their seats.

Bangalore grew rapidly each year, but you still didn't feel the crush of massed humanity as you did in the other four metropolitan cities. The place had a general middleclassness about it: the one city in India where people had found some respite from poverty, and where their sensibilities would not be abraded by constant exposure to dehumanizing poverty. The serene self-possession of young executives at Bangalore pubs could not have been shared by most of their Bombay compatriots, by people who daily drove through Dharavi to reach their places of work. The slums in Bangalore existed, but were out of sight, unlike Bombay where they cower beneath high-rise buildings in the poshest of localities. Presumably, the poor couldn't afford to live in Bangalore.

For one, they would have had a problem getting around the city. I made the discovery every time I came to Bangalore: it simply had no cheap public transport worth the name. The sullen auto-rickshaw driver consented to take you only after a lot of persuasion and then tried to overcharge you. In that way, Bangalore could still seem to lack the frictionless efficiency which even a place as overpopulated and chaotic as Bombay had.

'It's an attitude problem,' Shinde, a software expert from Pune, told me. 'The people who have been here from the beginning still don't think of themselves as living in a big city; they don't see themselves in the larger scheme of things.'

This may be true or untrue, but Bangalore, with its shopping malls, its new restaurants and five-star hotels, its health clubs and designer boutiques, sent out a different message to the rest of India. It claimed to be up with the Joneses; it claimed to be modern and efficient; it proposed itself as the model Indian settlement, a place other upcoming Indian towns could aspire to. Bangalore, it would begin to appear, was where their future lay.

The only hitch was that Bangalore's own future was not too clear. Its problems were growing as population multiplied, and more and more industries came up, and they were the same as faced by other cities: power and water shortages, lack of proper transport, congestion, pollution.

Serious, probably insurmountable, problems. But one could be easily deceived by what was generally known about the place. In recent years, a lot of imported notions had come to stand for Bangalore: India's Silicon Valley, India's electronics capital. They belonged to the world of abstract finance, of gung-ho businessmen ever ready to pounce upon lucrative new territories, and they could almost completely ignore ground realities. In that world of cosy certainties, it was easy to forget, after all the talk about Silicon Valley, that Bangalore was an Indian city with Indian problems, which, given the experience of other Indian cities, had the odds stacked against it. It wasn't pessimism but hard realism that made one see that only time was of consequence, and that one only had to wait before Bangalore went the way other Indian cities had gone before it, letting entropy do its slow inexorable thing, turn this once-elegant cantonment town into another Indian urban nightmare.

Bangalore:

A Short Story

Sherry Simon

CROSSING THE city could take more than an hour, and each of those moments in a rickshaw meant lungfuls of diesel exhaust, sudden swerves and painful bumps, so whenever Lakshmi or I crossed the city to see each other the very fact of the visit was already a huge debt incurred. Each treated the traveller with the respect due to one who has just undertaken a perilous journey, immediately offering water and a cool place to recover from dust, heat and the rickshaw—'auto', it was often called, the automated version of the human runner kind, of course an immense improvement, but still a source of indignity, both to the driver and passenger, a three-wheeled scooter with a passenger seat and hood added, not much in the way of suspension and so rebounding off every crack and swell in the pavement, open to dust, waves of water in the rainy season, and no real power or speed, the lowest in the hierarchy of vehicles on the streets of India, except for the bullock and the bicycle, always beeped at and overtaken by scooters, motorcycles, cars, buses and trucks. I lived in Malleswaram, a neighbourhood in the north end of the city, and she in Banashankari, in the very south end. And these were not the only two extremes of our coming together, but marked the difficulties of our encounters surely as much as the others, the divide of place from which we came. Yet across the divide ran the strips of our sameness, some of which counted and others that didn't, categories that fell into alignment, her family in perfect symmetry with mine, her job too, a life in a river of languages and the songs she sang with her daughter. Lakshmi teaches Sanskrit, I have come here to teach French. We meet at the

Originally published in *Translating Desire: The Politics of Gender and Culture in India*, edited by Brinda Bose, Katha, 2002.

university where we are office neighbours, and our families get together for Sunday breakfast in the Tiffin Room, a huge restaurant a block away from the Botanical Gardens, where they serve breakfasts of buttery dosa and sticky gulab jamun to families crowding large tables. To hear each other we have to shout, and so it is a relief to get out into the morning sun and stroll through the gardens, the men pairing off, the children forming a cheerful bunch, and the two of us falling behind the rest, my pale spareness beside her black and gold sari, and together paying only cursory attention to the mildewed pavilions of the Gardens, caught up rather by the spectacle of lithe, shy newly-weds who are taking their first Sunday stroll together.

We strike a silent pact, surrendering to a common desire to navigate the veins of our sameness, to clamber over the raw accidents of our difference, to know everything about each other's world. Instead of meeting at the university which is a collection of new brick squares plunked down outside the city, Lakshmi and I decide to explore the city together, spending mornings at Russell Market, watching the Muslim artisans make cane furniture, shuddering at the hunks of meat hidden in the back corner of the market, lingering at the mounds of cut flowers and choosing armfuls of irises to take home. Other days we go downtown to bookstores, soon ducking into a restaurant for a *biryani* or a coffee. But we tire of these excursions in the heat and prefer to see each other in the quiet of our homes. When the pace of our conversations starts to let up and we have finished tracing the crazy path that connects a Tamil village to a European settlement, completed our study of childhood smells (and some are the same, chalk and blackboard), remembered the same dreamy years when novels were life (only she was curled up in a hammock in the shade of the leafy garden, flies in her hair, and I was on a corduroy sofa by the television), once we have drawn up the lists of our favourite books and argued long and hard about the shortcomings of Western theory, we decide that it is time for us to work on a project together. We decide to translate a story.

There's a Tamil story by a popular author that she's particularly fond of. She'll give me a literal version of the Tamil as we go along, we'll work out the English together and then I'll put it into French. It's a story about a woman named Durga, a story without much plot, more like a portrait drawn with quick and untidy strokes. I find the story ragged, its sentences so loosely strung together that it feels like it will fall apart any time. Lakshmi, however, follows each thread with attention and respect, giving heed to every detail. I can see that Lakshmi identifies with the heroine. Durga is an 'ordinary' woman, says the first sentence, but only apparently so; really she is a free spirit, the very force of life. On the marriage night of their daughter, Durga and her husband are sitting outside in the warm night and she thinks back to her own wedding, remembering how hopeful she and her husband were. A young film-maker has now fallen in love with her. She is tempted by his love, but decides to remain faithful to her husband.

Lakshmi and I are sitting on the floor side by side, the book of short stories on her knees, my laptop on mine. We sometimes argue for quite a while over a word, the 'ordinary' of the first sentence, for instance, takes ages to find because the writer had phrased his sentence in the negative. 'She was not a special person,' he said, but of course we know that she is, and want a better way of marking the irony of the introduction. Lakshmi's knowledge of English is precise and mine feels rusty in comparison, as if English were my second language rather than my first. Her patience lasts longer than mine. She is consumed by the story, and loves caressing the grain of Tamil, a language she learnt late. She reads each sentence and then quickly, so quickly, comes up with a few sentences of English, moving around and then closer to the meaning she's looking for. Then there is room for my voice, questioning and rephrasing, wondering how much I can quietly push the story away from the attitudes I disapprove of—the film-maker wants to 'take possession' of Durga, her smile remains 'mysterious' and 'wise'. I don't like these set poses, the bits that sound too familiar to me.

I can visualize some of the events of the story, filling in the storyteller's silences with the bits of Indian culture I have begun to acquire. I see a semi-rural setting, huge leafy trees around a dark house and the benches where Durga and her husband fall asleep in the summer warmth, side by side, after the wedding festivities. Now that I've been to some Indian weddings I note the satisfaction and relief of the parents, and also their uncomfortable sensuality, the way they are at the same time distant and companionable. I put Durga in a gold-bordered wedding sari for this special evening, her husband in a Western shirt and silk dhoti. I also see the ox blood concrete floors and the crumbling green paint of the office where he works, the piles of ledgers, the cups of coffee carried in by the young boy at exactly ten in the morning.

There are other parts of the story I don't understand. Did Durga's husband give in to corruption or not? Lakshmi doesn't want to discuss the husband, she's much more interested in Durga. I too find myself aspirated by one of the characters. If Lakshmi is Durga, I am the film-maker who melts under Durga's gaze, who is made agonizingly aware of the 'dryness' of his work by those eyes, who, when he speaks of loving her, receives the response 'Do . . .'

When lunchtime comes, Lakshmi heats up some of the food she's prepared before breakfast, always rice and a vegetable dish, yogurt and pickle, sometimes chapattis and maybe a special dessert, a feast that is first offered and then pressed upon guests. What would you like followed by what you must have, a bit of this or that, always the same ritual words, the warm voice and insistent phrases as much a part of the meal as the metal vessels. We sit on the kitchen floor, the coolness of the hard surface under our crossed legs, me trying to eat correctly with my fingers.

Working through the afternoon is slower going. I want to rest my head in Lakshmi's wide lap, feel my cheek against her round arm. I can smell the coconut oil in her hair, and see the thickness of each strand of long black hair stretched tightly away from her face and then exploding in an exuberant spray down her back. Lakshmi is the best kind of translator. She's in no rush to interpret each sentence, or criticize the writer for not being more precise. It's her generous and attentive nature that speaks here, her loyalty too. There is no question for her about which side of the cultural divide she belongs to. Her real love is for the Tamil language and for this place. She is not a traveller, not an adventurer. The few times she travelled abroad, she was miserable with longing for home and cut her stay short.

Lakshmi was right to provide herself with a quick ticket home. She was not about to lose her points of reference, fall into any third spaces, get dizzy with the incessant comings and goings that unsettle familiar boundaries forever. Translators can easily get lost when they stay away too long, when they try to learn too much about the world on the other side of their language borders. She would never allow the frame that defined her reality to loosen, to become a lumpy, leaking thing.

When our sessions are over, we stroll over to the busy intersection to get a rickshaw. I don't usually stay for supper, that would mean a ride home in the dark by myself. Everybody says this is dangerous, and I had a taste of it when once I challenged local wisdom and got a rickshaw driver who took a totally unfamiliar route home, stopping several times for gas, oil, and betel, each time taking time to chat and not paying any attention to me. In the vast and black Bangalore night, the city is a stranger. There are neither lights nor friends to count on, only the headlights of passing vehicles that give grey substance to the oceans of exhaust that rise like floodwater over the main boulevards, only a few street lights, signalling here and there a familiar sight, but mostly waving you back into the black of a jumbled city, a labyrinth which defies maps, and you could be led anywhere.

When I arrive back at our apartment at night it is always a shock to find the watchman lying across the front step, asleep in a blanket and woollen cap. The obstacle of his body is guarding our building, one of the concrete high-rises filling my neighbourhood, Malleswaram, one of the oldest parts of Bangalore. The new buildings are interrupted here and there by the old houses, low, Turkish-looking houses with decorative wooden gables set back among groves of noble flowering trees. All these constructions are set at awkward angles to the street, many of them now owned by Indians abroad. I like my busy, noisy street, the boys playing cricket in the tiny courtyard every afternoon, the rheumy sunset from the balcony, the red glow deepened by the layers of grey dust. All day the clamour of traffic climbs and lashes at my closed windows, from the early morning ring of a solitary bicycle bell to the scream of horns that comes at peak hours, meek tooting from the little vehicles and get-out-of-the-way-otherwise-you'll-be-dead blasts from the trucks and buses, and added to the commotion of the street is the clutter of vessels being washed on the balconies and high-pitched conversations on the landings, but when I walk to the market the side streets are quiet and the floppy leaves wave at me as I pass. Sometimes I linger on the sidewalk to watch women buying batches of mangoes for pickles or a shoemaker setting up for work on the sidewalk, sharpening his tools and sending his son to get him a package of betel before he begins. When I get home I prepare a salad of silver pineapple, amber mangoes and papaya the colour of flame.

*

LAKSHMI AND I decide to interview the author of the short story to collect material for the preface we'll write. We have to go over to a part of town I don't know, a pleasant residential area where the streets are lined with gulmohars and ashokas. To get there we take the bus and, once we've battled our way on to the fat red giant (miles taller than the poor rickshaw), I watch the traffic scatter as we careen and hurtle ahead.

The author has a fleshy round face, a neat moustache and a magnificent smile that he mostly directs towards Lakshmi during our long talk. He is wearing modest white pyjamas and quite evidently enjoys the attention we are giving him. He is alternately hopeful and angry, explaining how important modernist ideas are for Tamil writing, dismissing the airy-fairy idealism of 'Ford-funded intellectuals', describing his relationship to Western literature and to the ancient traditions of Tamil. He writes his own stories in the local language, and has no dream of a vast English-speaking readership, preferring to modernize his own tradition against the conservative forces that drive writing towards folklore and entertainment.

Lakshmi is eloquent and incisive, phrasing her questions knowledgeably, smiling encouragement and pleasure, and continuously complimenting the author, showing the deference which I see is a sophisticated form of flirting. Lakshmi comes to life in this kind of conversation, thinking out her ideas in response to the author's musings, displaying the gifts that make her the excellent translator that she is, knowing how to go poking about in someone else's ideas and still find her way home. I enjoy the sturdiness of her back as she moves her gaze from the author to me and back again. She will never topple over into confusion . . .

The author talks about how he uses translation to nourish his own writing, taking as his own the voices of other writers. These outside voices, he says, lead him to discover new voices within himself. Cultural border guards are easily outsmarted, he boasts. I see that he and Lakshmi both think of translation as a quick dash over the border, the escapade of a clever smuggler. They're prepared to use whatever cultural goods will serve their purposes, using translation as a knife to scratch off the sticky label of origin.

Lakshmi and I are supposed to be conducting the interview together; she is careful not to fall into Tamil with the author, but I feel increasingly uncertain as the afternoon goes on, my body even more pale and insubstantial than usual, my voice thin and lacking conviction. Very little of what I know seems to be appropriate here and I'm uncomfortable trying to stay sitting cross-legged. There's not much of the intrepid explorer left in me.

My visit to India seems to be lasting too long. My family has gone back now, leaving me to finish my work, but every day I forget a bit more of the life I had at home, and why I had to do and know the things I did. I have joined the legion of travellers who are singed by the heat of India, who become heady and dazed by its dissonances. I'm beginning to see myself as a bit of debris which has just happened to wash up on to land, like the dolphin I once saw on the beach in Trivandrum, its naked jawbone jutting into the air, each wave sucking bits of rotten flesh off the carcass, licking the cockeyed mass into shudders of shame.

I make an effort to propel myself back into the interview and justify my presence here. I try to get the author to question what he means by his 'own' culture. Didn't he know that the novel form was imported into Indian languages, that the first novels in Bengali were copied from translations from English? Isn't he aware that his writing has to be in some way influenced by Western fashions? The author senses the provocation in my questions but remains unfazed. He has his own questions for me. What about the Indian tradition of storytelling? Hasn't this tradition influenced Western narrative? And anyway, what's the point of trying to win at the game of origins? If sometimes you can't separate idea from influence, if you can't tell where translation ends and writing begins, is this a problem?

The author's companion, his second wife, has been listening

respectfully to the whole interview, monitoring, I suspect, his interaction with Lakshmi. She makes no comments until she produces hot fried snacks and coffee, introducing soft eddies of good talk into the potentially dangerous waters of our conversation.

By the time we leave the author's house it is dusk, and Lakshmi and I are too tired to fight our way into a bus.

We stroll down the main street, enjoying the gentle evening air despite the hot breath of exhaust fumes. I insist on buying Lakshmi the plump brown *chikoo* that she loves, far too mushy and sweet for my taste. We walk arm in arm, and I look affectionately at the group of young boys loosely holding hands or slinging their arms around each others' shoulders. I admire the relaxed competent gaze of the women completing their shopping.

When we walk by a market we buy jasmine petals for our hair and I spend the rest of the evening lost in their perfume.

Tonight I give up on finding my way back to my part of town, and sleep in Lakshmi's house. Lying under my mosquito net, I listen to the soft breathing coming from beds placed here and there in the small apartment, the elderly parents in the next room, the children sleeping on cots in the hallway. I can guess the shape of Lakshmi's body, the grain of her skin in her warm night bed. I wonder if these firm surfaces are not deflecting me away from a more untidy story, if the geographies of daylight don't disappear for her too when the city turns black.

In my diary, I write the dates with increasing awe as the day of my departure approaches. It has been some weeks now since I saw my family off at the airport. By the time they left it was two in the morning and I was rushed back across the city in the hired car, the streets deserted, the driver seeming to have no thought for the bullock cart or the bicycle that might be waiting around the bend as he sped through each roundabout, giving me my revenge on the hectic city, on the press of traffic and the confusion of tiny streets. The airport was behind me, the heat and mosquitoes, the large crowds of family casting their final impress on the traveller. It was cool and fragrant in the car, and I felt very small on its springy seat, a fragment in this city where no one is alone.

The rainy season has begun, the trees shaking with surprise as the cold air suddenly chases the warm and slowly, very slowly, the hot air long trapped in the apartment is forced to renew itself. Children on the street shriek with joy as the first drops of rain arrive, but I'm wondering about the shanty town on the edge of the railway tracks. Those children will be sleeping in mud, slogging along water-soaked paths, and smelling the newly virulent trash.

The power cuts are getting longer, despite the promise of renewed water reserves. The huge cockroach I had seen in the kitchen turns up dead in the fridge, drowned by the sog from the melting freezer compartment. I've become used to feeling absent, a non-resident in my body. I have become lighter during my stay here, the burden of identity considerably lessened, not contained by language either but open to the airy currents of estrangement. It's as if I've exchanged the weight of selfhood for the thin surfaces of skin and fabric, the shell a reassuring foil for the absent kernel, the sound of words sufficient points of contact.

The teaching term is ending at the university and I have been told I must administer oral exams to the students in my French course. I'm not quite certain why any of the students want to learn this language. French is simply one more note in the thickly textured dissonance of idioms here, the Hindi, Kannada, Tamil, Telugu that you hear on the streets, not a triumphant language but an idiom of defeat, just like at home, the colonies in Canada and India handed over under the same Treaty of Paris to the doubly victorious British, and so the language makes no pretence to rivalling English, offering itself as a curiosity and the key to no particular door.

It's Usha's turn today and she presents her work with remarkable intensity. She's wearing jeans, one of the very few women students who don't wear saris. She's too thin, but her black eyes flash as she makes an impassioned and precise speech on the virtues of yoga.

She does away with Western illusions in a few lapidary formulations. Romantic love, she says, is 'as egotistical as it is ephemeral'. She will never, evidently, have any truck with such Western nonsense. Adoringly, she paints the landscape of yogic ideas and practices. I want to follow her there, walk barefoot along the paths of conviction, breathe in serenity with the perfume of the jackpines.

Upamanyu, a gentle slim boy, is equally self-assured in his little speech. But he surprises me with his anger. He has chosen to talk about the movie *M. Butterfly*. It's about a French diplomat working in Peking who falls in love with a Chinese opera singer. The singer turns out to be a transvestite and a spy, and the diplomat is sent to jail. Upamanyu sees an exhilarating lesson here. Finally, he says, a movie that shows how the ignorance of Western culture will lead to its downfall. The diplomat should have known that the women's roles in Chinese opera are always played by men. If he had known more about Chinese culture, he would have understood that he was being tricked. I try to argue with him, suddenly feeling intense sympathy for this diplomat who lost his cultural bearings and fell for the wrong object, this man for whom cultural confusion was the beginning of love. Upamanyu listens politely to my arguments but shows no indulgence.

Lakshmi and I rush to finish our story, using every minute we can together. We disagree about how the story is to end, the last sentence involving a subtle difference between 'going' and 'coming' home which I have difficulty understanding and even more difficulty finding a French equivalent for. Probably I'll have to shift the emphasis away from the verbs of movement to words for home, so Durga will be returning *'dans son foyer'*, *'dans sa famille'*, *'chez elle'* or *'à la maison'*, the sequence of those terms indicating an ever thinner attachment to that place and that part of her identity.

Though my translation is now virtually complete, I'm not at all sure of it. Lakshmi showed it to a colleague from France who found some of the French expressions awkward, and I sense that she has lost her confidence in me, wondering if all those hours have been wasted.

I'm not surprised that my text doesn't stand up to scrutiny. The task of a translator is to be a beacon guiding the text across the divides of difference. How can I do this when I have lost my own bearings in this cluttered city of words? It's true, as Lakshmi has told me, that every language focuses on some central point of being, here rather than there, home rather than away, one fixed and settled point to go away from and come back to and which permits the proper use of verbs of movement, or adverbs of location. Once you lose that point, you begin to stumble along muddy sidewalks that somehow all look the same, the line of horizon a dirty smudge against the pale sun. When I leave Lakshmi's flat for the last time, both of us know that I have failed. I have not been what she wanted, someone who is as strong in my place as she is in hers.

Instead, I have allowed the confusions of this place to enter the cracks of my being, force them wide open and crumble me bit by bit. Lakshmi walks me to the corner, even though it's raining hard. Finding a rickshaw tonight is more difficult than usual. The intersections are awash in water, the traffic nervous, rickshaws and scooters squashed into a dense pack moving jerkily forward, thrumming ahead whenever there is the tiniest space. The line of drivers presses against the tyranny of the red light, revving their motors, waiting to pounce as soon as the signal changes. Scooter passengers hold umbrellas in their free hands and the black canopies are a ragged roof over the angry swarm.

As I step into the rickshaw, Lakshmi begins a hurried speech of affection, offering wishes for my speedy return, but the words ring false and I turn away before she's finished. Splashing and lurching homewards, I suck in the damp grey air around me, coating my insides with the gritty memory of this place.

My Friend, Mani

P. Lankesh

Lankesh launched Lankesh Patrike, *the largest-selling Kannada weekly tabloid magazine, in 1980. It is still in print today. Over the years, it has enlisted the goodwill and talent of several leading fiction writers, poets and essayists. Lankesh became an icon for his staunch secular stand and anti-establishment viewpoint.*

THESE ARE times when newspapers and dailies are being born almost every day. The number of Kannada readers h́as also gone up. A newspaper can bring about an awakening in the people. People have come to realize that it doesn't take a millionaire to run a newspaper, but even someone with modest means can do the same. People heap praise on me and say that I'm instrumental in bringing about such an awareness in the community. Taken in by all the admiration that haś come my way, people have tried to start their own papers, burnt their fingers in the process, and then held me responsible for it.

With one look at a newspaper, its approach and ideology is obvious to the reader. No matter how much they criticize me, no matter how endlessly they extol their own achievements, and no matter what the amount of their offerings at the lotus feet of all their mysterious goddesses, every line in their newspaper will hold a mirror to their sincere or hypocritical ways. Even as I continue to be amused by the ways of the world, I will share this small piece of information. This particular newspaper, which damns me, is printed at the same press where I print mine. The first, most righteous (read sarcasm) act of theirs was to submit an application to the Registrar claiming that their circulation was humongous, and got 90 tonnes of paper

---

'Geleya Mani' is one of Lankesh's Kannada weekly columns titled 'Teeke Tippani'. It was originally published in *Lankesh Patrike* in the 1980s.

sanctioned. They sold it and made big money. So, now you know one of the secrets of running a newspaper.

Since I have nothing to hide, I'm going to tell you one of the key features of our *Patrike*. For all those spewing venom, answers can be found in the stance of the newspaper and not in my justification. If I had taken their slander seriously and made an attempt to give them a befitting reply, I'm sure my readers would have been very disappointed with me.

When we started our newspaper in July 1980, the first six issues were printed in a private cylinder press. It would take two full days for us to print 25,000 copies. I used to pay the press Rs 1000 to print every 1000 copies. I was in no financial position to set up a press of my own, so I was on the lookout for a printer who was courageous, as well as reasonable. It was around this time that someone gave me the details of the printing press where the paper *Lokavani* was being printed. In the process of finding the place, I met a printer by name Subramani. Since we hadn't met personally, he had assumed that our newspaper was rigging circulation figures, but was surprised to hear from me that it was actually 25,000! Unlike others, who would flatter him just to extract the favour of getting their papers printed on credit, I was professional and made my payments without any delay. Mani respected me for this. What Mani possessed was an ancient, flatbed rotary machine. This machine, which cost Rs 70,000, looked like a rickety old cart; but nevertheless it would print our *Patrike* in just a couple of hours. With this switchover, the cost of printing came down dramatically to a quarter of what I used to spend earlier.

Apart from this, it's also important to speak of the cordial relationship that Mani and I shared. There is an important incident to illustrate this, too. The Tamils of Bangalore were observing Kannada Rajyotsava and invited both Mani and me to be a part of the celebrations. That week, we had carried a story on the various activities of the Kannada activist Vatal Nagaraj in the *Patrike*. Even before I addressed the gathering, about twenty-five goondas rushed on to the stage and started thumping me. I fell to the ground and, just when they were going to thrash me, Mani stood with his legs across my body and began to shove them away. Mani was getting beaten in the process, but he wouldn't budge. The assailants, terrified by the look on Mani's face, ran out to bring in more people. Mani shouted a warning to them and dragged me away to safety.

Impressed by my persona and the manner in which I ran my newspaper, Mani began to learn Kannada. When I wrote against the Tamils or when I wrote in favour of the Gokak agitation,[1] not even once did Mani express his displeasure. What is significant is the fact that all those politicians and bureaucrats whom we wrote about in our paper brought tremendous pressure on Mani. 'All that you want is money, isn't it? We will give you money. Stop printing Lankesh's paper,' they cautioned him. 'I know how important *meshtru*'s paper is for the people. If he makes a request, the government will be more than willing to give him a loan to have his own press. But that's not what he wants. And I cannot stop printing his paper,' replied Mani, and stood his ground.

By then, Mani and I were great friends. Even when it came to business, I knew how generous, how naïve he was. Just as it was important for me to make money and keep the paper out of financial doldrums, it was equally important for me to keep all the people who worked for me comfortable. And so, out of curiosity I looked into the details of Mani's account books: electricity, ink, building rent, printer's remuneration. I calculated to find out how much he was spending on printing our *Patrike* and realized that at the end of every month, Mani was left with a paltry sum. I yelled at him for keeping me in the dark, and increased the fee by Rs 15 for every 1000 copies. I even suggested that he should increase the printer's fee.

Mani, who did eventually make some money from printing the *Patrike*, bought a new machine that cost him Rs 35 lakh. Just a couple of days before he bought the machine, I had contemplated buying it myself. But my friends had advised me against it, because I would be taking upon myself a huge financial burden. Moreover, Mani had bought the machine only after seeking my consent and it was impossible for me to let him down. We had, through strange circumstances, established that it was possible to print in a press not one's own, just as the dailies in England have done for years.

I will also tell you of the many incidents related to this. It was barely a few months after the Kannadigas had fought tooth and nail in the Gokak agitation. Some militant Kannada lovers came up with some dark, devious plans. For instance, the Gangadhar Mudaliar episode, the Bangalore bandh incident, diehard Kannadigas storming the Film Chamber and, in the middle of all this, *Patrike*'s Dharwad correspondents nurturing political ambitions. One of them, who had intentions of cleverly using the *Patrike*, suggested that I do a cover story on 200 Kannada language agitators contesting the elections. 'I can probably commit such mistakes as an individual, but I cannot put the paper's interests at stake,' I had said. Disappointed by my response, he took a stance contrary to that of the newspaper, and pronounced 'You shouldn't publish anything that the film lovers do. And that is the desire of the 3 crore Kannadigas.' 'The newspaper is familiar with the 3 crore Kannadigas; it doesn't have to take lessons from you,' I had admonished him and rejected the stories he had written for the *Patrike*. Following this, he and his friends started a malicious campaign against me.

I have to tell you of this incident, too. About a year and a half ago, we carried a report on Dr Rajkumar's birthday. In that report, we even said a few things about people who were responsible for the birthday bash. Infuriated by this, close associates of the actor stomped into our office and threatened us. They headed straight to the press and menacingly declared, 'If you publish this newspaper, we will set the whole building on fire.' Mani was out of station when this incident took place. His son, who was managing the press, went into a state of panic and called me. 'Let them, we'll see,' I had said. That put an end to all the bullying. Eventually, and rather strangely, these very people got their paper printed in the same press. I was open to all kinds of responses from the reading public. Hence, I didn't discuss this with Mani.

Translated from the Kannada by Deepa Ganesh

Note

1. The Gokak agitation was a successful language rights agitation in the 1980s that fought for the first-language status of the Kannada language in Karnataka. It was named after the committee headed by V.K. Gokak that recommended giving primacy to Kannada in state schools. The cine icon Rajkumar led the campaign.

Reworking Masculinities:

Rajkumar and the Kannada Public Sphere

Tejaswini Niranjana

The kidnapping of the seventy-one-year-old Kannada matinee idol Rajkumar on 30 July 2000, threw the city into a ferment for 108 days. His death on 12 April 2006 paralysed life on the street as lumpen elements took over. This article, published in December 2000, explores issues of identity within the context of the kidnapping by a forest bandit from neighbouring Tamil Nadu.

THE KIDNAPPING of Rajkumar by Veerappan has inspired new negotiations of the question of Kannada linguistic identity, of what being Kannadiga means today. The crisis has enabled a rearticulation of the anxieties and social tensions of the last few years. Central to these anxieties is the recurrent theme of masculinity in crisis.

The event of the kidnapping has produced various kinds of popular arguments for new cultural agendas in relation to the Kannada language, often seen as embodied in the star presence of Rajkumar ('My blood is Kannada, my life is Kannada, my heart and mind are Kannada'—these phrases circulate through his many film dialogues and his public speeches). A popular magazine, headlining the kidnap story, proclaimed that it was 'An axeblow (*kodali yetu*) to the very existence of the language' (*Taranga*, 14 September 2000). Why does the language issue appear so salient in the portrayal of an embattled Kannada identity in a way that is certainly different from assertions of Telugu or Malayalam identity? Why has Kannada linguistic pride

---

An extended version of this essay was originally published in the *Economic and Political Weekly* in December 2000.

often defined itself in opposition to and alongside Tamil pride? Is this phenomenon and the star culture associated with it more an issue for the southern Karnataka districts than elsewhere in the state?

The responses to the kidnapping have to be seen in relation to the aggressively masculinist public sphere which emerges in its present form in the 1990s in Bangalore. Crucial to the articulation of this new Kannada public sphere are phenomena like the hugely successful films of Upendra, in particular, *A* (1998), *Swastik* (1999) and *Upendra* (2000), and weekly tabloids like *Hi Bengalur!*, *Agni*, *Polisara Horata* (Police Struggle), *Crime News*, *Star of Bangalore*, or *Sanje Sphota* (Evening Explosion) which retail in equal measure political criticism and local scandal. The first two papers have a different profile from the rest, seeking unlike the others to make visible interventions in the public sphere and maintain connections with literary figures.[1]

The two tabloids I present here in some detail are *Hi Bengalur!* (*HB*), edited by Ravi Belagere, and *Agni*, edited by Shridhar. Both editors are fiction writers and essayists; the first is also a poet. Both are rumoured to have underworld connections; the latter openly flaunts his knowledge of 'the world of crime'. Peppered with references to Belagere's Zen, his Esteem and his new red Gypsy, deploying the slang of hip teenagers (e.g., the column 'Luv luvike'), *HB*, like *Agni*, often expresses anti-globalization sentiments; several articles by staffers project a pro-Kannada anti-'outsider' position. The outsider is always upper class, moneyed: businessmen and software professionals living in safe suburbs like Indiranagar or Jayanagar, college students from élite institutions who frequent the pubs on Brigade Road and M.G. Road. The poor outsiders, like the migrant Tamil labourers and street vendors who usually bear the brunt of pro-Kannada violence, are not singled out by the tabloid press, although the anti-Tamil pronouncements clearly include them as targets.

Newer and cheaper technology provides the wherewithal for a different kind of popular cultural artefact, the audio cassette, which for the first time in Kannada has moved out of the devotional, folk and mimicry genres into contemporary political commentary.[2] Eleven audio cassettes have been released in the wake of Rajkumar's kidnapping—nine in Kannada, one in Hindi and one in Urdu. Well-known comedians, mimics, playback singers and drama company actors provide the voices. The first cassette was released some ten days after the event, and the latest two months after. An article in *Lankesh Patrike* informs us that each audio company has released about 20–25,000 copies of each cassette into the market. One little music shop in Gandhibazar sells approximately 100 cassettes per week (Rs 25–30 each).[3] It is believed that retailers from Mysore, Kolar and other places come to Bangalore and buy about twenty copies of each cassette.

The structure of the cassette presentations is a relatively simple one, following the *harikathe* mode: we hear two men talking, one questioning, the other replying, with occasional interjections by others. Seldom do we have female characters, although the dialogues are often interspersed with songs, a few sung by women. The songs, unless composed for the occasion, are remixes of famous Rajkumar numbers, either picturized on him or sung by him. When the lyrics are changed (e.g., a song from the hit film *Yeradu Kanasu* [1974], where Rajkumar romances Manjula, goes 'I will never be able to live if I forget you', and is transformed into *'Endendu nimmanu maretu naaniralare/naanendu kannada bittu badukiralaare'* as Rajkumar now romances the *abhimani* and his language, in these words: 'I will never be able to live if I forget you / I will never be able to live if I leave Kannada' [*Mangana Kaiyalli Manikya*]). The words either relate to the current situation or reflect Rajkumar's love for his abhimanis. A couple of the cassettes are compilations of songs written for the occasion (*Nadina Anna Kadinalli* [The Land's Elder Brother in the Forest], *Rajanna Naadige Baaranna* [Come Back to the Land, Rajanna]); one uses the folk performance style known as *kamsale*; one employs the north Karnataka dialect; one claims to be in *janapada* (folk) style but actually has standard film tunes.

Significant similarities exist between the language and imagery of the cassettes and those of the newspaper articles and editorials. The difference in tone is noticeable, however: the seriousness and occasional sarcasm of the tabloids are counterpointed by the humour, and expressions of love for the star, in the cassettes. Inept politicians are blamed for the mess, and exhorted to action in the papers. The cassettes too pin the blame on politicians, from both Karnataka and Tamil Nadu. 'Why didn't Veerappan kidnap some of those politicians? The white elephants in the Vidhana Soudha who've swallowed up the World

Bank money; why didn't he kidnap them?' (*Aranyadalli Annavru*) (Annavru in the Forest). The answer usually is that the people don't care a fig about the politicians, and therefore it wouldn't serve Veerappan's purpose. The profile of the Kannadiga (and 'his' predicament) is crucial to how the present situation is configured in these narratives of loss and sorrow.

The brief of the cassettes appears to be the glorification of Rajkumar and the excoriation of his kidnapper. The picture of Rajkumar which emerges from the cassettes also helps us form a picture of the Kannadiga fan (the abhimani literally, one who holds someone in esteem). Rajkumar is hailed in call-and-response mode, with his titles called out one by one, and a chorus responding with '*Dr Raj avarige Jayavaagali*' or simply chanting 'Rajanna' as *Kannadada Kanteerava, Kannadada Kulatilaka* (community ornament/adornment), Kentucky Colonel (reference to a Kannada American award won by him), Dadasaheb Phalke *Vijeta, Badavara Bandhu* (friend of the poor), Padma Bhushana, *Kannadigara Dyavru* (God of the Kannadigas), *Bahadur Gandu* (Boss Man, reference to a famous Rajkumar film loosely based on *The Taming of the Shrew*). The expressions of outrage at the kidnapping of such a noble Kannadiga usually focus on two issues (although the tapes mention all of Veerappan's demands): Cauvery water, and the language question.

The Tamils and 'Us'

THE QUESTION of who is a Kannadiga is posed in relation to who he is not. An *HB* editorial of 25 August 2000 suggests that what the Tamils have is a bad pride (*durabhimana*) in their language, the excesses caused by this pride are contrasted with the bitter grief resulting from 'our' non-pride (*nirabhimana*). Unlike us, the Tamils are prone to suicide and anti-nationalism (their links with the LTTE and ISI are well known); we, on the other hand, are 'respectable' people. In this phase of his career, Veerappan comes to be identified as a Tamil, rather than merely as a poacher or brigand. While this reidentification is connected to Veerappan's allies and what some perceive to be a new kind of demand, and will clearly have its own effects in Tamil Nadu, what we are concerned with here are the implications for issues of

Kannada identity. 'Never before had the speakers of a different language laid hands on the very heart of Kannadigas, on their self-esteem,' says the 25 August *HB* editorial. A week later, on 1 September 2000, *HB* asks rhetorically: 'After all this has happened, must we still retain our helpless patience?' The editorial speaks of our unpreparedness in the face of Tamil terrorism, suggests a connection between Veerappan, Maran and Karunanidhi, the LTTE's heroin and arms trade; contrasts 'their' machine guns and landmines with 'our' pujas, bhajans and *urulu seve*; asks why the Kannadiga is slowly regressing to this totally helpless state. Even the water in our taps, warns *HB*, will soon be regulated by their gun barrels.

The Kannadiga's legendary tolerance is another recurring trope in the masculinist public sphere. As *HB* puts it, the Karnataka government runs 200 Tamil schools, and Bangalore alone has 12 Tamil corporators. 'There are several Tamils in the IAS, the police force and the legislature here. We have loved them all, we have tolerated them. But in the light of the changes in Tamil Nadu, should we continue to retain our helpless patience? This is the question we have to ask ourselves' (1 September 2000). One common example given in the cassettes and the tabloids to contrast Kannadigas with Tamils is as follows: 'Are there any Kannada slums in Chennai like there are Tamil slums in Bangalore?' The point is not that there are no Kannadigas in Tamil Nadu but that they have blended with the local population, unlike the recalcitrant Tamils in Karnataka.

In an editorial on 25 August 2000, *Agni* discusses the carpenter Shanmugams and contractor Annamalais: 'Their ancestors might have come from Tamil Nadu, but they have a right to be here; and we have to create the conditions which will make them Kannadigas; we should create a situation where no one in Kannada Naadu can live here without learning and using Kannada.' The perception that it is the fault of the state as well as civil society that has led to an enfeebled Kannada is widespread. In response to Veerappan's demand to make Tamil the second official language in Karnataka, a cassette character exclaims: 'We're struggling even to be able to make Kannada the first language, and he wants Tamil to be another official language!'[4]

As the crisis wears on, a specifically Kannada helplessness becomes a defining feature of the state's response to the situation. An *HB* editorial of 15 September 2000, is sombre: 'The Tamils look upon Kannadigas as figures of fun. Rajkumar might forget one day his 40 [sic] days in the jungle, but the Kannadiga will never forget the humiliation meted out to him by Tamils. It has become the daily routine of the Kannadiga to sit at home and look forward to the moment of victory. And you [S.M. Krishna, chief minister of Karnataka] have been sitting more helplessly than all of us. This shouldn't happen, sir. History will not forgive any of us.'

Kannada Masculinity

THE 18 AUGUST 2000, editorial of *Agni* gave a call for people to go into the forest to rescue Rajkumar. Remarking that thousands of young men phoned in their readiness, editor Shridhar criticized those few who urged caution (*Agni*, 25 August): 'Let not peace/nonviolence become cowardice'. A month later, readers were still being exhorted: 'Leave fear behind, do not become sheep' (22 September).

A 25 August article in *Agni* by Shridhar, 'Not a Tiger but a Eunuch', continues to define by opposition. 'Who is a really masculine man?' asks the writer. There are two pictures of Veerappan, one with moustaches, one without, in addition to other photographs taken in the forest. 'Does he have true manly [in English] virtues, and masculinity? Let us examine this question with an open mind. You know my experience and knowledge of the world of crime. One who's truly manly doesn't glorify his acts, he forgets them. Only the weak and cowardly boast of their deeds. [Among other things, Shridhar asks whether walking 50 km a day or knowing the forest well constitutes manliness, says anyone can walk that distance even without practice, and every tribal who lives in the forest knows it well, why is it a special virtue?] . . . Hitler was a eunuch. If he had even a little manliness, he wouldn't have been so violent. What then should we call Veerappan? Effeminate, transvestite, a genderless person? With one voice our boys said: Chakka (eunuch).'[5] Nowhere in this article is Rajkumar mentioned, but he is clearly the implicit reference point in the discussion of Veerappan's manliness. A distinct feature of Veerappan's appearance, his large moustache, becomes a convenient peg for the discussion of masculinity. The moustache features centrally in a long dialogue between Rajkumar and his captor, ventriloquized in the cassette *Kaadinalli Kannada Ratna*.

The gentle and avuncular-looking Rajkumar, who embodies Kannadaness and the potential of Kannada masculinity, is the same figure who also holds back the *abhimani* from violence, from the attainment of a conventionally understood masculine potential. It is almost as though the persona of the older present-day Rajkumar prevails in his contemporary public image over the personae of the CID films, the romances or the historicals. In the cassettes and tabloids, there are innumerable references to his taped request not to engage in violent acts, or to his family's plea to the *abhimanis* to observe restraint. While reiterating these requests, the characters in the cassettes add that Rajkumar's wishes are the only constraints on their willingness to turn violent, either in the city or in the jungle.

Yet another series of cassettes further elaborates the question of masculinity. The references are to Veerappan and Rajkumar as representing *kaadu* (forest) and *naadu* (usually land, but here it can also refer to city). Brute force is contrasted with refinement, explosive aggressiveness with stoicism, bloodthirstiness with gentleness. A cassette song, '*Tumbida madakeyu tulukademba maatide, ninna baalu maatige naija chitravaagide*' (There is a proverb that the full pot does not spill over / Your life is a true illustration of this saying), refers admiringly to Rajkumar's *shanti mantra*, a fitting response to Veerappan's violent life.[6]

In evidence in the kidnap discourse is Rajkumar's body, one which has been worked upon, like his speech, his gestures. His body is described as 'a body that's been in the *garadi (akhada)*'.[7] He is presented as a hatha yoga expert, one who has cleansed his *maimanassu*, mind and body. One cassette has a suggestive tale about the significance of knowing yoga. In the forest, Veerappan tries to teach Rajkumar how to do the suryanamaskara. Rajkumar smiles gently, and embarks on a series of asanas. By the time he has finished rolling his stomach muscles 'as though he were stirring ragi porridge', and letting the water in and out of his nostrils, Veerappan falls at his feet, acknowledging his mastery.[8] Seemingly in sharp contrast to this picture, we have the constant reiteration of the childlike nature of Rajkumar, as in the following allusions: Father of the state, elder brother of the abhimanis, a little child in his innocence, gem, pearl, god, dove. His mind, says a character in *Adaviyalli Annavru*, is like milk (*haalinantha manassu*), clean and pure.

The burden of expressions of Kannadaness at this time, when the compulsion is to speak in the name of a unified Kannada identity, is to suture together the abhimani's desire for violent action and the yogic iconicity of Veerappan's famous prisoner. That the attempt to bring these disparate elements together is not always bound to succeed, that the process of the reformation of masculinities is so evidently a confused and unstable one, is perhaps enough cause for optimism.

Author's note: The material used in this article is from the Media and Culture Archive of the Centre for the Study of Culture and Society, Bangalore. For assistance and encouragement, I am grateful to Ashish Rajadhyaksha, M. Madhava Prasad, S.V. Srinivas, P. Radhika and A. Raju.

Notes

1. *HB,* which started publication in 1995, claimed a readership of 18 lakh per issue in 2000! Reliable sources estimated the print run at just below 1 lakh.

2. Peter Manuel's discussion of how the advent of the cassette proletarianized the production and circulation of music in northern India would also be relevant in the south. See Peter Manuel, *Cassette Culture: Popular Music and Technology in North India* (Chicago, 1993).

3. Basavaraju: *Raj in the Forest, Veerappan in Song, Lankesh Patrike,* 20 September 2000, p. 15.

4. From the audio cassette *Katthegenu Gotthu Kasturi Kampu.*

5. It is widely believed that the well-known poet Prathibha Nandakumar, who has been with the newspaper since its inception, and who writes several articles in each issue under her own byline, also contributes substantially to the discussions about the issue's content. Her contribution seems to become invisible in a context in which Shridhar invokes 'our boys'.

6. In *Kaadugalla Kadda Mutthu.*

7. In a memorable opening sequence in *Immadi Pulakeshi* (1967), Rajkumar, playing a young chieftain, uses his body to save the princess of the realm from an enormous falling log of wood, an early visual representation of his image as *homo nationalis*.

8. *Narahantakana Baleyalli Karunadina Hridaya.*

Mapping Bangalore

Shashi Deshpande

WHEN WE first came to Bangalore, it was still part of Mysore State; Karnataka would be born a few months later. To us, Bangalore was part of a twinned entity called Bengaluru–Mysuru, the duller sibling, the commoner, as opposed to royal Mysore. Though we came here ten years after Independence, it was still incredibly feudal and loyal to its portly Maharaja and people said 'Namma Maharajaru' reverently, with folded hands. It was a time when more *jhutkas* plied on the roads than buses and autorickshaws, two-wheelers meant bicycles, girls wore long skirts (rudely called parachutes, because of their billowing capacity) and almost every woman wore flowers in her hair.

The year was 1956. My father had been appointed as Drama Producer in All India Radio. He had come here before us, and perhaps my mother had hoped he would have a home ready for us when we arrived. Instead, we were whisked off to a hotel, the Modern Hindu Hotel at Ananda Rao Circle. We didn't know it then, but we had gone straight to the heart of the city; we were only a stone's throw away from the railway station, from Gandhinagar, and, most important of all, from the area called Majestic, the hub of the city. In the hotel itself, we imbibed the essence of Bangalore—a melange of aromas, of agarbatti and flowers, of coffee and sambar and *sagu* masalas. And there was the distinctive Kannada, peppered with Swamis, Sirs and Ammas. A strange Kannada, we thought it, studded with English words. What was galling was that they thought it was *our* Kannada that was strange and incomprehensible. In just a few months there would be an influx of government servants from other regions into Bangalore, and the newly created Rajajinagar would soon be flooded with Joshis, Kattis, Kulkarnis and Patils speaking this Kannada. But, to our chagrin, we would remain outsiders until the city found other outsiders to contend with.

To go back to 1956, my father must have realized that a hotel was not the place for his family, for we quickly moved into a temporary home. A colleague of his offered us the use of some rooms on the first floor of a relative's house in nearby Nehrunagar. The road was parallel to the railway line and, sitting on the large balcony above the portico, we could wave to the passengers of the trains that clattered past. I remember the beautiful red polished floor of that house, so typical of Bangalore houses then, of how it shone, almost like a mirror, and how cool it was under our feet when it rained. It was an intriguing household; our host had 'married' a second time to get a child and an astrologer had promised that a child would 'soon come'. Unfortunately, we were not to know if that happened, for in a fortnight or so we left the place and moved into our first real home in Bangalore. This house, in Kumara Park, was like the innumerable Housing Board houses scattered through the city and had, in the landlord's terminology, one 'hall-u', two 'rooms-u', a 'kitchen-u' and a 'bathroom-u'. The entrance was a small, grilled space, from where you could see who your visitors were, as well as watch the world go by. It was also the place where family and visitors shed their footwear when they entered. I remember that when my father once had a reading of his play, which took place in the 'hall-u', someone carried away all the footwear, ours, as well as the visitors,' while the reading was going on. A whole lot of theatre enthusiasts walked home in their bare feet that evening!

We lived here for nearly two years, but scarcely came to know any neighbours, except our landlord and the couple who lived behind us. People in Bangalore, we realized, didn't believe in neighbourliness; they preferred to stare out of their windows when you passed by, to give you a blank stare when you met. During festival times, however, unknown little girls in long skirts came with invitations. Accepting these invitations meant that we were now met by occasional smiles and my mother with the inevitable inane question, '*Oota aytaa?*' ('Have you eaten?') Nevertheless, the houses were so close that we were often granted intimate glimpses of our neighbours' lives. Living in such close proximity to others was a strange new experience for me; before this, we had lived in Dharwad, where our closest neighbours were beyond shouting distance. It was here that I saw the repetitiveness of women's lives, heard their conversations in the afternoon when their morning chores were done, noting the cadences in their voices as they spoke. Sounds that came back to me years later, when I began writing.

Opposite our home were the tall walls of a boys' hostel, a place which came to life in summer when it was rented out for weddings. Through the long summer months, we listened to film songs in Kannada and Tamil blaring out on the loudspeaker. I soon got to know most of the popular film songs of the day—my introduction to the movie culture in the city. I had come from Bombay, *the* film city; nevertheless, I was overwhelmed by my first sight of Kempe Gowda Road (K.G. Road to the locals. Bangalore had a penchant for abbreviation. I soon learnt to say K.R. Circle, N.R. Circle, etc.) More amazing than the number of theatres on the road were the posters outside them. Huge outsize posters with lush garlands nailed round the heroes' faces on the first day, heroes with pudgy faces and luxuriant moustaches, some trying to look dashing in tights, cloaks or masks, with swords in their hands. There was the same kind of fleshy opulence about the heroines, who had mounds of flowers in their sleek hair. This was before Kannada activism and fanaticism began; no one questioned the fact that Tamil movies predominated. Only a couple of theatres showed Hindi films. One of them was Majestic, the theatre which gave the entire locality its name. I remember seeing *C.I.D.* there. Kempe Gowda theatre, which also showed Hindi films, was a dark and dingy theatre, but my memories of it are forever coloured by a carefree, debonair Dilip Kumar singing 'Suhana safar . . .' in *Madhumati*.

This area, Majestic, soon became a part of my life when I joined the Government Law College at the Mysore Bank Circle. Classes were in the morning. In my memory it was always cool and fresh when I walked along Seshadripuram Park, past the school where a huge pandal would spring up during Ramanavami to hold the head-nodding, thigh-clapping music aficionados. Past the usual 'lodge' with men's underwear and wet towels hanging on the railing, on which the young men leaned, calling out comments as I walked past, head held high, trying to ignore them. Waiting for my bus, opposite the Swastik theatre, I could smell flowers from the market behind me, horse dung from the jhutka stand, I could hear the bells from the temple nearby. I'm sure it rained sometimes, it must have been cold and hot as well, but I don't remember ever carrying an umbrella or wearing a sweater.

Life was peaceful and innocent and the people quaintly old-fashioned. Yet, incongruously, there were plenty of wine shops. People here drank, something that seemed to us, coming from Morarji Desai's Bombay, shocking.

By now, I had settled into the rhythm of this city, its gentle pace more familiar, so that I learnt to amble rather than trot. I had begun to cope with the indolence of the people, the 'doesn't matter' attitude, to appreciate the leisurely pace of shopping in the city. When we went to a jeweller on Avenue Road just before my wedding to get some jewellery made, I remember that we sat there for two entire days, my mother and I, picking out the best stones for a necklace, stones of the right shape, size and colour. And this in an open shop, with people on the road walking past, within touching distance of the precious stones! I think of that when I see the dazzling glass-fronted jewellery shops today, swarming with security and closed circuit televisions. Sari-shopping in those days was mainly in Chickpet, with the added attraction of a stop in a Balepet eating place, where you got the best dosas in town. Shivaram Karanth, it was said, stayed here when he came to Bangalore. The Cantonment was another world altogether, foreign territory which we visited occasionally for English movies, for loafing on South Parade (M.G. Road to newcomers!) or Commercial Street, or for rare family treats in Koshy's. Cubbon Park, with its spectacular flowering trees and its air of peace, was a slice of heaven. I can remember a time when my father lost his way in Cubbon Park. It was dark, a fine mist-like rain was falling, and there was not a person or vehicle around. We drove round and round in circles, until he accidentally found his way out.

We moved house an amazing number of times in those early years. Looking back, all the moves seem painless and easy to me. Perhaps they were, for we had minimal possessions and my mother, very competently, and without any fuss, coped with every change. But when my father announced that we were to move to Malleswaram, my heart sank. Until then we had lived mostly in the area around Kumara Park, in the newer and posher areas. Malleswaram seemed incredibly old-fashioned and dowdy. But of course, we did move there; this was to be my father's last move.

Malleswaram was like a snooty old lady; stately houses in large compounds with stone walls looked as if they had been there forever. The names at the gates, to our awe, said 'Zemindar of this' or 'Raja of that'. We never saw any of them, though, nor did anyone take note of us; there were no curtain-whisking neighbours here. Our house was a doll's house among giants. But it was here that my father found his place in Bangalore, our house becoming a hub for theatre, as well as literary people. I can remember Masti Venkatesh Iyengar beaming kindly at me, V. Sitaramiah impeccably dressed in the old Mysore style, Dr Shivaram's booming voice and jokes. The Niranjans, then a young literary couple, visited us and I can remember an even younger Girish Kasaravalli, who came to invite my father to his wedding.

The Sixth Main Road, on which we lived, was a quiet shady street, just a few roads away from the market and temple area on one side and the railway station on the other. The sound of trains hooting when I went to sleep and when I woke up became familiar in a while. In fact, the quaint little station became part of our lives. When I came back with my children, we took them there to see the trains go by. And my parents, in their later years, regularly walked there every morning, timing themselves by the trains. My bus stop was on Margosa Road, a short distance from the market area. Going to college in the mornings, I walked under a canopy of the gulmohar, passed the ubiquitous old man plucking flowers with the crook of his walking stick from others' gardens, inhaled the aroma of freshly roasted and ground coffee from the one shop that was open at the time. On the rare occasions when I came home a little late in the evenings, the roads were almost deserted and I walked home at a rapid, almost running pace, nervously watching my own shadow growing longer and shorter between the few street lights. Malleswaram was a place where one walked. My friends and I walked every evening to the 18th Cross and beyond, my parents walked to the city railway station, to Gandhinagar and Rajajinagar. We walked to the post office, to the banks, to the market, to the well, one just walked everywhere.

When I left for Bombay after marriage, I little thought I would come back to Bangalore. But fourteen years later, when my husband was offered a job in NIMHANS, we returned. Both Bangalore and I had changed; I was no longer a girl, but a woman with two children. And Bangalore had begun its march ahead, though it was still a steady decorous progress through planned suburbs. We were to live in the NIMHANS campus, a place which had been, as the cemeteries which we passed before we got to it indicated, outside the town. At first, I didn't realize the slight odium attached to living there. 'NIMHANS', I would say to the bus conductor, to be met by a blank stare and then a grinning '*Ucch aspatre-aa*? Why didn't you say so?' Nobody, it seemed, was willing to call it NIMHANS; it continued to be '*ucch aspatre*' the Mental Hospital. Our houses in the campus were in the midst of nowhere. We tried to civilize our surroundings, we got rid of thorny weeds and parthenium, we grew papayas and bananas, planted a cassia, a sampige. But for long it remained a wilderness. Once, before our houses were fenced in, our neighbour, an early riser, found that he could not get out of his house one morning; it had been bolted from the outside. Looking out of a window, he saw a group of huddled sleepers in the portico. When he called out, one tousled head was raised and a sleepy voice said, '*So jao*.' Our neighbour, a man who enjoyed the unusual, did just that. When they woke up, the door had been unbolted and the group of nomads had gone. We had an unbidden guest too, a recalcitrant snake in our backyard, which defied all our efforts to get rid of it and refused to leave. Even the snake-catcher went away, defeated. Finally, we left it alone, being careful not to go there at night. But we saw it once or twice when it came out to sun itself, a beautiful shining cobra.

We were surrounded by hospitals and localities with names I had never heard. Byrasandra, Lakkasandra, Hombegowda Nagar, Audogodi. I was fascinated by the dark broody Christian cemeteries on the Audogodi road where branches of lush trees drooped heavily and protectively over the ancient graves and tombstones. A symbiotic relationship, for the trees grew so huge, they seemed to be enriched by the dead. I promised myself that I would go and wander among the graves one day, read the names etched on the tombstones, find out who those dead were.

But it was not to be. My husband gave up his job in NIMHANS and once again we packed our belongings and set off for another house, this in a distant (it seemed so then) suburb, Banashankari, a place I had never seen. Those were the monsoon months and my memories of that year are of constant heavy rains, a very rare thing in

Bangalore. Our house was damp, dismal and full of cockroaches; once again we were in a row of back-to-back houses, in a street of curtain-twitching neighbours. I took long walks in the evening, during which I saw a new locality taking shape. Houses were coming up everywhere. But my own creativity seemed at a standstill; I could not write. The greatest solace of my life was to go up on the terrace and look at the hills in the far distance, to watch the monsoon clouds and feel the breeze on my face. Far away, I could see a lone bus plying on a road that seemed to lead to nowhere; that way, I was told, lay Padmanabha Nagar, soon to become a new layout. The small street with its cheek-by-jowl houses was claustrophobic and I was glad when we moved out in just a few months, first to a house near Ashoka Pillar in Jayanagar, and then back to Malleswaram, to the apartment my father had built above his house. A totally changed Malleswaram. Unknown cars drove past with people from the new apartment blocks that had come up in the past few years in place of the old bungalows. Only the old bungalow opposite ours held steadfast, its large compound and all the trees in it intact. A new generation of children were throwing stones at the mangoes on the trees along the stone wall. Not urchins now, but students of a school on the next road, who, having no playground, came here during their breaks to play cricket. All morning, while I sat at my table trying to write, I heard raucous cries of 'out', 'not out' or a triumphantly strident 'four!' or 'sixer!' In the evenings my father sat out, looking anxiously at the sky, waiting for rains, fanning himself with a piece of paper. Where were the clouds? Where had the rains gone? And what was happening to the traffic? It was becoming increasingly difficult for my husband to travel all the way to South End Circle and back, something that pushed us into taking a decision: the time had come to possess our own little bit of land in Bangalore.

We built a house and moved to Jayanagar. A suburb where every fifth house had a name plate that said 'Retd Chief Engineer' and where more people spoke Kannada than elsewhere. Like all householders in Bangalore, we planted trees. Frangipani and parijaat within our compound, a neem and gulmohar outside. And as they let down their roots, so did we. By the time the frangipani flowered, the gulmohar stretched across the road and the parijaat shed its flowers to create a white and red carpet every morning, we had learnt to say

'Kamplexu' for the shopping complex, to call the row of parks 'Rose Gardens'. We got to know the places for the best dosas, masala and chutney powders. I travelled every Sunday to Malleswaram to visit my mother. The drive through the quiet roads on Sunday mornings was like a journey to the past. The roads were so familiar I could have driven with my eyes closed. With my mother's death, my links to Malleswaram snapped. Jayanagar was truly home. But like a spider's web, a fine tracery of lines began to connect us to the rest of the city, to family and friends—Defence Colony and Banashankari, Mathikere and Koramangala, Sanjaynagar and J.P. Nagar.

How much land does a man need, Tolstoy asked. A forty by sixty piece of land seemed enough to knit us into this city.

Romance of the Cantonment

Geeta Doctor

THERE WAS a time when the whole city of Bangalore with its bouquets of gardens, ribbons of newly laid streets culminating in the broad band of South Parade (now known as Mahatma Gandhi Road), knelt at her feet. She was after all Alexandrina Victoria, Queen of Great Britain and Ireland, and from 1876, Empress of India. Even the Sunday visitors to St Mark's Cathedral opposite, correct in their top hats and frock coats, in their well-sprung landaus and broughams, with their parasoled partners by their side, would involuntarily slow down as they trotted past her marble likeness. Queen Victoria's statue represented the reason and the symbol of their continued existence there, and if the sculptor in his enthusiasm had added a touch of Roman imperialism to her profile that ill accorded with the plum pudding plainness of the rest of her personality, it was only to be expected. That very state was designed to put 'natives' in their place.

Queen Victoria continues to stare today, but only in horrified astonishment. Noisome yellow scooters fly past her on every side, tall towers leer at her from a distance, tourist buses disgorge their passengers from every corner of the country, if not the world, with alarming regularity at the entrance to Cubbon Park. And at nights, the transformation that takes place with the neon lights advertising 'Sexy Sheila' and 'Naughty Niloufer' and innumerable bars, nightclubs and restaurants, is such, that it would have left 'dear Albert' sleepless for months.

It is only in the early mornings that one can ask: where is the Bangalore that Queen Victoria first saw? Where are the Infantry Barracks, the Parade Ground, the Cavalry Road, the Residency where the Commissioner lived, and all the other symbols of power and permanence with which the British first stamped their right over

This essay was originally published in *The Taj Magazine*.

Bangalore? In the crisp early morning light, pink-purple still with the edges of darkness around it, the old names that the British carved out for themselves—Benson Town, Richmond Town, Frazer Town, Cooke Town, Knoxpet and all the others—stare out whitely from their name boards.

Bangalore Cantonment was founded in the early nineteenth century. The first of the barracks was built south of the Ulsoor village and it was only much later that the usual regimental-style station was laid out. The Parade Ground which survives today as a greatly diminished one in size, though not in importance, lay a mile long with Infantry Barracks to the north of it. In some of the most evocative passages on army life, described as the Soldiers' Paradise in India, *Plain Tales from the Raj* gives an account of what some of these parades were like: 'You paraded for your meals. You paraded to see the doctor. You paraded to draw your rations. You paraded to draw your stores. You paraded to draw your ammunition. You paraded on Sundays because Church Parade was compulsory. It was parades 365 days a year. Any hour of the day or night, the call would come up: *On Parade. On Parade.*

To the memory hunter, each halting step down South Parade (or M.G. Road) is a corridor leading into the past, and so fast are the changes taking place that even as he walks, a whole era has probably been buried under the rubble of an estate developer. Only the names remain, as in the Barton of Barton Court, which is now a hotel. One name which has stubbornly resisted change is the small but popular ice-cream parlour called 'Lake View'. It belonged, so the story goes, to an Englishman whose dairy, which supplied the main ingredients, overlooked the Ulsoor Lake, which provided the inspiration for the name. When the gentleman left in 1947, he gave both the name and the tradition to the present owner.

Another one of the old timers is the Dias Music Saloon which sells the pianos that were once a part of every decent parlour and the bane of every child with a musically minded mother. It was opened in 1927 by Jose Marianna Dias who spent his life either in front or behind some musical instrument, playing it as a band leader at the popular balls at the Bowring Institute or selling it at his shop. When the Charlie Chaplin era was ushered in at the Globe, Dias and his band were there, filling in the awkward pauses between the soundless scenes or tracking every pratfall. His daughter Irene Lemos and her husband now wait for the stray customer who might wander in, lusting after a Grand Piano.

The Deccan Herald building, which is more often than not protected by a posse of riot police to fend off slogan shouters who feel it their democratic duty to oppose anything that might be printed, even though they may not be able to read it, has withstood these attacks and those made by the passing of years, remarkably well. As with many newspaper offices that cherish every cobweb and layer of dust like precious heirlooms that must be zealously guarded, the dominant impression is that time has stood still here, lingering over the ink-stained floors, the lofty ceilings, wooden staircases and ancient courtyards. Nothing could be more deceptive, of course. The *Deccan Herald* is one of the livelier papers of the south with an excellent press, questing reporters and a very active devil in the printer's section. Perhaps it is but the ghost of a reveller from the days when the place was a popular restaurant named Funnels, famous for its fish 'n' chips as also the dancing and the drinking.

Nearby down Brigade Road, old age has almost caught up with Wren Bennett and Company, which was split into three. One part now forms the popular somewhat soporific Cauvery Government Arts and Crafts Emporium that is a haven for the imagination of the craftsmen who specialize in inlaid wood and ivory work, as well as the best place to buy the once-famous Mysore Sandal soaps and agarbattis. Next door, Enayeth Brothers and Spinker and Company linger like twin ghosts with their high ceilings supported on iron pillars and see-through glass cupboards. Spinker and Co. was founded in 1896 by Govindarajulu Naidu who, feeling this name might not be the sort that would easily trip off people's tongues, settled for Spinker.

Mr Mekhir, one of the present owners of Enayeth Brothers, which has been subdivided again, remembers the old days when few Indians were allowed to stray into that area. He especially recalls how he had always to be in full business suit attire to attend to his British customers and complains that working in shirtsleeves left him feeling positively naked. At the time when the whole area was connected to a mere 140 telephone lines, Enayeth Brothers had the distinction of being number 128.

Bangalore would not be Bangalore without its cinema halls, then or now. The early theatres were unabashedly named after the taste of the empire builders, the Globe, or Empire. In 1943, the owners thought it prudent to change the Globe into Liberty, and Liberty it remained with its hard wooden seats, torn covers and small fans to deter the mosquitoes, until one morning, or so it seemed, a multi-storeyed building was found to have gobbled it up.

The Plaza came in later with its first show on 30 March 1936. The theatre had a dance floor, which in the days when all Bangalore just had to be at a ball on Christmas Eve or New Year's, was the number one attraction. There was also the Three Musketeers Ball, which again was a must. All such occasions usually ended with a grand turnout of the revellers along South Parade, with a girl on either arm, a bottle inside the shirt, and one at the lips. Not surprisingly, the prescriptions that followed such binges were candid as to their intent—'Henry's curers', 'Sufferer's friends', 'Lampblough's peptic saline', and if all else failed there was the ritual dunking in the Ulsoor Tank, unsullied and inviolate as it was in those days.

The theatre at the Rex, named it is said after one Paul, had a curious feature which apparently fuelled the ardour of the young men who escorted their partners to the movies. It was reputed to have a broad tunnel that passed beneath the seats, with an outlet at each end, through which air could apparently be pumped with bellows to help cool down the customers. With so many skirts flying up, however, it is to be presumed that the effect was just the opposite.

Cubbon Park, which was named after Sir Mark Cubbon, the longest serving Commissioner at Bangalore and laid out by Major General Sankey, R.E., has been lovingly sculpted to give a variety of different experiences. There are bamboo groves with a mournful aspect, formal gardens, bordering wide expanses of curving lawns, carriageways that pass by flowering trees or cross out in the open along broad roads flanked on either side, as far as the eye can see, with rows of bright cannas.

The bandstand, which was a gift of the Maharaja of the time, was a natural gathering place for the 'paterfamilias' to parade his brood on Sunday, particularly in the days when the Model T Ford had made such outings a pleasant adventure. On such occasions, the band with its brass shining and the tassels of the bagpiper flying would play famous English marches and ballads.

On every side, Cubbon Park plays host to some of the oldest and most elegant of the buildings of Bangalore. Most famous amongst these is the long red silhouette of the 640 feet long High Court buildings known as the Attara Kacheri, which the people of Bangalore are trying hard to protect from demolition. Dominating even this imposing structure is the best-known landmark of Bangalore, the Vidhana Soudha, built by Sri Kengal Hanumanthaiah, the chief minister of Karnataka, soon after Independence, in a style that manages to out-empire anything that the British might have dreamt up.

The architecture of Anglo-India, comments Charles Allen in *Plain Tales* again, had a tendency for grandiose structure that mixed the Gothic with the Saracenic, or that strived for an Indiana Jones-in-India look or that used 'Tuscan columns and round Renaissance style arches'. Bangalore is fortunate in having escaped the horrors of the first and preferred to adapt the lofty spaciousness of the other two styles in both its public and private buildings. Around the environs of Cubbon Park may be seen the buildings of the Museum, the Public Library, the Century Club, which was the 'chief social centre in the city', and other government buildings.

Of the older ones, Mayo Hall was built as the office of the British Resident to perpetuate the memory of Lord Mayo (who was assassinated in the Andamans) by public subscription at a cost of Rs 40,301. In 1939 it was made over to the Resident of Mysore on the condition that 'at all proper times the upper storey be made available to the public for meetings of a public nature, free of charge'.

The name of Lewin Bowring has been immortalized in the Bowring Institute, though it is known today for its tennis courts and tournaments. Bowring was one of the most energetic of the commissioners, who made several changes in the field of health and education. It was during his tenure that the Attara Kacheri was built in 1864. But he will perhaps be best remembered for bringing the railway line up to Bangalore from Madras. When Bowring first came to Bangalore, he had a rough journey from Jolarpet, where the train came to a stop, and complained how he had to endure 'severe jolting in a hearse-like transit carriage to reach here'. As a result of this, within two years the railway lines were built up to the Cantonment.

Of the many churches in Bangalore, none is perhaps as satisfying to contemplate than the beautifully preserved St Mark's Cathedral. Fondly called the garrison chapel when it was opened in 1812 for the use of the British troops stationed there, it did not excite much admiration and was described by one source as 'the ugliest ecclesiastical building ever erected'. Almost a hundred years later, the original dome and spire of the church collapsed and two decades later a raging fire completed the rest of the damage. When it was rebuilt, however, the parishioners saw to it that they got the best. Not only was it constructed as a smaller version of St Paul's Cathedral in London, but elaborate carvings, stained glass windows and a marble pulpit and font were specially brought in from England and Italy. The silk bookmarkers embroidered with liturgical colours and the sacred High Altar were executed to go with the Renaissance style that pervades the whole structure.

Since Bangalore started out as a military base, there has been a tendency to lay out further extensions on a strictly chessboard plan. This is a feature that prevails even today and makes each new 'nagar' look exactly like the previous one, except that now the squares have shrunk into minute blocks of cement and concrete. The only exceptions are the old bungalows in the areas favoured by the British and Anglo-Indians in the old days.

The main feature in all these buildings was an imposing gate through which could be glimpsed a wide curving drive and a house, most often painted cream and white, with a portico. Aside from the trees, some of these establishments also had tennis courts, croquet lawns and clock golf. Ferneries were made, sometimes an aviary, and ladies gathered fresh roses every morning from the rose garden. Some of these fine old houses with their thick whitewashed walls and elaborate façades are still maintained with all their old glory.

To pass through the imposing portals of such a home, with its carved chairs with cane bottoms and antimacassars, its old-style armchair in one corner with fold-out leg-rests, its portraits on the walls of hunting dogs and racing horses done in *petit point*, its glass showcases with pieces of porcelain from Limoges and souvenirs of Brighton, is to pass through the barriers of time itself. In such surroundings, Queen Victoria herself would have lowered her marble gaze and nodded. It was after a way of life to which she had given her name, the Victorian age, in which there was, in the words of one writer 'plenty of space—a spacious world'.

(*with Geeta Abraham*)

The Serious Purpose of Life

Winston S. Churchill

THE GREAT triangular plateau of southern India comprises the domains of the Nizam and the Maharaja of Mysore. The tranquillity of these regions, together about the size of France, is assured in the ultimate resort by two British garrisons of two or three thousand troops apiece at Bangalore and Secunderabad. In each case, there is added almost double the number of Indian troops that sufficient forces of all arms are permanently available for every purpose of training and manoeuvre. The British lines or cantonments are in accordance with invariable practice placed five or six miles from the populous cities which they guard; and in the intervening space lie the lines of the Indian regiments. The British troops are housed in large, cool, colonnaded barracks. Here forethought and order have been denied neither time nor space in the laying out of their plans. Splendid roads, endless double avenues of shady trees, abundant supplies of pure water; imposing offices, hospitals and institutions; ample parade grounds and riding schools characterize these centres of the collective life of considerable white communities.

The climate of Bangalore, at more than 3000 feet above sea level, is excellent. Although the sun strikes with torrid power, the nights except in the hottest months are cool and fresh. The roses of Europe in innumerable large pots attain the highest perfection of fragrance and colour. Flowers, flowering shrubs and creepers blossom in glorious profusion. Snipe (and snakes) abound in the marshes; brilliant butterflies dance in the sunshine, and nautch girls by the light of the moon.

No quarters are provided for the officers. They draw instead a lodging allowance which together with their pay and other incidentals

From *My Early Life: The Early Life of the Greatest Englishman*, originally published by Fontana Monarchs, Great Britain (1930).

fills each month with silver rupees a string net bag as big as a prize turnip. All around the Cavalry Mess lies a suburb of roomy one-storeyed bungalows standing in their own walled grounds and gardens. The subaltern receives his bag of silver at the end of each month of duty, canters home with it to his bungalow, throws it to his beaming butler, and then in theory has no further material cares. It was, however, better in a cavalry regiment in those days to supplement the generous rewards of the Queen Empress by an allowance from home three or four times as great. Altogether we received for our services about fourteen shillings a day, with about three pounds a month on which to keep two horses. This, together with 500 pounds a year paid quarterly, was my sole means of support: all the rest had to be borrowed at usurious rates of interest from the all-too-accommodating native bankers. Every officer was warned against these gentlemen. I always found them most agreeable; very fat, very urbane, quite honest and mercilessly rapacious. All you had to do was to sign little bits of paper, and produce a polo pony as if by magic. The smiling financier rose to his feet, covered his face with his hands, replaced his slippers, and trotted off contentedly till that day three months. They only charged *two per cent a month* and made quite a good living out of it, considering they hardly ever had a bad debt.

We three, Reginald Barnes, Hugo Baring and I, pooling all our resources, took a palatial bungalow, all pink and white, with heavy tiled roof and deep verandas sustained by white plaster columns, wreathed in purple bougainvillaea. It stood in a compound or ground of perhaps two acres. We took over from the late occupant about a hundred and fifty splendid standard roses: Marechal Niel, La France, Gloire de Dijon, etc. We built a large tiled barn with mud walls, containing stabling for thirty horses or ponies. Our three butlers formed a triumvirate in which no internal dissensions ever appeared. We paid an equal contribution into the pot; and thus freed of mundane cares, devoted ourselves to the serious purpose of life.

This was expressed in one word—Polo. It was upon this, apart from duty, that all our interest was concentrated. But before you could play polo, you must have ponies. We had formed on the voyage a regimental polo club, which in return for moderate but regular subscriptions from all the officers (polo players and non-polo players alike) offered substantial credit facilities for the procuring of these indispensable allies. A regiment coming from home was never expected to count in the Indian polo world for a couple of years. It took that time to get a proper stud of ponies together. However, the president of our polo club and the senior officers, after prolonged and anxious discussions, determined upon a bold and novel stroke. The Bycullah stables at Bombay form the main emporium through which Arab horses and ponies are imported to India. The Poona Light Horse, a native regiment strongly officered by the British, had in virtue of its permanent station an obvious advantage in the purchase of Arabian ponies. On our way through Poona, we had tried their ponies, and had entered into deeply important negotiations with them. Finally, it was decided that the regimental polo club should purchase the entire polo stud of twenty-five ponies possessed by the Poona Light Horse; so that these ponies should form the nucleus around which we could gather the means of future victory in the Inter-Regimental Tournament. I can hardly describe the sustained intensity of purpose with which we threw ourselves into this audacious and colossal undertaking. Never in the history of Indian polo had a cavalry regiment from southern India won the Inter-Regimental Cup. We knew it would take two or three years of sacrifice, contrivance and effort. But if all other diversions were put aside, we did not believe that success was beyond our compass. To this task then we settled down with complete absorption.

I must not forget to say that there were of course also a great many military duties. Just before dawn, every morning, one was awakened by a dusty figure with a clammy hand adroitly lifting one's chin and applying a gleaming razor to a lathered and defenceless throat. By six o'clock, the regiment was on parade, and we rode to a wide plain and there drilled and manoeuvred for an hour and a half. We then returned to baths at the bungalow and breakfast in the Mess. Then at nine stables and orderly room till about half-past ten; then home to the bungalow before the sun attained its fiercest ray. All the distances in the spread-out cantonment were so great that walking was impossible. We cantered on hacks from one place to another. But the noonday sun asserted his tyrannical authority, and long before eleven all white men were in shelter. We nipped across to luncheon at half-past one in the blistering heat and then returned to sleep till five o'clock. Now the station begins to live again. It is the hour of Polo. It is the hour for which we have been living all day long. I was accustomed in those days to play every chukka I could get into. The whole system was elaborately organized for the garrison during the morning; and a smart little peon collected the names of all the officers together with the number of chukkas they wished to play. These were averaged out so as to secure 'the greatest good of the greatest number'. I very rarely played less than eight and more often ten or twelve.

As the shadows lengthened over the polo ground, we ambled back perspiring and exhausted to hot baths, rest, and at 8.30 dinner, to the strains of the regimental band and the clinking of ice in well-filled glasses. Thereafter those who were not so unlucky as to be caught by the senior officers to play a tiresome game then in vogue called 'Whist', sat smoking in the moonlight till half-past ten or eleven at the latest signalled the 'And so to bed'. Such was 'the long, long Indian day' as I knew it for three years; and not such a bad day either.

Follow My Bangalorey Man

Traditional Nursery Rhyme

Anonymous

This traditional Mother Goose nursery rhyme dates back to the middle of the nineteenth century, when Bangalore Cantonment came into existence. That's when hundreds of young British women sailed out to India to find suitable matches among the uniformed Tommies. These words capture the mindset of these 'English roses' on their single-minded mission. Many of them finally sailed back home on ships that, in popular parlance, were termed the 'returned empties'.

Follow my Bangalorey Man;
Follow my Bangalorey Man;
I'll do all what ever I can
To follow my Bangalorey Man.
We'll borrow a horse, and steal a gig,
And round the world we'll do a jig,
And I'll do all that ever I can
To follow my Bangalorey Man.

A Rose Petal Life

Anita Nair

INSIDE MISS Flanagan's garden, you will find Miss Flanagan's house which holds captive Miss Flanagan's secret self—gutsy, controlled, exquisite. This is no place for trespassers. It is a protected realm, where the bold and the brave know not to tread. Even the family keeps its distance. Like any woman of substance, Miss Flanagan is hard to know. If she does let anyone know her, it is only what she chooses to reveal.

I have heard Miss Flanagan tales ever since I moved to Bangalore six years ago. In photo albums, I have glimpsed some of her fabulous creations. I have even been acquainted myself with the fringes of her world. And have admired from a distance the dignity and deeply ingrained deportment that at ninety allows her to walk with her shoulders held straight, her chest pushed out and her belly sucked in.

Here is a woman who has eaten, drunk and driven through change. Here is a woman who has continued to weave her own little magic with flowers, persevering under punishing physical conditions, declining any offer of balm or respite. Here is a woman who encapsulates within her the spirit of the roaring 1920s. The Flapper, who rejected the lethargy of a suburban debutante, bobbed her hair, put on her choicest hat and a great deal of audacity and went into the battle of life. She refused to be bored, chiefly because she wasn't boring. She was conscious that the things she did were the things she had always wanted to do.

Seeking Miss Flanagan's home was like delving into her mind. It took me the whole of two mornings and some degree of hope to wander through the many streets of Richmond Town looking for a

This essay was originally published in the *Saturday Times, The Times of India*, Bangalore, 1995.

bungalow with a pitched roof, monkey tops, a trellised veranda and a signboard that said 'Verdon Ville'.

Even the gates of Miss Flanagan's home are an indication of the precise and thorough person she is. 'Please do not enter before calling,' it warns. I call once, twice, several times. When there is no response, I take a chance and walk in. A dog gives a cursory bark and then puts its head back on its paws.

There is a brief driveway from the gate to the front door. The garden is overgrown. Ferns and wandering jews. Weeds and grass. Crotons and calendulas, creepers and succulents. A couple of gnarled old trees, a bower on which ivy runs amok, a stone bench and a brilliant blue barrow, all coexist in harmony, even if incongruously.

The driveway, now more a path, curves to lead into a veranda where an ancient weather-beaten table and two faded rattan chairs rest. The elaborate trellis work, painted green, creates a pattern of light and shadow on the floor. I knock on the door cut into the window mesh. It opens and a maid pokes her head out to enquire who I am.

When I am led in, it is as I expected it to be. A parlour with chintz curtains, china ornaments, an occasional table, dry floral arrangements, deep upholstered sofas, a piano, and numerous sepia-toned photographs. Two table lamps throw two pools of light in a room otherwise wreathed in shadow. A room that echoes the *koi hai*, cucumber sandwiches, and glories of the Raj.

She is impeccably dressed, right down to the scalloped-edged handkerchief tucked into her sleeve. A warm, musty smell greets me. The smell of a room where dogs frolic. Suddenly, Miss Flanagan doesn't seem so formidable any more.

We get on fine. I am the friendly inquisitor, who prods her gently and then buffets the intrusion with apology, hoping to perform a painless extraction. When I ask her about her origins, she deflects the question, saying, 'My people were Irish. They came down to India and I was born here in the deep south.'

'Where?' I probe.

'Trichinopoly. But do you have to mention all that?' There is annoyance in the query.

Her gait is measured, her patience is not. Her memory is long, and she meanders through history, remembering. But when it comes to private conversations, her mind is fleet, dexterous and artful, so as to not give anything but the necessary away.

According to legend, she doesn't hand over the bride's bouquet to anyone except the Best Man. And, then, only if he arrives in a car. No motorbikes with coat-tails flapping and the wind winnowing the flowers. Yet another legend claims that Miss Flanagan accepts no orders on the Queen's birthday. Again and again, I discover that the royal family of Britain is the nucleus around which Miss Flanagan spins her cocoon of memorable moments. The sorrow when King Edward abdicated. The joy at the fairy-tale romance of Prince Charles and Lady Diana. The shock at their separation. The horror at changing values. Both in England that is home and in Bangalore that is surrogate home. There is pride in her carelessness.

'The queen writes to me, you know.'

I nod.

She continues, 'I sent her a card on her birthday and she wrote back, saying she remembers the bouquet.'

I piece together a scatty history of the life and times of Miss Flanagan. Of how she and her family came to Bangalore first in 1921 to this bungalow, left to them by relatives. Of working with Krumbiegel, the renowned economist, botanist and landscapist at Lalbagh. Of the years devoted to the Horticultural Society in Bangalore and elsewhere. And, of course of that proud day—21 February 1961—when a bouquet crafted with love and pride by Miss Flanagan was presented to the Queen in front of the Bible House.

Miss Flanagan has a name. Gladys. In and around Verdon Ville is evidence of her talents. Floral arrangements, sketches, photographs. But it is flowers that make Miss Flanagan's heart sing. Summer orchids with the fragrance of summer wine fill her with a strange happiness. They blossom for her in her own garden.

And then, there is the car. A 1927 Chevrolet shipped brand new from London to Bangalore almost eight decades ago. Star of several Raj movies—*A Passage to India, Jewel in the Crown* and even *Gandhi* (Sir Richard Attenborough is said to have sat in it and certified its smooth running) and winner of several vintage rallies, it rests in the garage, on a jack. A faint tinge of sadness colours Miss Flanagan's voice when she says, 'Running the car isn't so easy any more. For one thing, the tyres need to be imported. For which I need to write several letters to the Indian government attaching proof of letters from Indian tyre manufacturers saying that they don't make such tyres to validate my request. And then, when they arrive, I have to pay exorbitant customs duties here. Even the tyres were a gift from the British tyre manufacturers, you see.'

There are people who remember Miss Flanagan in her brand-new Chevrolet. There are people who have seen Miss Flanagan in a classic Chevrolet, head held erect, wearing a hat and a gauzy scarf, driving down a sedate South Parade. And there are people who have glimpsed a lady in a vintage Chevrolet, managing to keep her pace even amidst the burgeoning traffic on M.G. Road. But time, like traffic lights, doesn't stand still, and so Miss Flanagan had to stop driving.

But even time hasn't been able to still the magic of Miss Flanagan's fingers. Real flowers and ferns, silk flowers and satin leaves, pearls and ribbons, accessories for the bride, bridesmaids and flower girls. Horseshoe decorations for the car. Thingummies for the pew, fat little shimmery satin hearts for the rings, dainty little niceties wrapped in tissue paper and stored in neatly labelled cartons.

'Do you see all that?' Teresa, nurse and companion, whispers. 'That's what she does after they've locked the doors and barred the gates in the evening.' I had voiced my curiosity to Teresa. What does she do in the evenings? A television was conspicuous by its absence.

Miss Flanagan is in the veranda, discussing a bouquet with a bride-to-be. The bride's sister had her bouquet made by Miss Flanagan. I gather it is a sort of tradition in the family, even though they are not residents of Bangalore. The bride describes her sari for Miss Flanagan's benefit. Yellow and gold. The bride says she would like lilies of the valley. Miss Flanagan's eyebrows arch a little. Lilies are, after all, funeral flowers. The bride fishes out a copy of *Brides* magazine and points to a flowing arrangement which is a perfect foil for the tall and svelte model in a lacy white wedding gown. The bride is portly and pint-sized. Miss Flanagan tries to dissuade her.

Teresa mumbles, 'If only they would let her choose the flowers and the bouquet style. She knows best.'

I understand Teresa's irritation. After all, it is like taking a copy of

'How to write poetry in twelve different steps' to T.S. Eliot, and asking him to follow it. To compensate for the bride's insensitivity, I ask Miss Flanagan to choose for me a wreath from her accessories collection.

But I take with me more than a wreath of salmon pink roses and grey-green leaves as a keepsake. I take with me a picture of a moment frozen in time. Of a parlour where light plays hide-and-seek and age has collected in plump pouches of darkness. Of Miss Flanagan sitting on her sofa, hands held loosely in her lap, legs crossed at the ankles. The dogs, Dinky and Tommy, lie on the faded carpet at her feet. Teresa is marking some labels. Miss Flanagan's sister Lily sits alongside on another sofa, while her mind wanders through the intricacies of a trip to Canada. Lily is the dreamer.

I wonder as the day fades what Miss Flanagan has scheduled for the evening. Will she talk to her parrot Pittoo, caress her white doves, or throw a handful of grain to the fowl clucking outside? Or maybe she'll write a few letters and make some notes. After all, she chairs so many committees.

Or she might indulge in a little nostalgia. Think of those days of beaus, dances and evening dresses. Tennis matches and strawberry teas. And balmy, bright days when Bangalore was like the Home Counties. Or, maybe she would just go back to her haven and comfort. Her world of flowers. And continue where she left off the previous night when she had retired to bed with a cup of Horlicks.

Oh, Come to Gandhibazar!

S. Diwakar

AROUND THE year 1960, a collection of poems by a new poet was published. The name of this collection was *Manassu Gandhibazaru*. Navya poetry was already at its zenith, but at that point, this collection added its own distinct voice. I, for one, was so thrilled by the very name of the collection that, in the days that followed, I couldn't help but go looking for the poet, K.S. Nissar Ahmed. I met him, spoke to him, and felt blessed. Though I lived in Bangalore at that time, I had never been to Gandhibazar. In the next two years or so, I came to live very close to the locality and it all seems like sheer serendipity.

> The mind, Gandhibazar
> Where hundreds of thoughts surge
> Like a brakeless car . . .

Now, thirty years later, if I still say my memories of Gandhibazar surge like a 'brakeless car', I'm not resorting to exaggeration.

That evening, when Kanakanahalli Gopi made his presence felt on the streets of Gandhibazar, despite the sunshine there was a persistent, light drizzle. In those days, Gopi worked as an assistant to Girish Karnad, who was making a film. We, a group of three or four friends, were ambling towards Gandhibazar circle when Kanakanahalli Gopi spotted this very charming girl, who had strangely gone unnoticed by the rest of us. She was a vegetable seller. Gopi straightaway walked up to her and switching to a typical rural dialect, asked her, 'What *ammo*, how about acting in a film? If you wish to, tell me, I'll get you a chance.' We assumed that such an unexpected question would startle

This essay was originally published in *Naapatteyaada Gramaaphonu* (The gramophone which has disappeared), Akshara Prakashana, Heggodu, 2005.

her as much as it had startled us. 'Ah hahaha . . . you want to find me a chance in the films, do you, oh revered one?' she said in a pseudo-refined tone, dunked in sarcasm. Without more ado, she called out to the woman seated in the opposite row. '*Dyamavvo* . . . is there a broom around you? This man needs to be whacked,' she belted out in her full-bodied, fearless voice. The next instant, I caught myself darting away in panic. My entire body had broken into a sweat. Was I scared by the words she had used? Or did I feel nervous that someone I knew would spot me as part of this foolhardy act? Now, I can't be too definite why I reacted in that manner. But the fact is I didn't venture out in that direction for the next seven to eight days.

The manner in which I was drawn to Gandhibazar is curious. It wasn't too crowded then; one could comfortably walk on the footpath. You were bound to meet at least one known person as you strolled on its streets. Ba. Ki. Na., a dear friend of budding writers, had started his printing press on the road adjoining the Gandhibazar main road. Then, there was the already famous Vidyarthi Bhavan. The very thought of their made-to-perfection dosa is mouth-watering. I'm indeed grateful to this dosa that made it possible for many a relationship to flower. If I got close to people like YNK,[1] the Vidyarthi Bhavan dosa was the facilitator.

At dusk, the Gandhibazar main road filled your being; it wore the charm of a bashful young girl. At one end was the Ramakrishna Ashram; the other end had Tagore Park with B.P. Wadia Road to its rear. On either side of the road were gigantic trees. One evening, as these trees treated us to their green splendour, B.G.L. Swamy[2] sauntered on the streets of Gandhibazar. Just as we had failed to notice the trees that provided shade to us all along, we had failed to notice B.G.L. Swamy, who strolled by in a half-sleeved shirt and shorts, with a cloth bag slung over his shoulder. In and around Gandhibazar, there lived so many personalities who have gone into the pages of history. In the neighbouring Gavipuram lived Masti, in an adjoining street was P.R. Ramaiah, the editor of *Tayinadu* newspaper, and very close to his house lived M.S. Puttanna,[3] among the most important novelists of the Navodaya period. While D.V. Gundappa lived on Nagasandra Road, A.R. Krishna Shastri[4] lived on Surveyor Street, adjacent to the National College, which was well known from pre-Independence times, and not to forget the driving force of the institution, Dr H. Narasimhaiah.[5] If there was the Indian Institute of World Culture started by the Theosophical Society, on par with it was the Gokhale Institute of Public Affairs started by DVG. The entire locality was teeming with artistes like A.N. Subba Rao and musicians such as Anooru Ramakrishna, L. Raja Rao and R.K. Suryanarayana. The individual achievements of all these artistes collectively gave Gandhibazar its cultural importance.

By nature, we as a people are not in the habit of recording our cultural heritage. Therefore, the likes of me, who know this location fairly well, feel anxious about the steady loss of its edifying past. It's no surprise that Gandhibazar, an integral part of my emotional being, now remains in me as a symbol of an era gone by.

In the present, when I think of Gandhibazar, what comes to mind is Masti. Masti used to go to the Basavanagudi Club to play cards every evening. At the stroke of five, come rain or shine, Masti would appear on the streets of Gandhibazar. In summer, he wore a dhoti and a snuff-coloured coat. In winter, he wore trousers and an overcoat that went down to his knees. His cap and umbrella, however, were a constant. As was his childlike laughter. Whenever I think of him what conjures up before my mind's eye is how, when he bumped into children, he would immediately rummage in his pocket for chocolates to stuff into their little hands. Though hundreds of people walked on the road, Masti's presence was always special.

Around 7.15 p.m., he would walk back home. Curiously, even when it wasn't raining, Masti chose to keep his umbrella open and it never failed to surprise us. Once, one of my friends asked him, 'Sir, you don't need an umbrella in this weather, do you?' Pat came his winning answer: 'This is to shield myself from bird droppings. Do I have a choice? I'm no Dharmavyadha.'[6]

This very Masti once gave some twenty or thirty rupees to two old women who sat all curled up in one corner of the stone platform in front of Canara Bank. 'There was a time when these bright women lived well . . . but their own kith and kin robbed them of all their money and drove them out into the streets. Now, even I'm unable to identify their house in this Gandhibazar, which is so familiar to me,' Masti had told us. After that day, for several days, I noticed those old women in the same place. They sat there silently without blinking, gazing in one direction. These women with their unkempt hair and tattered clothes (as the old song goes, 'Deenanathara, dukhitaranyara'), who knows what the Gandhibazar of their perception was?

In the 1970s, the poet Sumatheendra Nadig used to run a bookshop in Gandhibazar. But it is now history. He had just returned from America then and would interact with each and everyone. Even to an acquaintance, he would quickly pull out a poem from his pocket, scribbled on a piece of paper, and read it out. He was unflustered by his thick crop of shining silver hair that refused to stay in place, no matter how hard he tried. It seemed as if the word 'embarrassment' didn't exist for this writer, who spoke in a brash, unrefined manner, even to the elderly. He had shattered all our notions about America and about people who had visited America. So much so, we friends often wondered if he had visited America at all. One of us remarked: 'I don't think he has gone to America. If he had, would he behave in such a manner?'

I say 'we' because we were a collective: short-story writer Gopalakrishna Pai, occasionally Ba. Ki. Na. of the Lipi press, film lyricist M.N. Vyasa Rao, A.N. Prasanna, who was quite famous for his stories and plays, and I. Sometimes, Nadig's friend Lankesh (he hadn't yet started *Lankesh Patrike* then), Nissar Ahmed, and N.S. Lakshminarayana Bhatta would show up, too. Thanks to Nadig, I met not one or two, but hundreds of people. For someone like me, with a deep, abiding passion for literature, terribly frightened of writing, and with an overall touch-me-not attitude, it was in this Gandhibazar that I was able to interact with litterateurs. For the first time, I met writers like Chaduranga, Yashawanta Chittala, Shantinath Desai, M. Shankar, T.G. Raghava, M.S. Prabhakar, who wrote under the pen-name Kamaroopi, and G. Rajshekhar. I became close to some of them.

The coming of poet Gopalakrishna Adiga to Gandhibazar was undoubtedly an 'extraordinary act of destiny'. As if drawn by the notes of an unknown flute, like the opening line of his outstanding poem *Yaava Mohana murali kareyito*, for the next three to three and a half years, he came to see us every day from his home in Jayanagar. This, I must say, is our good fortune, carried forward from our previous births. No sooner would he get off an auto, than Gopalakrishna Pai and I would be ready to receive him. We would walk towards Sanman Café to have coffee. Here, we would be joined by our other friends. Adiga would light a cigarette, offer it to those who smoked among us and, as soon as the coffee arrived, he would set the day's discussion in motion. Who's written what, Indira Gandhi's administration, an analysis of Eliot's poetry, Brezhnev's autocratic ways, the prevailing price of coconut, the static state of this country, where even a matchstick fails to ignite . . . Anything under the sun could become a subject of our discussion. We would talk, talk, and talk.

I was greatly taken by his alert political consciousness and intellectual conviction. Though I was a journalist, it was from Adiga that I learnt the nuances of reading the newspaper. My proximity to him only augmented my desire to expand my world of experience. I realized how important it was to have an interest in every aspect of life, including politics, to nurture the ability to think independently, and to question every single thing. I was privileged enough to read Adiga's writings in their manuscript form. Of them I remember *Moolaka Mahashayaru, Battalarada Gange, Chintamaniyalli Kanda Mukha* and *Shantaveriya Ashanta Santha.* It was here, in this very Gandhibazar, that we suggested that he bring out his complete poems. And I'm convinced that publishing it was a milestone in Kannada literature.

Now, in retrospect, I feel that Gandhibazar, which charmed many eminent literary figures, did play a role in nurturing Navya poetry. Personally, it is because of Gandhibazar that I realize how bad a writer I was. It taught me the modes through which people must be understood and how life had to be envisioned, if one has to be a good writer. The poet D.R. Bendre talks of how 'a chunk of the *Nandana* (paradise) has descended' into his own home in 'Sadhanakeri'. And so, in that sense, Gandhibazar is my Nandana. But now, this Nandana doesn't exist outside of me as a physical space, but resides in my very moral fibre, as a metaphysical space.

Two days ago, I visited my dear Gandhibazar yet again. The sight of this little road distressed me deeply. It has become a casualty to globalization. The competitive consumeristic culture of pizzas and Coca-Cola has destroyed the tranquil, pleasant and cultured veneer of the Gandhibazar of yesteryears. Trees that had managed to survive now looked like 'phantasmal witnesses' of a past. I had to force myself to believe that Masti, Adiga and Lankesh, who added enormous charm to this street, were no longer there. Today's Gandhibazar is like a gloomy book that speaks only about ancient vestiges. Then, it had myriad things, but now has nothing.

Masti, Adiga and Lankesh are writers of three generations. The literature they created became the three main streams of Kannada literature. When we say they are no longer there, it also means that the Gandhibazar in which they wandered around has ceased to exist. Like that famous line, 'Where have those days gone?'

Translated from the Kannada by Deepa Ganesh

Notes

1. YNK, the pen-name of Y.N. Krishna Murthy, a well-known journalist and humorist. He was the editor of the largest-circulated Kannada dailies like *Prajavani* and *Kannada Prabha*. He did much to popularize modern Kannada literature, new theatre and new-wave cinema.
2. B.G.L. Swamy, a renowned botanist, wrote several books on plants and trees. His works read like fiction.
3. M.S. Puttanna was one of the earliest Kannada novelists.
4. D.V. Gundappa, A.R. Krishna Shastry and Masti Venkatesh Iyengar are among the doyens of Kannada literature.
5. H. Narasimhaiah, a Gandhian and an educationist, was the founder of the prestigious National College.
6. Dharmavyadha was an ancient sage whose gaze burnt a bird to ashes when he saw on his own person the droppings of the bird.

Turning Crimson at Premier's

Ramachandra Guha

THERE ARE two surefire ways to distinguish an old Bangalorean from the recent immigrant: where he (or she) buys his (or her) books, and the name by which he (or she) knows a well-loved café on St Mark's Road. Those who have lived long enough in this city always buy their books at Premier's, and they always drink their coffee at Parade's (which they never call 'Koshy's').

Happily for the old Bangalorean, Premier's and Parade's are a cricket pitch's distance away from one another. In between lies Variety News, where one can buy magazines in all the languages of the Eighth Schedule (and then some). The usual drill is to start at the bookshop, proceed to the newsagent, and end in the café, where one places the material newly acquired lovingly on a chair, before ordering a coffee and perhaps a patty to go with it. (The routine used to be more elaborate and more fulfilling in the days when the floor above Parade's was occupied by the British Library.)

I first began to patronize Premier's in the 1970s, at a time when, unbeknownst to me, the lady who is now my wife began to patronize it as well. My first clear memory of the bookshop is of a day in January 1980 when my wife, then my girlfriend, took me there to buy a parting gift. I was off to begin a Ph.D. in Calcutta, and she was due to rejoin her design school in Ahmedabad. At my request, she bought me a copy of Isaiah Berlin's biography of Karl Marx. Somewhere before or after buying the book she gave me a gentle peck on the cheek. By the standards of contemporary Bangalore this was positively genteel. However, by the social norms then prevailing, it was outrageously provocative. Unfortunately, she was caught in the act by the bookshop's owner, who turned a deep shade of red in consequence.

I was back in Premier's on my first holiday from graduate school. It took longer for my girlfriend to return, not because her love of books was any less, but because it took her a while to overcome the embarrassment of that perceived transgression. Even so, we usually went there separately. In any case we had and have different tastes, she reading literary fiction and a little poetry, me going in for history and the harder or more boring stuff. Fortunately, Premier's had plenty to suit us both. In time, our children began going there as well, to develop as keen a sense of ownership as we had.

Among Premier's lesser attractions is that the shop gives decent discounts; 10 per cent to the first-time visitor, 15 per cent to the regular, and a hefty 20 per cent to the true old-timer. Among its greater charms is the charm of the owner himself. His name is T.S. Shanbhag, and he learnt his trade from his uncle, the legendary Mr T.N. Shanbhag of Strand Book Stall, Bombay. Our Shanbhag first set up shop in Bangalore in 1971, opposite the Technological Museum on Kasturba Gandhi Road. A year later he moved to his present location, which is off Church Street in the very heart of the city.

T.S. Shanbhag is of medium height, with a round face. He is clean shaven and does not wear spectacles. For as long as I have known him he has not had a hair on his head. He is a reticent man, who says just enough to let you understand that he knows a great deal. He has a sly wit, infrequently expressed verbally, but doubtless always at work in words thought, if unspoken. As it is, most of what he says is about books, usually to alert you to a new arrival that his experience suggests might be of especial interest to you specifically.

Also among Premier's attractions are the wild eccentricities of its layout. The shop extends over a single room, this 25 feet long and 15 feet wide. In the centre is a mountain of books, seven or eight layers deep, these representing the sediment of knowledge discarded or scorned by Bangaloreans down the years. The last layer of the mound, the only one that is visible, showcases modern classics: Graham Greene, Gabriel García Márquez, P.G. Wodehouse, and the like. One has to walk around the hill to view the other books on display: set in piles against the walls of the shop. As one enters one sees, first of all, the new hardbacks, these carefully chosen: not books on cheese and chicken soup but, rather, works of history and biography that Mr Shanbhag feels will attract the more elevated among his readers.

Then one begins a ritual circumambulation of the mountain. The wall to the left features, as one goes along, first, fiction; then sociology and political science; then history and economics and ecology. Now it is time to walk around the mound, to consult, on the other wall, first, children's books; then books on nature; then works of spirituality and resting appropriately next to them, of science; and last of all, paperbacks on current affairs and military history.

There is a method to this mayhem, but one needs to have years of experience to know it. Still, even if one were to find a book on one's own, without Mr Shanbhag, one cannot easily take it off the shelf; else, dozens of other books will tumble down with it. There are frequent traffic jams as one goes around the hump in the middle. This happens when visitors ignore the shop's unspoken rule, which is that walks of discovery be undertaken clockwise only.

The crowd of customers and the cramped quarters are, however, redeemed by the character of the man in charge. Once, I went to buy some books for a friend in America who wanted to acquaint himself, long distance, with modern India. I ordered Sunil Khilnani's *The Idea of India* and a volume of *Subaltern Studies*. Assessing the train of my thought, Mr Shanbhag then pulled out a breezy book on India by a not-unknown Indian. 'Not that,' I said, 'I am looking for *serious* stuff.' 'Wait a minute,' said Mr Shanbhag, 'we don't want any more fights in *The Hindu*.' Titters of laughter broke out from the men and women in the shop who had caught the put-down, which referred to a bloody polemic which I had then just started in the pages of that newspaper. Now, it was *my* turn to turn crimson at Premier's.

In January 2001, my wife and I threw a party to celebrate thirty years in the life of Bangalore's best-loved bookshop (and bookseller). She had printed a card with a photo of the shop's inner circle, looking even madder than we had imagined it. Those who were invited all intimated that they would attend, but I was very nervous that the chief guest would not show up. The party was scheduled for a Sunday, on which day Mr Shanbhag usually kept his shop open in the mornings. I was there at 9.30, chewing my nails until he arrived. He came at 10, and for the next two hours I hovered around him. At noon he gave in, closed his shop, and drove his car behind mine to our home.

The scientist C.V. Raman liked to say that his greatest discovery was the weather of Bangalore. Fortunately, the day of our Premier party was in keeping with this—a cloudless sky, a gentle breeze blowing, and the green barbet calling in the middle distance. After the bisi bele had been consumed, it was time for the speeches. All, mercifully, were short, and most were witty as well.

The first tribute was offered by Chiranjiv Singh, a Kannada scholar of Sikh extraction, and one of the state's outstanding civil servants. Chiranjiv recalled how he and his venerable senior in the service, Christopher Lynn, built the Secretariat library more or less from the selection at Premier's. Then he added: 'There is one thing that I want to tell you about Mr Shanbhag, which speaks of the kind of man, or businessman, that he is. He has *never* entered a government office.'

Following Chiranjiv was another pillar of Bangalore, Tara Chandavarkar, for long one-half of the city's most reputed architectural firm, for long also a great patron of music, and servant of the suffering and the elderly. 'Those of you present here,' began Mrs Chandavarkar, 'know of Premier's as a bookshop. But I have also known it as a crèche run for charity.' Apparently, in her early days as a professional, she would leave her little children in Mr Shanbhag's shop while she herself went off for a meeting with a client.

Other speakers that day included Narendra Pani and Janaki Nair, who remembered how Mr Shanbhag would allow them, as impecunious students, to take away books and pay when they could. (Now they are established authors, and Premier's proudly displays, and sells, books written by them.) In the end, though, it was the sly old man who had the last word. As the party dispersed he commanded us to wait, disappeared into his car, and returned with a gift for each of us; this, of course, a book.

At the risk of sounding snobbish, I should say that Premier's has the most cultivated tastes of all the bookshops I know in India. It is only here that works of literature and history outnumber (and outsell) books designed to augment your bank balance or cure your soul. When it comes to fiction, Mr Shanbhag stocks not merely the latest Booker winner but the back-list of the author (if he has one). When J.M. Coetzee won that prize, even the pavement seller was selling *Disgrace*, but only in Premier's would one find *The Master of St. Petersburg* as well. Mr Shanbhag keeps more, and better, hardback history than any other Indian shop I know; more, and better, literary fiction; and more, and better, translations.

The quality of his stock is, as I have said, enhanced by the quality of the man himself. One winter I was in and out of Bangalore, one week in town, the next week out of it. Taking a plane back home, I suddenly remembered that I owed Mr Shanbhag five hundred rupees. The next morning I went into the shop to pay it back. Mr Shanbhag denied that I was in the red; to the contrary, he said it was he who owed me the money. In his version he did not have the change for a larger note, which I had said I would collect the next time around. I was certain that the debt ran the other way. We argued back and forth, till ultimately I gave in. I still think I owed him the money. However, my guilt at having done so was substantially exceeded by the embarrassment felt by Mr Shanbhag at the mere possibility that it was he who was the debtor. The entire conversation was conducted to the growing bemusement of the customers present. Which other shopkeeper would refuse an offer of money owed, and claim that it was he who had to settle accounts instead?

Sadly, the Bangalore that T.S. Shanbhag represents appears to be dying. Recently, a journalist rang to ask me to recommend a book that all Bangaloreans should read, 'You know, like all people from Los Angeles must read *The Wrath of Grapes*.' I told her that the novel was actually called *The Grapes of Wrath*, and that it was set in rural California, not LA. She persisted: 'But Mahesh Dattani says when a group of Bangaloreans meet they should read Maya Jayapal's *Bangalore: Portrait of a City*. Next I will ask Anita Nair. *Please* give me your choice.'

We seem to live in an age where more books are sold, but fewer books read, than ever before. Books are bought to gift as presents and adorn drawing room tables, but not, it seems, to read or discuss. To be fair, the journalist's question seemed to display an almost guilty awareness of this. It might even have been the product of a desire to uplift and educate, to promote the idea that Bangaloreans should not merely drink alcohol or write computer software, but also improve their minds. Perhaps she thought: let me get a group of writers to each recommend one book that 'every Bangalorean *must* read' and read collectively, around a table stacked with beer cans. In time they might even come to read books alone, in their rooms.

However, that the question was asked at all shows a depressing lack of familiarity with the most civilized pocket of what was once a very civilized city. So long as T.S. Shanbhag is around, and selling books, residents of Bangalore have no reason not to know of the works of John Steinbeck, and of other great writers past such as Ivan Turgenev and Evelyn Waugh or present such as Milan Kundera and Ian McEwan or home-grown such as R.K. Narayan and Shivarama Karanth.

The Karaga Festival:[1]

A Performative Archive of an

Alternative Urban Ecology

Smriti Srinivas

IN THE new millennium, with a population of about 6.5 million, Bangalore's demographic and spatial growth continues to eat up old villages, water bodies, or agricultural land whether through the construction of high-rise apartments, suburban 'villas', Devanahalli international airport, roads, software companies, call centres, or shopping malls. As new spaces of consumption, production, mobility and residence erase older landmarks, boundaries and places at a fast clip and Bangalore seeks to imitate Singapore, troubling questions arise about the past and future of the city.

Whose city is this new Bangalore? What is the relationship of the thousands of factory labourers, textile workers, informal service providers and the poor to the high-tech, 'Silicon Valley of India'? Can older histories, spaces and practices survive in the new dispensation or will they be inexorably replaced and forgotten? In the past, the city has been the scene of riots and violence arising from issues such as the sharing of Cauvery river water with neighbouring Tamil Nadu or the expansion of Urdu language broadcasts on Doordarshan, raising questions about how these are related to the mapping of, and struggles over, urban space.

The annual Karaga festival (*jatre*) occurring in March or April in the Old City (*pete*) has a great deal to contribute to these questions and issues. The festival is Bangalore's most dramatic event and is said to attract about 200,000 people on the final day alone. Residents of the crowded streets of the City and adjoining neighbourhoods have witnessed or participated in the Karaga festival at one time or the other, while many spectators have come from the suburbs or watched the final day's procession, often attended by politicians and dignitaries, on television. All the ritual players are 'Vahnikula Kshatriyas', commonly known as 'Tigalas', a term used to refer to Tamil speakers whose ancestors migrated to Bangalore in several waves, chiefly from the Arcot districts of Tamil Nadu. Traditionally gardeners by occupation, some of them are now workers in factories or in the informal economy, while others belong to the petty bourgeois social stratum or work as government servants and professionals. The apex of their festival is the incarnation of Draupadi, the polyandrous wife of the five Pandava brothers of the Mahabharata. She manifests herself first in the form of a sacred icon, and second within the body of a male priest from the Vahnikula Kshatriya community, who becomes conjoint with her by carrying this icon.

Many who live in new residential areas and outer suburbs of Bangalore barely know that this vibrant festival occurs annually or that it has been part of Bangalore's history since the early 1800s, if not earlier, when the Dharmaraja temple on the eastern side of the Old City, called Tigalarapet because of its association with the Tigalas, received a large donation of land from the Wodeyar king. Smaller Karaga festivals also take place in other urban neighbourhoods that were erstwhile villages such as Doopanahalli in Indiranagar and in nearby towns such as Hoskote or Devanahalli. The festival, as I discovered during the course of my research, has become more popular as Bangalore has expanded, drawing larger numbers and also spreading to new sites. Its significance is enhanced, however, if we consider its intimate cultural relationship to Bangalore's history and its environmental base.

Kempe Gowda (c. 1510–70), a local warlord, is believed to have founded Bangalore or 'Bengaluru' as a fortified market town in 1537. The location of the town was based on the availability of water through artificial lakes or tanks (*kere*) such as the Kempambudi, the Dharmambudi, and the Sampangi tanks. Outside the city walls were smaller settlements, forests, gardens, shrines and fields, linked to the fort and bazaars through a variety of economic and cultural transactions. By the seventeenth century, Bangalore was part of the expanding kingdom of the Wodeyar kings from Mysore, later falling under the authority of General Hyder Ali (1722–82) and his son, Tipu Sultan (1753–99). Water bodies continued to play an important role: Lalbagh tank on the south side of the city, for example, was associated with a pleasure garden called Lalbagh laid out by Hyder Ali in the second half of the eighteenth century. The British East India Company, however, overran Bangalore in 1799 and reinstalled the Wodeyar kings, who allowed the British to maintain a military cantonment north-east of the Old City. The British continued to excavate small lakes in Bangalore such as the Miller and Sankey tanks. At the turn of the twentieth century, with a population of about 228,000, this industrializing city, girded by hundreds of tanks, was known for its numerous horticultural gardens, the Persian-style Lalbagh, and the nineteenth-century reserve called Cubbon Park. In this way was born the myth of Bangalore as a 'garden city'.

Until India's independence in 1947, most of the state of Karnataka fell under the independent princely state of Mysore, a monarchy that allowed its technocratic bureaucracy considerable freedom to implement modern, industrial planning models and to establish some of India's earliest electrification and communication infrastructures. In 1956, with the linguistic reorganization of the Indian states, Mysore expanded its boundaries and adopted Kannada as its official language, and in the 1960s adopted its current name. One of the most spectacular and well-known features of subsequent economic change was the explosive growth of the state capital, Bangalore, which became the sixth largest Indian city. In 1951, the population of the city was 991,000 while in 1991 it had risen to 4,086,000, with a projected increase to 5,800,000 in 2001.[2] As the site of extensive industrial production in textiles, machinery and electrical equipment, and the home of the state administration and several scientific and engineering institutions, Bangalore was well positioned by the early 1990s to move into software production that gave it the reputation of 'India's Silicon Valley'.

The degradation of Bangalore's environmental base has been one of the most important subtexts of the city's transformation. In 1985, for example, the Government of Karnataka set up the Lakshman Rau Committee, so named after its chairman, to make recommendations with respect to the tanks in the city area.[3] The committee reported that of the 390 tanks within the jurisdiction of the Bangalore Development Authority (BDA), 127 tanks lay within the conurbation limits; of these only 81 tanks were 'live', the others having been breached after Independence due to various 'development' activities. A report published in 1993 by the Centre for Science and Technology, a non-governmental organization in Bangalore, noted that of the 127 tanks under the purview of the Lakshman Rau Committee, three tanks had already been converted by the BDA into residential layouts and a further seven tanks could not be traced. Of the other tanks, eight had completely changed their use and were converted to residential and commercial properties, 18 were undergoing transformation into slums and housing for the poorer strata, some through government schemes, and seven had been leased to various parties, public and private, for the purpose of building housing colonies, bus depots, schools, hospitals and colleges. The BDA had encroached on 27 tank beds for the creation of housing layouts. In addition, 23 tanks were threatened because of mud lifting and brick making; there was solid waste dumping in 25 tanks; domestic waste flows in 56 tanks; and industrial effluents in 14 tanks.[4]

While civic amnesia accompanies the drastic loss of tanks as spatial markers which have disappeared (how many citizens recall any more that the National Games Village constructed in 1997 was the site of a tank?), Bangalore's tank culture is still remembered and evoked in the Karaga festival. For instance, the annual 'birth' of the sacred icon occurs every year on the seventh night of the festival at Upnirinakunte (salt water pond) in Cubbon Park bordering the Kanteerava Stadium. Ritual specialists bring the icon to a small pillared hall adjacent to the Kanteerava sports complex. This icon is surrounded by 'hero-sons' (*Virakumaras*), sword-bearing men of the Vahnikula Kshatriya community, who act as protectors of the Karaga priest. It is unveiled late at night to the gathering of devotees and citizens, who eagerly await the birth of Draupadi's power (*shakti*). Two days later, the procession of the priest with the Karaga on his head under a jasmine headdress leaves the Dharmaraja temple for a tour of the Old City. Apart from stops at various temples, the procession moves through enormous crowds, festive streets and decorated markets to pay a respectful visit to the tomb of the Sufi master Hazrat Tawakkul Mastan Baba.

Today the Upnirinakunte is merely a small covered well, easily ignored by passers-by, and it is indeed hard to remember that the site of the Karaga's unveiling was formerly the large Sampangi tank. Yet every year, the Vahnikula Kshatriyas who have trained to conduct the sacred festivities, return to the locations of several water bodies in Bangalore to perform rituals over nine days. Tragically, none of the central tanks really exist any more: the Dharmambudi tank (where my grandfather used to occasionally swim) is now the central bus stop of the city, the Sampangi tank has disappeared under the sports complex, and the Kempambudi is partially choked by sewage and urban construction.

The Karaga festival is also the occasion for a recitation of the *Karaga Purana* or *Vahni Purana* near a goddess temple known as the Elusuttinakote within the grounds of the Bangalore City Corporation offices. Although barely fifty people are gathered to hear it after the final Karaga procession the night before, the *Karaga Purana*, a mixture of song and prose, is the source of a unique Mahabharata story describing the origin of the Vahnikula Kshatriyas from Draupadi. Some of the characters present in the *Karaga Purana* are common to the Sanskrit epic attributed to Vyasa, but many themes found in it are independent of the classical version, such as the formation of an alliance between the Pandavas and a local ruler, Potha Raja. The central characters of the *Karaga Purana* are Draupadi and Potha Raja, rather than Krishna and the Pandava brothers, although Bhima provides an important bridge between the sections involving Draupadi and those about Potha Raja. The two languages of the *Karaga Purana* are Tamil (for the songs) and Telugu (for the prose). For about three hours or so, the family of the Gante Pujari, ritual officiants of the Elusuttinakote and key players in the Karaga festival, recites a tale that can be summarized as follows:

After losing their kingdom to the Kauravas, the Pandavas go into exile in the forest. In their eleventh year of exile, the gods petition them to fight against two demons, Ambasura and Timirasura. Shiva imprisons Ambasura in a cave but Draupadi saves him and he agrees to follow her in her fight against Timirasura. During the battle, the Virakumaras and other ritual officiants are born from her to help in her fight against the demon. As Draupadi shoots arrows against

Timirasura, his falling blood gives rise to hundreds of other warriors. So Draupadi assumes her cosmic form as the Primal Goddess (*adi shakti*): she lifts one lip to the sky and another to the underworld. She spreads her tongue on the earth and swallows the demon and his warriors! She then resumes her previous form and enjoins the Virakumaras to become gardeners. The scene then shifts to the fort-city of Shivananda Pattana. Shivalinga Raju and Kalyani Devi, rulers of the city, adopt Ambasura, now called Potha Raja. At the age of twelve, Potha Raja begins to rule the kingdom. One day Bhima arrives in the city in search of food and is imprisoned by Potha Raja. Krishna and Arjuna, dressed as nomad women, arrive there to save him; Potha Raja is enamoured by the young girl (Arjuna) and agrees to free Bhima if she satisfies his desire. However, the two trick him and instead a battle ensues between Bhima and Potha Raja. It is finally resolved when a marriage alliance is struck between the Pandavas and Potha Raja: Dharmaraja, the eldest Pandava brother, is married to Potha Raja's sister, Nagalamuddamma, and Potha Raja marries a sister of the Pandavas, Shankavalli, cementing a pattern of sister exchange common to many communities in south India.

There are several interesting aspects of this recitation of which I shall mention two. First, in the context of the city and a diverse audience, the *Karaga Purana* appeals to different sectarian and textual traditions. For example, echoes are struck with Villi's or Pampa's Mahabharata or Telugu oral epics. Draupadi appears like the fierce goddess of the *Devi Mahatmya,* and links are created to both Shaiva and Vaishnava deities. Second, although the *Karaga Purana* mentions Hastinapura and the Pandavas in north India, it quickly moves to a forest and fort-city network that seems south Indian in its scope. It is clear at least that we are provided a vision of interconnections and transactions between the forest and the city.

The Karaga festival in its two aspects—nine days of rituals culminating in a procession through the city and the recitation of the *Karaga Purana*—is an important archive of Bangalore's past and a model for its possible future. It reminds us that communalism and violence are not the only ways in which religion inhabits the city and that ritual exchanges (for instance, between the Sufi and the goddess) or mutuality between different traditions are living practices. It also suggests that the contemporary urban plans for Bangalore need to be seriously critiqued and a more radical rethinking of urban planning—where nature is seen as an integral element of urban space (rather than simply functionally as 'lung-space', as a drinking water source, or a green belt on the city's outskirts)—needs to emerge. The Karaga festival reveals that not only were water bodies a central feature of Bangalore's history, but that they have multiple material and symbolic roles in everyday life and ritual processes of neighbourhood communities. Further, oral epics such as the *Karaga Purana* contain important historical themes, such as the intertwining of cities and forests in South Asia, and testify to the vitality and plurality of narrative and linguistic traditions in the contemporary Indian city.

Notes

1. This material is based on my book, *Landscapes of Urban Memory: The Sacred and the Civic in India's High-Tech City* (Minneapolis, University of Minnesota Press, 2001), published in an Indian edition by Orient Longman (2004).

2. See *Comprehensive Development Plan* (Revised) Bangalore Report, Bangalore: Bangalore Development Authority, 1995.

3. Report of the Expert Committee Constituted by the Government for Submitting Proposals for Preservation, Restoration or Otherwise of the Existing Tanks in the Bangalore Metropolitan Area.

4. See K.V. Narendra, *Lakes of Bangalore: The Current Scenario*, Bangalore: Centre for Science and Technology, 1993.

Gopalaswamy Iyer Hostel

Siddalingaiah

MY MOTHER admitted me to R. Gopalaswamy Iyer Dalit Hostel in Srirampura. She worked as a sweeper at the hostel, and that gave me some courage. I used to feel bad when boys spoke to her roughly. My father, who was poverty personified, visited our hostel once in a while. The hostel was huge, with a 4-acre field in front. Across the road were a government primary school and a police station. At night, we heard weird cries from the police station. The police would be beating up those in custody. Hostel life gave me new experiences. Three hundred students stayed there. Anywhere between ten and thirty slept in a room. Eczema was rampant. Boys applying ointment and warming themselves in the sun was a common sight. The students came from various districts, and spoke different kinds of Kannada. Boys from Kollegala and Mamballi said, 'Baruda, hoguda' for 'Ba, hogu' (come, go), and those from the Malavalli region said, 'Baruja, hoguja'. The moment the four or five of us from Bangalore opened our mouths, foul words came out. Older students played good volleyball. They called themselves the Ambedkar Volleyball Team. Some players even made it to the state team. Many people came to watch them practise. Once, the ball knocked our warden off his chair. He had to be hospitalized. In another part of the field, the Kennedy Kabaddi Team played good kabaddi. They had defeated many rivals.

*

The ghost who woke up students for prayer

ALL STUDENTS had to go for prayers immediately after bathing. The hall could seat three to four hundred. It had a wide platform.

From Siddalingaiah's autobiography, *Ooru Keri*, Sahitya Akademi (2003).

One morning, a boy rushed in, screaming '*Ayyayyo*'. The warden was startled, and said, 'Stop the prayer.' We were mortified. The warden enquired what his problem was. The boy said he hadn't been getting up to have the usual cold water bath and so had missed the prayer. Instead he had continued to sleep in his room. He had been doing this for a long time, and no one had caught him out. That day, someone had said, 'Get up for your prayers.' He had flung aside his blanket, thinking it was the warden, but it wasn't. This man's feet were on the floor, near the mat, but his head was high up, near the roof! The boy had never seen anyone like that. It hadn't taken him long to realize it was a ghost. He had leapt up and rushed, screaming, into the prayer hall. When the warden heard this story, he thrashed the boy and made him sit down. The boy's shivers did not stop. Our prayers continued.

Life in a cupboard

PERHAPS BECAUSE it was enforced, I developed an aversion towards prayer. I longed to sleep on, but was not prepared to lose my meal. I would sneak out just before the warden came on his rounds, and sleep in someone else's bed, covering myself with a blanket. He would write down that student's name, and push him out of the dining hall later in the day, not believing a word of his pleas. Several students went hungry because I overslept. Soon, however, the sight of the warden driving them out began to bother me. I stopped sleeping in other boys' beds. Each room had a cupboard for plates and tumblers. I was lean and short, and sneaked into the cupboard like a monkey as soon as the others left. Friends would lock me in before they left for their prayers. I would sleep inside for hours, breathing with the help of a small opening. My friends came back after the prayers and the drill, opened the lock, and let me out. I slept this way for months. I gave up the practice when the warden got wind of it.

Fighting for food

THE FOOD served at the hostel just wasn't enough. At the end of the meal, the boys would rush, holding their plates, for the leftover *mudde* and *saaru*. The man serving us would hold the vessels high above his head to protect himself. Regardless of how tight and how high he held the vessel, it would turn over and the saaru would spill all over the clamouring boys. It would give their heads, shirts and shorts a special colour. If there was any mudde left, the practice was to serve it to all those sitting in line. This was called 'extra'. Very young boys refused the extra serving. Seniors made friends with such juniors, reserved seats, and invited them to sit by their side. They would tell the juniors not to refuse the 'extra', and to give it to them later. The seniors had much use for juniors. I was so short that I could be called the youngest among the juniors. A huge boy called me to his side very affectionately. He told me to accept the 'extra' and hand it over to him. I turned him down, saying I could eat the extra mudde myself. He was surprised and disheartened.

Non-vegetarian trouble

ON CERTAIN Sundays and holidays, the warden handed us gunny sacks and sent us to City Market. We would stand in front of the shops, and beg for food grains and vegetables. Some shopkeepers gave generously. Others gave rotten vegetables, equally generously. We carried everything and returned to the hostel by evening. When three hundred of us walked by in a procession, traffic was sometimes disturbed, but passers-by usually appreciated our discipline. Once, when we returned to the hostel, we were in for a surprise. A heap of bones lay in the dining hall. Students got angry that someone had eaten non-vegetarian food while we were away trying to get vegetables. Non-vegetarian food had never been served at the hostel. The boys demanded to know who had eaten meat that day. Is it right to do so in a hostel named after R. Gopalaswamy Iyer, the boys screamed. Iyer's name has been insulted, and should be removed from the board, some demanded. They refused to eat unless this was done. The elderly Venkataiah arrived, begged the students' forgiveness, and put an end to the row.

God who got a *dichchi*

I WAS in Room No. 24, 10 feet wide and 50 feet long. Forty students stayed in it. Each of us had a mat and a trunk. We usually sat on the mat, beside the trunk, reading or doing something. One evening, the mat I was sitting on started swelling in the middle. It rose high and

was about to tear. My neighbour was using all his strength to push his
huge trunk against it. I lost my temper, and asked him to stop. He
was older and stronger; he just sniggered and continued to encroach
on my space. I didn't know what to do. The condition of the mat was
worrying me. Boys of Srirampura were known to deliver a *dichchi* before
they fought anyone. Only then would they make contact with their
hands. I had observed a lot of dichchi giving. One grabs the collar of
the opponent, rears up, and rams his nose hard with the forehead.
This is what they call a dichchi. Blood streams down the opponent's
nose. A *dichchi* meant the beginning of a fight in this neighbourhood. I
wondered if I should try a dichchi on this fellow. As soon as I picked
up a quarrel with him, he pounced on me. Being shorter, I leapt up
and gave him a dichchi. He hadn't anticipated one. He had planned
to bash me up. He was not well versed in the dichchi technique.
Blood oozed out of his nose. He was shell-shocked. Instead of hitting
me back, he started dancing about strangely. He ground his teeth,
making a 'nora nora' sound. He started shrieking and making noises
like 'Ha ho'. His body shook wildly. A friend from his town saw what
was happening, and cried out, 'He is possessed!' Many boys gathered
around us. They said he was often possessed back home. Because of
my *dichchi*, the deity had come over him that day. The boys helped him
to sit and begged his forgiveness. They lit incense sticks. He continued
shaking. I stood around in a daze. My friends told me to come back
after a while, and not to worry as they were on my side. I loitered
around and returned to the room after a few hours. The possession
had left him. Many seniors at the hostel were from the possessed
boy's town. They called a student jury to hand out justice. They led
me into the room as an offender. Three friends, my roommates,
followed me. They were Srirampura students, who also happened to
be dichchi experts. They told me not to lose heart and promised to
give anyone who dared to raise a hand against me a taste of their
dichchi skills. The seniors interrogated me. I explained what had
happened to my mat. Was he possessed when he pushed the mat? I
told them he wasn't. Didn't you give him a dichchi when he was
possessed? I said no. They were convinced I had not insulted the
deity. They warned me that my neighbour was holy, and let me go.

Translated from the Kannada by S.R. Ramakrishna

Corners and Other Childhood Spaces

Janaki Nair

ON THE sun-warmed yellowing granite of the steps before the Tract and Book Society, my brother and I played, while Anthony, spread out over several steps, shut his watchful eye. We ran races and jumped between its blistering green wooden doors and those of the Haberdashery Store opposite. On Sundays, the street was ours, a playground into which only the occasional cycle or cycle rickshaw intruded. Car numbers were carefully noted in a little book, and crossed out if they passed twice. The rain tree shed its plentiful jammy fruit, from which hard balls were fashioned.

We had our pick of playgrounds at the meeting of St Mark's Road and Church Street, above which our house was perched. There was Church Street itself, where our father's gleaming Vauxhall car stood, all alone. The big parking lot of Aerflow opposite was more strictly guarded than the lovely wooded grounds of Bowring Institute where we learned to cycle, batted several jammy balls into the undergrowth, hollowed boats from seed pods, and collected 'piss-kois' (the bladders of the spathodea) to squirt at distracted passers-by. Further afield was the splendid tarmac of Cash Bazaar, ideal for the afternoon cycle ride. But on Sundays we claimed St Mark's Road itself, and we knew the afternoons were ending when a chattering crocodile of girls from Bishop Cotton passed by on their weekend walk and Mr Pinto's saxophone pierced the deafening Sunday stillness.

C. Pinto ran the most popular cycle shop, renting cycles for 25p or 50p an hour, depending on your size. Cycles shared space with a piano in the little front room, and sometimes his daughters played tunes that made up for what our untutored ears heard only as noise from the saxophone. We knew him in all his guises, in his workday clothes, fixing a cycle with a cheroot between his lips, in his striped underpants, and in his tuxedo, playing the saxophone for the Bowring Band. He was as alert as we were to our 'petty pilfering of minutes', renting the cycle at 5 minutes to 2 and returning it at 10 past 3. He was easily the most loved of all the shopkeepers at our end of Church Street.

The dark narrow staircase to our house was squeezed between Vittal Rao and Sons, the tailors and the Haberdashery Store. The homoeopathic clinic of Dr Peters, who was a hearty announcement of good health, and immaculate in his suit and bow tie, completed the set of shops below the house. Nothing in Vittal Rao's mild indulgent manner, not even the wickedly large scissors he wielded, betrayed the violent inclinations so proudly claimed on his board: The Late Cutter of Agnes. He was a stark contrast to the owner of Haberdashery Store, Inayethullah Khan. The Haberdashery Store sold everything from thimbles and rick-rack to stockings and cloth. Inayeth Khan ruled its dark interior, obsequious in his dark clothes and brimless hat to the woman looking for stockings, but never hesitating to bring his wooden yard rule down on our sticky fingers if we handled the satin ribbon for too long. Ibrahim and Mohammed Sait who ran the Furniture House next door were far more gracious, allowing us to fidget on the plump sofas, open and shut chests of drawers, hide in cupboards and make faces in the mirrors.

We learned early to watch out for too much friendliness, of the kind offered by 'he of the wandering hands' who worked at the Tract and Book Society. But the attractions of the books at that shop were more than outdone when the British Council Library was started opposite us, a space that was so different from anything we had seen. Deep armchairs and tables were interspersed between shelves groaning under the weight of books. Children were served a wide range of books and magazines. From the pages of *Good Housekeeping*, we chose many a sleek blonde table to replicate out of jungle wood and nails. *Lettice Leaf* and *Eagle* brought English worlds alive long before Archie and Richie Rich took us to America.

But this great treasure trove was not so easily plundered. The rite of passage was the Silent Reading test. After haunting the children's section for several days when it first opened, I was told by the librarian to bring an elder in for a chat. 'Until she learns to Read Silently,' my sister was told, 'she cannot use the library.' I smarted from the humiliation for more than a year, and when I felt bold enough to sneak past the librarian, heart thumping, I don't think he put my face to the memory of loud vowels.

Of the many small pleasures of our block was the race around it, only briefly pausing to twitch the long black curtains of New Empire and be stunned by the sudden looming face of Nargis or Madhubala. We only briefly lingered, propelled past the pretty grey house on the corner, where a beautiful Goan woman lived, and then the ugly row of small shops and restaurants back to our own familiar space.

The way back home passed the family that lived on Church Street, leaning on and playing around their gunny-bagged belongings. Copper-haired children ran about and occasionally begged, but over all the years we spent sharing the street, we never learnt their names. Other passers-by and residents alike we rudely christened, according to what we thought appropriate. Uncle Joe was the man who ran the scooter garage, a dashing young Anglo-Indian. Mother Hen descended from her cycle rickshaw to make her purchases of lace or maybe curtains. But the most intriguing of passers-by was the pair of Parsi women whom we called the Paper Pickers. They passed by at about 8 p.m. each night, scrupulously picking up every scrap of paper as they made their way down a deserted Church Street. We never knew why, but that did not stop our wild speculations. Nor did we hesitate to experiment. Sometimes, we would add to their arduous labours by helpfully scattering more paper. Other times we cleared the short stretch, convinced that they looked dismayed by this deprivation.

People who came and went from Parade Café, as Koshy's was known then, provided some variety from the monotony of the regulars. A woman on a motorcycle came there for her cup of coffee. A few straggling lawyers, a stream of foreigners, and others who photographed the monkeys on our terrace made up a fair clientele. In the racing season, the 'Original Vel Race Book' was pressed on these visitors by young boys. But Koshy's itself was out of bounds to us, and a peek through the windows was the only glimpse of what was forbidden, where who knew what dangers lurked! In all the years we lived opposite we may have stepped in once, for what I distinctly remember as tomato ice cream.

All this changed when we grew up and away from our beloved corner of Church Street and St Mark's Road. Offices sprang up and took the place of houses, drably towering over an increasingly busy street. There was no room for nostalgia, since smart new cement buildings were a good deal better than sagging verandas with monkey tops and broken tiles. The arrival of Premier Bookshop added to the attractions of the new commercial area, and more than amply made up for the dull descent of the British Library into a technologized information source. The taciturn Shanbhag replaced Mr Pinto as the favourite shopkeeper, especially since he gave generous credit, and played the role of postmaster in the time before the invasive mobile phone, transmitting messages between friends, lovers and other argumentative Indians. At the impressionable age of eighteen, it only needed an IIT friend to mention Buckminster Fuller's *Utopia or Oblivion* for it to be bought and prominently propped over coffee at Koshy's. By this time, Koshy's had shed its dark mystique and had become an important traffic junction for Marxists, socialists and aspiring writers and artists. There was nothing but a wonderful elegance to the silver sugar bowls and unhurried coffees. Looking out of the big glass windows of Koshy's became a far more interesting pastime than looking in. We had, after all, become the People Our Parents Had Warned Us About.

A tiny art gallery called Krithika opened across the road from Koshy's, and by the 1980s, introduced us to the work of many Indian artists without the needless distractions of beer-drenched openings. More art, displayed along the tables at K.C. Das, became the backdrop to the sale and consumption of Bengali sweets. Koshy's resisted this trend towards multiple uses of space, and kept away from opening an oxygen bar. It remained a unique space offered equally to the people of the City and the Cantonment, a place of reconciliation in what was once a divided city.

When draught beer replaced coffee as the preferred beverage, what must have been Bangalore's first pub serving Khoday's beer on the tap sprang to life right next to Premier's in 1984. Quarrelsome journalists and writers could afford to drink at a price that matched the Press Club without digging too deep into the purse. Noisy talk rather than deafening music joined the smoke in filling the air. Then they could lurch into the Ginza Restaurant that served Chinese food to evening shift journos. Premier's had acquired a rotating Picador bookshelf, and many thronged the store between drinks and dinner. How many were the grand thoughts and schemes that were hatched, nurtured or savagely critiqued on the corners of Church Street and St Mark's Road, a furlong that teemed with ideas.

As each passing year pressed more shops and restaurants on to that small space, as the Pintos, Gaffoors, Regos, Rosses and Rodrigues moved away, and as the jostling on the streets for parking space replaced thoughts of revolution with unvarnished rage, it looked pretty much as if Buckminster Fuller's *Oblivion* was being realized. Premier's and Koshy's still provided the much needed and increasingly beleagured spaces for meetings and now, deals. The rows of books in Premier's had climbed to three, and Shanbhag had to dig deep, though with unerring accuracy, to find Richard Sennett's *Flesh and Stone*. Many of Shanbhag's early debtors had become authors, anxiously seeking their own books on the front shelf, and if fortunate, were favoured with the small miracle of a purchase before their eyes. For very long, Shanbhag stubbornly resisted the credit systems of the New Economy, preferring to trust his memory over the machine, until he was reluctantly dragged into swiping cards. By this time, it was positively dangerous to enter the store, since even the loud hailing of a friend could bring down a tottering pile of books.

Money spoke, and rather loudly in this small stretch. Designers and event managers were replacing scruffy intellectuals on the corners of the streets, and there was no guarantee that you would find a single familiar person to thump on the back at Premier's. There were still some constants such as the fruit sellers who clung to their trade before the far more fickle fortunes of the Tract and Book Society, where records, then coffee, and finally beer began to be sold. The fruit sellers always fondly remembered my father, two decades after he had died, and always asked the same question: '*Anna yeppide irikirango? Annavaa, thambiyaa?*' (How is your older brother? Is he older or younger to you?) as if, in time, he would achieve the feat of reversing the process of ageing.

I did not grieve for what had once been, only avoided the tedium of finding a space in the traffic to cross the road and walk the crowds.

I did not grieve until one morning in 2000, I saw that the bright shining wealth of the new millennium had not in fact evicted the oldest residents of Church Street. Rigged up on the corner of the pavement diagonally across from Premier's was a makeshift bier, and a few straggling flowers, between the gunny bundles. Copper-haired children played around it, and in the eyes of the thinner, older woman sorting paper, alongside the dead member of that family who was laid out, there was a flicker of recognition. They alone had watched the street change hands, and they alone remained untouched by the promiscuous trafficking in properties. Even the small traffic island at our end of the street, over which my father sometimes drove his Vauxhall, had been 'sponsored' before yielding place to the road divider. If only the money that marked each inch of Church Street had offered this family a better chance: instead, they alone remained like a harsh reminder of the corners of our childhood, and all that success had blinded us to. It was a small and painful jolt to those memories of another time, but I still could not bring myself to find out their names, these people who had shared the street from when we were young, and to whom death came as a welcome eviction.

Majestic: The Place of
Constant Return

Zac O'Yeah

THE OFFICE rains always catch me off guard and so I wade up the *gali* which has turned into a small river, up the slope from the computer paraphernalia bazaar of S.P. Road, with my loot for the day, locally made printer cartridges, a 1GB memory chip, or an audio cable with unusual features, tucked away inside my shirt. I try to feel happy about the fact that as long as it rains I won't need to breathe in the dust of years of bullock poop ground into the asphalt, though I do worry a bit about the glue keeping my soles attached to the bottom of my shoes. If my karma is really bad my shoes (or parts of them) might swim down one of those semi-open drains and clog the municipal sewers, causing unnecessary bother to some of my fellow city dwellers.

Perhaps my lack of precaution stems from the fact that, as a writer, I don't have an office to go to, from which it follows that I have no natural way of timing the arrival of the surprisingly punctual late afternoon monsoon showers that are a daily nuisance for everybody else who leaves office at this particular hour.

In Majestic, the man about town might find refuge on higher ground in a seedy first-floor bar, chomping away on garlicky Gobi Manchurian (and wondering what the Chinese might think of this unauthorized official dish of our cosmopolitan city) or that distinctive red-paint-covered, deep-fried, miscellaneous roadkill called Chicken Kabab, another local contribution to the universe of bad eating habits. Or I might escape into a covered market that defies all laws of copyright and brings to us the best of world cinema, another proof of this city's borderless cosmopolitanism, and with the gutter-water squishing in my boots browse through French Noir and Japanese Horror, side by side with cineastes ranging from leading film critics to general culture vultures like myself.

But on this particular day I run past the august Majestic Talkies, festooned with huge cut-out stars getting soggy under the open skies, climb some nearby steps and find myself in an odd little currency recycling shop. Buying torn bank notes at less than their nominal value, the shopkeeper gets his assistants to paste them together and passes them off to some European tourist or the other in one of those massive wads of hundred rupee notes that they get in exchange for their euros. However, my great discovery was a counter full of ancient coins, so ancient that they could no longer be passed off as legal tender, unless one happens in one of Majestic's backstreets to find a convenient time warp to the founding days of the city, that is to say, to 1537.

Some coins were even more ancient than that: Sangam or Kushan period. All coins, pre- or postcolonial, were up for sale and the shopkeeper turned out to be a leading coin collector (his numismatic hobby being an extension of his job), so he knew pretty well exactly from where each coin came. I bought a Kashmiri coin from circa AD 56 for fifty rupees (no great appreciation of value there) and an equally old Roman coin swept up by a tributary to the Cauvery, not far from Tiruchirappalli, for six hundred rupees (which might suggest a bit of inflation in Italy in the last two millennia). The shopkeeper even had a good explanation as to how the Roman coin had ended up in a south Indian river: it had been sacrificed in the way one might flip a coin into a wishing well. Apparently, if you do this in Fontana di Trevi it guarantees that you'll return to Italy in good health. Some Roman trader, I assume, must have wanted very badly to return to south India. Finally, through this miraculous little shop the coin got a second life, reincarnated as a collector's item.

Now, this was the moment that made me think. In the middle of a modern city, just a couple of blocks from the computer bazaar, I am holding in my hand a human artefact, a tiny coin, which has witnessed, albeit in hazy visions from beneath the mud of a river bed approximately as much history as most of our history books put together.

There it was: that momentous feeling of being in one time and glimpsing or touching, if ever so fleetingly, another era. It is important that we are able to recognize history when we see it, but unfortunately we're often too busy with other things. When I communicate with history, willingly or not, I often find myself in Majestic.

I still recall, in vivid wide-angle Technicolor remembrance, the day I first set foot in this particular corner of the world: how I got off the train and walked across the footbridge wrapped in the blue fumes of the buses in that inverted anthill of a bus station, and breathed the slightly dry and nippy December air of the Deccan. Revisiting Majestic I am sometimes able to relocate the hotel I checked into that day, and sometimes I have no clue where it is. It wasn't obviously the best in town, but exuded a feeling of 'this is your home too', which is fairly unusual for hotels. And at eighty-five rupees a night, well, I wasn't going to complain.

I'd for some time been carrying my life around in a backpack: apart from clothes, I had a couple of books and a typewriter. The road ahead just seemed to get longer, the more I covered of it, so this sudden feeling of being at home came as a pleasant surprise as I sat every morning reading *The Hindu, Deccan Herald*, the (as yet unsplit) *Indian Express*, having my coffee and *vadai*. It felt as if I was heading for home when I walked through Cubbon Park in the evening with books from Premier or Gangarams, or from performances at Ravindra Kalakshetra. It never occurred to me that I should upgrade myself to a fancier hotel in M.G. Road.

How can I explain that sense of belonging I felt in the streets of Majestic, where I had my dinner in restaurants so dimly lit that I could barely read my newly bought books, and which have now either been pulled down (to make way for brightly lit malls) or are still there, more decrepit than ever and smelling as if I forgot to flush the loo fifteen years ago and nobody bothered after me?

Only years later, after I had properly moved to Bangalore, did I find out that Majestic was supposedly a 'bad' area, shunned by better-off travellers, and pretty much *terra incognita* even to many Bangaloreans except those who lived or worked there. After my backpacker days, from 1992 to 1994, which resulted in my first book, I thought I might not see the city again, but the law of karma has its own way of operating and brought me back in 1996 for the Sahitya Akademi's Festival of Letters. The following year I returned as a commissioned writer for a travel magazine and, when I finally left Europe at the turn of the millennium, it so happened that my wife-to-be was a Bangalorean.

Call it chance, call it karma, but ever since then Majestic remains my particular piece of urban nostalgia: the derelict offices of film distributors with their poster-plastered walls; homely migrant-run restaurants where one can try any Indian cuisine from Bengali fish thalis to Kerala appam and ishtew without spending more than thirty rupees; or the Navkarnataka bookshop that arbitrarily gives me a discount (or doesn't); the Photo Guide where I buy all my camera equipment; the luggage expert not far from the railway station who has spare parts, such as extra handles, for any type of suitcase; the bazaars filled with everything from antique gramophone parts to cashew nuts to business card printers to bitter gourd pickles to grey market Sony tape recorders to concrete blenders to rudraksha beads to *burqas* to bathroom tiles to Circo's Coffee, freshly ground at the charmingly named Mahatma Sugar Candy Works, to books that deal with the cultural relationship between India and . . . Bulgaria?

Majestic is a strangely organic area, a high-calorie version of urbanization, the bitter pill of civilization, where every other shop was founded in 1925 or 1948, yet everything appears to be in a constant state of renewal, reconstruction and renovation, and, simultaneously, in decay. Everything is partly demolished and partly rebuilt: some shops have gleaming glass fronts but if one happens to pass behind the same shops one might be forgiven for feeling that one missed the morning's headlines about a low-impact localized war or a meteorite crash. Everything speaks of unvarying flux, a perpetual remaking of the city along lines unknown to any modern theory of town planning. Its roads packed with the residue of an ever-growing world trace the boundaries of cities and forests that have long ceased to exist; they lead not only to a future that came and went, but which is constantly coming and going. Yet it remains an utterly recognizable area: I've been coming here for fifteen years, but might as well have spent a century roaming these ever-changing streets of no fixed identity, which by itself has become their identity.

It is a place for both business and pleasure, the embodiment of the wonderful and the weird, and looking around, which I strongly recommend everybody to do once in a while, you'll find anything you need from branded stores with the real McCoy or, if that's too costly, the McPloy in the next stall; the Jepson cartridge, which Epson warns against, will print almost as well as the expensive original; a pair of Elvi's jeans will fit almost as perfectly as Levi's. Speaking of which, I've even found pants branded as Bofors, presumably for the guy with the biggest self-esteem. Being a migrant from Sweden, I just had to try them on and I must say they were surprisingly tight.

Majestic conforms to the Universal Critical Mass Theory, according to which areas located next to major railway stations develop a certain identity: an arrival and departure point, a gateway clocking passages at a hysterical rhythm, a doormat spelling out the words 'Well' and 'Come' on two separate lines. Crowded with phirang backpackers wearing the beach bum paraphernalia they wore yesterday in Goa, but also, on any given day, thousands of job-seekers entering the city from Andhra Pradesh, Kerala, Tamil Nadu, Tulunad, Malnad, everywhere and anywhere and an equal number being drained away by buses and trains that might take you via Kolhapur or Howrah to the end of the world, it is both a traveller's dream and nightmare.

If we looked at sweet Majestic from the moon, we'd find that it occupies a truly interesting position: it lies immediately north of what used to be the original Bangalore, a walled-in medieval city, still identifiably shaped like a toppled-over boiled egg in a pot of biryani. That commercial extension of Kempe Gowda's mud fort remains majestically pre-eminent among the city's bazaars; if you want to go there you just tell your rickshaw driver: 'Market!' As we are looking at it from the moon, we'll even recognize the winding bazaars of an ancient map—there's Balepet and Chickpet and Doddapet and Halsurpet and even a stretch of old fort wall to the south. Kempe Gowda Road, which cuts straight through, almost certainly represents the moat outside the northern city wall, and is with its endless stream of buses almost as treacherous as a crocodile-filled river.

The Europeans came in the early nineteenth century, setting up their Commissioner's Residency on Residency Road: Majestic lies immediately to the south of their Race Course (Sir Cubbon was fond of horses) and west of Cubbon Park (laid out in 1864, after Sir Cubbon died, but simultaneously with Central Park in New York. With its bandstand and rich flora, it is as pretty as its New World cousin). The great park was undoubtedly meant to serve as a border and quarantine area between the old town and the British Cantonment, where roads named for brigades and infantries tried to create another kind of home away from home—from the point of view of the colonialists, who had just survived the 1857 war and like all Englishmen believed that 'My home is my castle' and 'My lip is very stiff', probably a rational measure.

Between these entities the old market town and the Cantonment area remained a mysterious piece of wasteland, a place of neither here nor there. Fast forwarding to a 1920s map we see that the bus station was a lake, back then when Bangalore was a city of lakes and parks, and nearby was the Central Jail (now demolished), and apart from that nothing else, just a great emptiness. This was what became Majestic, fertilized by its uncertain parentage, an amalgam of the popular and the élite, the kitsch and the profound, the beauty and the beast, the pride and the prejudice, the vadai and the sambar, the bars and the Brahmins, the chaat shops and the chic shops, the temples for devotion and for cinema . . .

Once upon a time, Majestic had the greatest number of cinema halls per square kilometre anywhere in the world, unless I am being led by the nose, as I usually am, but it remains to me a significant clue to this area's nature that Majestic is formally named Gandhinagar after the father of our nation and, yet, we all call it by the name of one particular cinema.

But naturally.

PART IV

COFFEE BREAK 2

City cartoons by Maya Kamath

DON'T WORRY ABOUT CONTAMINATION, MADAM.
THE SEWAGE STAYS ABSOLUTELY PURE.

PART V

CITY SCAN

Meditation on Postal Colony

Anjum Hasan

O POSTAL Colony, where the garbage collection is whimsical
and the electricity supply erratic and the roads smeared with
cow shit and the mustard eternally frying in hot oil. Vacant
plots whose prices run to middle-age lakhs lie hidden under muck
and weeds, and men shrivelled as their vegetables walk the noon
streets begging us to buy their drumsticks, beans, slices of giant
white pumpkins, modest cauliflowers, again, again, again.
For weddings, the choultry whose every marriage party
sounds and smells and looks the same, for wrinkled clothes
the ironing man under his cassia tree halfway down sloping
6th Main, for music somebody's Carnatic tape playing or
the gypsy nadeswaram wallahs splitting quiet mornings into two
halves of pleasure and pain. For amusement, kids dreaming
aloud about the makes of every imagined car they own, for nature,
the jacaranda flowering in February and the sky darkening in May.
(A brief interlude concerning the houses of Postal Colony. The oldest
were built with the savings of men who worked decades in the Post
and Telegraph Department to earn their rewards: gaze at a tree
they'd planted, scrub the veranda at dawn, go looking for Gangiah,
the telephone mechanic, write complaints to the water supply
and sewerage board. The newer ones have cake-icing colours and
cheap architectural frills, or are apartments with monkey grilles around
balconies where washing dries and children do their homework.)
Our neighbours are the nice dinosaur-skinned man who lives
for months in the USA with his children and their children
('It's a baby-sitting arrangement,' he says); a group of nameless
housewives; an infantile boy trapped in the body of a healthy adolescent,
addressing himself in broken howls; Srinivas, retired, member
of a laughing club, grandfather to a devious six year old;
and a very superstitious lawyer who will only take right turns to reach

the main road even if it means turning superfluously again, again,
again.
O Postal Colony: decrepit, friendly, staid. I'd like to believe that
nothing will change in these lanes where grandmothers feed
the placid cows from across their gates each morning, and at night
the kids rev up their motor-bikes, couples discuss land prices
and children are bathed. I'd like to feel peaceful in the way of those
so completely inside the skin of their lives, who ask each other
at all hours of the day: 'Had your lunch?' I sit here looking out,
and a crow might take off from a palm frond or an afternoon rain
could suddenly soak every terrace, wash every cloudy pane.

Through the Mahatma's Eyes

Rajmohan Gandhi

AS FAR as I can see, the Mahatma made his first visit to Bangalore in August 1920—a 'flying visit', as he would describe it later, though made by train. During the few hours he spent in the city on 21 August 1920, he spoke at the Idgah, asking Muslims and Hindus to non-cooperate with the Raj.

Seven years later, a fifty-eight-year-old Gandhi spent almost four months in Nandi Hills, Bangalore, from about the middle of April to the middle of August 1927, recuperating from an illness (contracted in western India) that had left him totally exhausted. Between these 1920 and 1927 visits to Bangalore, Gandhi had led, and after two years suspended, a nationwide defiance of the Empire. Along with tens of thousands, he had spent time in the Raj's prisons.

In the summer of 1927, he was marking time. The Mysore maharaja, Krishna Raja Wodeyar IV, provided spaces for Gandhi and his party, both at Nandi Hills and in Bangalore, but did not meet his guest face to face. The Raj would have disapproved.

But the Maharaja's Dewan, Sir Mirza Ismail, and a former Dewan, Sir M. Visweswaraya, called on Gandhi, as did the Right Honourable V.S. Srinivasa Sastri, who was a bridge between the Raj and Gandhi, and Srinivasa Iyengar, the Congress president for 1926–27.

Letters that Gandhi wrote reveal delight in his Nandi Hills and Bangalore surroundings. But, as we will see towards the end of this piece, this spell in the south also produced a surprise for Gandhi.

To Raihana Tyabji, daughter of the Gujarat jurist Abbas Tyabji, Gandhi wrote (19 July 1927): 'I have not got the poetic language to describe the weather here, but it is really fine at this time of the year in Bangalore.' Raihana's father, older than Gandhi, was both a political colleague and a close friend. He and Gandhi called each other 'BHRRR'. I don't quite know why—perhaps they had first met during a cold morning.

To Abbas Tyabji (21 June 1927) from Kumara Park, Bangalore: 'My dear BHRRR, I am still gathering strength and I am not likely to leave the South for another two months. It must therefore be some time before I shall have the pleasure of hugging you and touching your silvery beard and chatting on all matters important and unimportant. Raihana must be allowed to grow in her own way. With love to you all, Yours sincerely, M.K. Gandhi.'

Bangalore was praised (19 June 1927) to another very close friend, C.F. Andrews, who was in South Africa at the time: 'My dear Charlie, How I wish you were with me in Bangalore. You would have . . . enjoyed the glorious weather here.' To another white friend, the American Richard Gregg, who had recommended a book on vitamins, Gandhi wrote from Nandi Hills (13 May 1927): 'If you had given me the name of the book and the author, I would have tried to procure it in Bangalore which I am sure has very good bookshops.'

Sure of the quality of Bangalore's bookshops in 1927, Gandhi was also aware of the preference the Raj invariably gave to the Cantonment, in comparison with the City. Informing Mira Behn (Madeleine Slade) that 'Coomara Park will very probably be (his Bangalore) address', Gandhi added (29 May 1927): 'You will say Bangalore City because there are two watertight divisions, Cantonment and City, and unless "City" is mentioned, the letters first go to the Cantonment, as they do all over India where there is also a Cantonment.'

At Nandi Hills and in Bangalore, the Mahatma tried out some yoga _asanas_ in addition to continuing breathing exercises. As he wrote from Nandi Hills to Satis Dasgupta, the Bengali inventor who had become a follower (17 May 1927): 'I am taking gentle exercise by way of some of these _asanas_ and am eager to take more as I become stronger.' But astrology was different from _asanas_. To Dr M.S. Kelkar of Poona (as it then was), Gandhi wrote (28 May 1927): 'I respect your partiality for astrology. But I cannot get rid of my scepticism about it.'

He was grateful to 'Drs. Subbarao and Krishnaswami Rao, who have been kindly attending on me' and who had assessed that Gandhi could soon resume touring the country for khadi and against untouchability. To Satis Dasgupta, the Mahatma wrote (31 May 1927) that he was being careful, adding: 'I shall be taking soundings as the tour progresses. What is more, the ever kind and the ever vigilant Nature will give warning betimes of any danger that may be lurking. And then, in spite of all the extraordinary precautions, she will one day send her messenger who like a thief in the night will steal in *some day* and unperceived by anybody administer the dose which will send me to long sleep. Yours, Bapu.'

Also in his thoughts was Hermann Kallenbach, the German Jew whose life in South Africa had been changed through contact with Gandhi and who had placed a 1000-acre farm near Johannesburg at Gandhi's disposal. With Kallenbach, Gandhi was at his frankest:

'I am glad you are having short spells of Andrews's company. I have not come across a humbler or more God-fearing man throughout my varied experience . . . I am at the present moment taking my cure in a little hill in the State of Mysore, where an army of devoted volunteers and many of my closest co-workers are looking after me. Mrs. Gandhi and Devadas are with me . . .

'This loss of strength came in the twinkling of an eye. Latterly I had put such terrific strain upon the brain . . . But God seemed to say, "I shall demolish your pride before you recognise your mad method and show you that you were utterly wrong in rushing as you have been doing, thinking that it was all well because it was 'for a good cause. You fool, you thought that you would work wonders. Have your lesson now and learn whilst there is yet time that God alone is to wonder-work and He uses whom He pleases as His instrument." I am taking the chastisement I hope in due humility' (13 May 1927, from Nandi Hills).

His ability to smile at himself and his predicaments, which at this point included high blood pressure, comes across in a letter to Andrews written from Kumara Park, Bangalore, on 6 June 1927: 'Though I seem to be on the road to recovery, the head still remains silly and becomes refractory under the slightest pressure. However, I pray and grin and bear it.'

To someone called H. Harcourt, who had sent a book, Gandhi wrote an amusing letter from Bangalore (22 June 1927) that summed up his philosophy: 'Having the leisure of a convalescent, I went through the book from end to end . . . I liked your humorous touches especially with reference to *the complainant who the accused said in his evidence had struck the latter's fist with his nose.* I have remembered that joke well because you have unwittingly summed up my own belief. I have certainly run up my nose against many a fist, and have hitherto come out unhurt. I have found in my experience that when instead of putting up your nose for the man with the fist to play with, you try to ward off his play by holding it back, you really get the knock-out blow.'

Though it was a period of rest, inevitably more of the philosophy was also spelt out. In *Young India* (2 June 1927) Gandhi wrote from Nandi Hills: 'The distinguishing characteristic of modern civilisation is an indefinite multiplicity of human wants. The characteristic of ancient civilisation is an imperative restriction upon and a strict regulating of those wants.'

To sisters in his Sabarmati Ashram he wrote (5 June 1927) that handspun yarn was an ornament as well: 'One can put as much art and colour into a yarn bangle as one likes. And I am sure that the innocent pleasure one gets from wearing a thing prepared with careful art by one's own hand can never be had by putting on even a jewel-studded bangle costing thousands of rupees.'

Popularizing khadi went with recuperation. The thousands who came to Gandhi's daily Kumara Park prayer meetings (which became an institution and were remembered for long) were told about the cloth that tied India's better-off to poor spinners and weavers. When they came again to Gandhi's prayer meeting, many wore the new khadi they had bought.

July 1927 saw an elaborate khadi exhibition in Bangalore, organized by two of Gandhi's closest southern colleagues, CR (Chakravarti Rajagopalachari) and Gangadharrao Deshpande of Belgaum. CR had also acted as Gandhi's 'jailor' in Nandi Hills and in Bangalore, regulating visitors and terminating interviews.

At the exhibition, spinners from Karnataka competed before onlookers and received prizes. In remarks at the exhibition on 8 July Gandhi asked the onlookers to compare the spinners, who did 'not know the distinctions between Brahmin and non-Brahmin, Hindus and Mussalmans' and were united by 'the poverty of this land', to competitors better known to the onlookers.

What would you feel, Gandhi asked the élite of Bangalore, if champions in cricket or from the race course were present here amidst you? 'I know how enthusiastic you will feel.' He felt that way now, Gandhi added, among the spinning stars, poor as they were. Saying this, Gandhi broke down.

He spoke also at meetings organized by Dalits in Nandi Hills, Chikballapur and Bangalore, to industrial workers, and at the Indian Institute of Science, where scientists were encouraged to ask themselves if 'all the discoveries you make have the welfare of the poor as the end in view'.

Politics was not wholly forgotten, however. Gandhi took care, while in Bangalore, to sort out the question of the next Congress president. Motilal Nehru wanted Jawaharlal chosen, but Gandhi felt that Jawaharlal's time had not come yet, and that the honour should go to Dr Mukhtar Ahmed Ansari of Delhi, who had never forsaken his faith in Hindu–Muslim partnership.

When K. Srinivasan, editor of *The Hindu*, called on Gandhi, he was told: 'If I am spared, I shall certainly enter again the political arena. It will then be a fight to the finish.'

Visiting Mysore later in July, Gandhi said he was delighted to see the beautiful city of Mysore with its palaces and mansions, its broad and well-kept roads, gardens and parks. But when he considered the other side, the poor in the city and in the villages steeped in misery and pain, his heart was touched. It was not, he added, that he hated palaces and mansions, or gardens and parks.

When he met Mysore's Adi Karnatakas, he said (21 July): 'I am both happy and unhappy to meet you. I am happy because I have had occasion to purify myself by having met you, but I am unhappy that for health and other reasons I have to reconcile myself to staying in palaces, although I know full well the miserable conditions in which you live.'

Kasturba and their fourth (and youngest) son Devadas were in Karnataka with Gandhi, who wrote several letters during this period to his second son Manilal and third son Ramdas, and to Kumi, sister-in-law of his estranged eldest son, Harilal. Kumi was looking after Harilal's children, who had recently lost their mother.

But it was Devadas who came up with a startling idea. The twenty-seven-year-old son said he wished to marry Lakshmi, CR's daughter, who was also in Bangalore.

CR, too, was taken aback. Not because he and his daughter were Brahmins and Devadas a Bania. His objection was that Lakshmi was only fifteen.

This was Gandhi's concern too. Could she really know her mind at that age? Well, she thought she did. Devadas had in fact proposed to her in a park in Bangalore, and she had accepted. But she added that she would not marry until her father approved.

The fathers said that the two young persons would have to prove their love over time. If, without meeting or writing to each other for five years they still wanted to marry, they could.

The two youngsters proved their love. In 1933, a year before Gandhi was again in Bangalore in 1934, they were married, but not before Devadas nearly died in a prison of the Raj, and not before a new wave of defiance, sparked off by the Salt March, had spread across the land.

Gandhi's 1934 visit to Bangalore, a short one, was primarily to fight untouchability. Two years later he came again, and once more spent time at Nandi Hills and in Bangalore—a month in all. Tyabji and Ansari again figured in letters he wrote from Bangalore. But they had both died, and Gandhi was mourning their departure.

The Wholly Raman Empire:

Bangalore's Emergence as a Centre of Science

Shobhana Narasimhan

ON 28 December 2005, a shooting attack at the Indian Institute of Science (IISc) in Bangalore killed one scientist and injured others. Though none of the attackers was ever caught, it is generally presumed that terrorists targeted the institute because of its iconic status as a symbol of the perceived strengths of the new, globalized India—science, industry and high technology. Indeed, science and technology play a significant role in defining the ethos of Bangalore, just as government does for Delhi, or finance and films for Mumbai.

The roots of Bangalore's transformation from genteel cantonment city to Mecca of the hi-tech world can arguably be traced back to 1900, when Sir William Ramsay made a whistle-stop tour of British India. A distinguished Scottish chemist, famous for having discovered the rare gas elements argon, krypton, helium, neon and xenon, Ramsay visited India to advise on where to set up the 'Indian University of Research' that J.N. Tata had suggested be established to help Indians catch up with Western advances in science and technology. Ramsay recommended Bangalore, partly because of its pleasant climate, and partly because of a promised donation of land by the Maharaja of Mysore. Despite the strong lobbying for Roorkee, it was nine years before the Indian Institute of Science was set up on several hundred acres of jungle land at the northern tip of the then-new suburb of Malleswaram in Bangalore. Ramsay's assistant Morris Travers came out to India as the first director of the institute.

However, the institute signally failed to show much evidence of scientific achievement and progress in its early years. Instead, it became known as 'a quiet, sleepy place where little work was done by a number of well-paid people'. It was staffed mostly by mediocre British expatriates, who had been attracted by the high salaries (supplemented by generous overseas allowances) and low professional demands that the institute offered. The little research that was done consisted primarily of applied science, rather than basic science, and the institute did not even possess a department of physics (but it did possess—and still does—gardens laid out in the shape of the Union Jack).

Things began to change in 1933, with C.V. Raman's appointment as the director of the institute. Just forty-five years old, with the discovery of his eponymous effect, a knighthood and a Nobel Prize already under his belt, Raman had seemed the obvious choice to be the first Indian to head the institute. However, the irruption on to the Bangalorean scene of this brilliant, irascible, energetic and arrogant physicist was to create an uproar amongst the urbanely undistinguished colonial types who were then enjoying their peaceful sinecures at the institute. The resulting brouhaha would, ironically, turn the eyes of the international scientific community towards Bangalore for the first time.

Raman's arrival in Bangalore coincided with the rise to power of the Nazis in Germany. Large numbers of talented German Jewish scientists were desperate to flee elsewhere. To Raman, this seemed like the ideal opportunity to attract brilliant minds to Bangalore, and he proposed making job offers to a list of truly outstanding physicists (including Erwin Schrödinger, Max Born, Rudolf Peierls and Paul Peter Ewald), any one of whom the institute ought to have been privileged to get. The proposal wasn't entirely outlandish—at that time, a professor in Bangalore earned a higher salary than one in Cambridge, and 'the land of the Upanishads' held additional appeal for those educated in the Orientalist Romantic German tradition.

In 1935, one German professor, the legendary Max Born, accepted Raman's invitation and came to Bangalore with his wife, intending to stay. It is not clear whether Born's arrival was genuinely resented by the definitely anti-German and probably anti-Semitic Englishmen at the institute, or whether it merely provided a convenient stick with which to beat the abhorred native director, whose sweeping administrative changes already had them seething. Protests against Born's appointment were led by a newly arrived electrical engineering professor called Aston, who, it was rumoured, had been sent out to

Bangalore with the specific mission of getting rid of Raman. Raman attempted to rally support from his connections amongst the British scientific elite (there was a flurry of telegrams between Bangalore and Cambridge) but, at a tumultuous faculty meeting, Aston's argument that the institute did not need 'a second rate foreigner driven out from his own country' carried the day, and Born's job offer was withdrawn. Born left, despondent, for Scotland (two decades later, he would have the last laugh by winning the Nobel Prize for Physics), and Raman resigned as director.

Instead of fleeing the site of his humiliation, Raman stayed on at the institute. He retreated to his laboratory in the newly established physics department, from where—touchy, imperious and driven—he pursued his research, inspired and terrified generations of awed students, fought protracted feuds with scientific rivals, and attempted to shape the course of Indian science. One cannot help speculating wistfully about how this course would have been altered if Raman had been successful in his attempt to lure German scientists to Bangalore. The city could conceivably have, overnight, leapfrogged its way to being the world's pre-eminent centre of physics; after all, the American dominance in physics in the post-war years was largely fuelled and catalysed by the influx of large numbers of German refugee scientists. (Needless to say, after the Born debacle, none of them considered moving to India.) Instead, Bangalore's scientific evolution was to be a slower progress.

Most of Raman's research was in optics and acoustics, the science of light and sound. He is best known for the discovery of the 'Raman effect', where light waves change frequency upon striking a liquid or solid, because of either giving up energy to, or gaining energy from, atomic vibrations in the medium. He was particularly fascinated by the optical properties of minerals and the acoustics of musical instruments. He was an aficionado of south Indian classical music, and reportedly decided to marry his wife after hearing her playing the veena and singing. His acuity of vision and hearing were renowned. It is said that he did not need the aid of scientific instruments such as spectroscopes or sound meters to detect changes in the frequency of light or sound in his experiments, while his keen sight also helped him spot (even from a distance, and out of the corner of his eye) male students chatting to one of the rare female students on campus, whereupon, shocked, he would mutter, 'Scandalous!'

Photographs of Raman show an intense, ascetic face, with dark eyes glowering from beneath his trademark turban. The wife of a foreign scientist described him as being 'black as coal, with a beautiful Scotch accent', while another exclaimed that, in his elegant Nehruvian outfits, he fit her idea of a fairy-tale prince. He was an intriguing mix of the traditional and the iconoclastic, retaining the characteristic *kudumi* or topknot of the south Indian Brahmin (concealed beneath his turban), and remaining a teetotaller and strict vegetarian, despite being 'the most untraditional person you can imagine'. A well-known story has him declaring, while declining an offer of champagne after the Nobel Prize ceremony, 'Sir, you have seen the Raman effect on alcohol, but no one has seen the alcohol effect on Raman!' This appears to have been a favourite joke of his, since many people from many countries report hearing him tell versions of it, including in Bordeaux, where the shocked audience took it to be an aspersion on their local wines.

Despite never having studied in England—a doctor had declared him too frail to withstand the rigours of the British climate—Raman was, in many ways, in the mould of the Victorian gentleman-scientist. He lacked formal training, and his early experiments were performed as hobbies, in his spare time from his job as a civil servant. He had a passion for being a collector: he assembled a famous collection of geological samples, and an even more famous collection of diamonds. These were acquired not as jewellery of course, but for optical experiments, and were sourced from everywhere—from unscrupulous gem merchants to friendly maharajas.

Raman's temper was legendary. One anecdote has it that he was so infuriated when he overheard a comment that a bust of his resembled an administrator at the institute more than him, that he smashed the statue to pieces with the metal ferrule of his walking stick. Bangalore owes at least one scientific academy and one institute to Raman's impatience and ticklish *amour propre*: dissatisfied with attempts to set up a national academy of sciences elsewhere in India, he proceeded to set up his own Indian Academy of Sciences in Bangalore, which flourishes to this day. Similarly, enraged by what he perceived as 'humiliating conditions' attached to Nehru's offer to create an institute for him on his retirement from the Indian Institute of Science, he moved a few blocks down the road and established his own institute, the Raman Research Institute (RRI), thus setting a pioneering example that was to lead to the proliferation of scientific institutes in Bangalore.

A now well-known French physicist recalls visiting the Indian Institute of Science as a young man, and being summoned to take tea with Raman at RRI. Before the meeting, he was carefully primed as to etiquette and protocol. Amongst other things, he was warned to address Raman only as 'Professor'. (There is a story about a visiting American, who, desiring to get on friendly terms with Raman, asked him what his first name was, and received the reply that it was 'Sir'!) The French student was also cautioned against saying anything about his visit to the 'rival' institute, or even mentioning the word 'phonon'. (Phonons are quantized atomic vibrations, which, to physicists today, are practically synonymous with the 'Raman effect', but Raman himself did not believe in their existence, having an alternative and ultimately discredited theory of vibrations.) After quizzing him about his research work (which, alas, was all about phonons), Raman offered the young Frenchman a choice of two treats: 'Would you like to see my collection of awards or my collection of diamonds?' Upon receiving the reply, 'The diamonds, please!' he was rather displeased, but then gruffly conceded, 'In that case, I will show you both collections!'

Today, Raman's collections are carefully preserved at RRI, and can be seen by appointment. There are several rooms full of mineralogical specimens and fossils, reposing in glass cases amidst assiduously typewritten labels and the occasional lizard droppings. The curator proudly announces that not one specimen has been moved from Raman's days, except for the opals, which are occasionally removed to be dipped in water or milk, which is supposed to help preserve them. Raman's diamonds are stashed away in formidable green almirahs that line the walls, but the location of Raman's Nobel Prize medal is now kept secret, to protect it from thieves like those who stole Rabindranath Tagore's Nobel Prize medal from Santiniketan in 2004.

Sadly, Raman's scientific work in his Bangalore years never quite matched the brilliance of his early work, and over the years, he became increasingly marginalized and embittered. While most of the famous scientists who visited Bangalore would, prompted by respect and curiosity, dutifully call on the grand old man in his lair at RRI, Raman was perceived as not having kept up to date with the latest developments and fashions in physics, and the 1960s were to witness the decline, if not fall, of the Raman empire. The movers and shakers of Indian science, who had the ear of the government and helped shape policy, were mostly younger men, more politically savvy and sophisticated than Raman, such as Homi Bhabha and Vikram Sarabhai (both of whom had, incidentally, put in stints at the Indian Institute of Science in their youth as glamorous anglicized playboys).

Arguably, Raman's biggest contribution to the scientific culture of Bangalore was in the shape of his relatives. For a start, he possessed four remarkable physicist nephews. One was the legendary astrophysicist Chandrasekhar, who emigrated to America and won a Nobel Prize. A second nephew, also named Chandrasekhar, was a student of Raman's. He made significant discoveries in the field of liquid crystals, for which he was elected a Fellow of the Royal Society, and he founded the Centre for Liquid Crystal Research in Bangalore. A third nephew, Ramaseshan, also a student of Raman's, went on to become a distinguished X-ray crystallographer, and did one better than his uncle, by successfully completing his tenure as director of the Indian Institute of Science. A fourth nephew and student, Pancharatnam, who is credited with discovering the now-famous 'geometric phases' in physics, was picked by Raman to be his successor, but he chose instead to move to Oxford, where he died young.

If Raman was a daunting uncle to possess, he was an even sterner father. One of his sons, Radhakrishnan, 'could not wait to leave the country to sample the world', and left home as a young man. However, by a curious series of events, despite having little formal training in physics (like his father), he ended up becoming a physicist and, upon Raman's death, succeeded him as director at RRI. There, however, any resemblance between father and son ends. 'Rad', clad usually in T-shirt, jeans and flip-flops, appears to delight in the role of maverick, builds boats and flies planes, insists on informality and, in vivid contrast to his father, refuses to answer to the title of 'Professor'. While Rad and the quartet of nephews are particularly well known, an astonishing number of other distinguished Indian scientists turn out, on closer examination, to be related to Raman. In fact, the Raman family was to so dominate Bangalore scientific circles for several decades, that they came to be referred to, only half tongue in cheek, as the 'first family' of Bangalore.

Raman died in 1970, and was cremated on the lawns of the Raman Research Institute. Today, a spectacular Mexican *prima vera* tree marks the spot. He was the first scientist of truly international stature to set up shop in Bangalore. To this day, despite the much-vaunted subsequent progress of Indian science, he remains India's only genuinely indigenous Nobel Prize winner in science. Unfortunately, Raman did not live to see Bangalore become a byword for India's hi-tech expertise. Nor did he live to hear British Prime Minister Tony Blair lecture to the Royal Society . . . the very same Royal Society that had sent William Ramsay out on his scouting mission to Bangalore a century before, the same Royal Society that Raman was a Fellow of, and indeed the same Royal Society that he later resigned from in a huff over an imagined slight . . .

Laying out his commitment to scientific research, Blair was to tell the Fellows of the Royal Society in 2002: 'The idea of making this speech has been in my mind for some time. The final prompt for it came, curiously enough, when I was in Bangalore in January. I met a group of academics who were also in business . . . they said to me bluntly: Europe has gone soft on science; we are going to leapfrog you and you will miss out . . . They saw us as completely overrun by protestors and pressure groups who used emotion to drive out reason. And they didn't think we had the political will to stand up for proper science.'

Raman, who used to bemoan the Indian tendency to 'cling . . . to the coat-tails of European Civilisation' would probably have derived some grim satisfaction from the irony of the situation: It may have been a long time coming, but the colonized have had their revenge.

In Search of the Star of David

Nemichandra

IT WAS 1995. Passing through Goripalya, a densely populated area where underprivileged Hindu and Muslim people live in close proximity in narrow lanes and bylanes, I noticed a small inscription that read: 'Jewish Burial Ground'. It was next to a Muslim cemetery on Mysore Road.

Curious, I stepped into the cemetery. I found tombs buried deep in the ground, covered by thick grass, bearing inscriptions in Hebrew. Some of them were a hundred years old! I was surprised. I had never heard of a Jewish community in Bangalore. Our city had no synagogue. Even today, there is none. I set out to find out more. It took me almost two years to trace the history of Jews in Bangalore. They were a thriving community under the British, but emigrated after the formation of Israel in 1948.

As a former student of the city's prestigious Indian Institute of Science, I knew that Sir C.V. Raman, the Nobel laureate in physics, had persuaded some Jewish scientists fleeing Hitler's tyranny to come to this institute.

Standing amidst the tombs, a sudden vision passed through my mind. I could see a Jewish scientist fleeing Nazi Germany, arriving in Bangalore with his little daughter Hannah. In that instant, I realized it could be the plot for my novel yet unborn.

My novel *Yad Vashem*, to begin in the 1940s, is about a little Jewish girl growing up in a Hindu family in old Bangalore. Her later search for her lost family would take her through Germany, America and, ultimately, Israel—in the midst of the Israel–Palestine conflict.

Ours is the land of a million gods, worshipped in all forms, celebrated by a million names. How would it impact young Hannah, from a culture and religion which commands: 'Thou shalt not take the name of the Lord thy God in vain, thou shalt not make unto thee a graven image, nor any manner of likeness.'

I had decided that the first half of my novel would be about how Hannah grows up in Bangalore, absorbing the essence of India, even as her past haunts her.

Over the next eight years, I researched my story in depth. By 1997, I had saved up enough to visit Berlin, Munich and the Dachau Nazi labour camp in Germany, which was not an extermination camp. Over 32,000 Jews lost their lives there. In 2001, I made a trip to the Holocaust Museum in Washington DC and the Museum of Tolerance in Los Angeles. Finally, in 2002, I found myself in front of the 'Wailing Wall' at Jerusalem in Israel, where my novel reaches its climax.

On the way to Jerusalem, I had asked our driver about Palestine. His reply was curt, 'Young lady, there is no Palestine, and there never was one.' It stunned me.

Meanwhile, I had also met the Jewish community in Cochin and the Rabbi of the Judah Hyam synagogue at Delhi. It felt like the right time for me to find out about the Jewish history of Bangalore because my novel was to engage with the city's past.

I had to go back to a time when M.G. Road was called South Parade, when Nrupathunga Road was Cenotaph Road. That's when a cenotaph stood in place of the statue of Kempe Gowda that today looms in front of the City Corporation building.

Many of the older generation in Bangalore, in their eighties and nineties, helped me to turn the clock back, to visualize the Bangalore of the 1940s. Various gazettes and old books assisted me, too.

When I was in Israel, I had gone through the telephone directory, noting down popular Jewish names like Rubin, Moses, Benjamin and Solomon. The directory in Bangalore had a long list of Jewish-sounding names. Each day, I'd call ten to fifteen persons with names that sounded Jewish. 'Sorry, we're Christians' was a constant reply I heard. Thus, in time, I met Reverend Jacob Reuben, who shared so much of Jewish history with me, and helped me to understand the Old Testament, which is common to Jews and Christians.

In 2003, I decided to visit the Jewish cemetery on Mysore Road again, after a gap of eight years. I noticed a new tomb there—that of Maurice Moses, who had expired in 2001. I rushed home. Flipping through the pages of the 2001 directory, I searched out his address: Maurice Moses, 19, Cavalry Road. I guessed it would be somewhere in the Cantonment area.

I spent a whole day walking through Cubbon Road, Brigade Road, Infantry Road, Main Guard Road and even M.G. Road. I could find no trace of Cavalry Road. Finally, late in the evening, I was walking down Kamaraj Road, which connects Brigade Road with Commercial Street. I stopped at a traffic signal and asked the policeman, 'Can you tell me where Cavalry Road is?' He smiled and said, 'This is Cavalry Road; it is now called Kamaraj Road'!

I tried to trace house No. 19. As Cavalry Road entered the Commercial Street area, I found that the shops on both sides bore three-digit numbers. I wondered how I would find a two-digit house number here. But just a little further down the road, to the right, stood an old building bearing the number 19. It was no longer a home; it was called Eastern Lodge. I recognized it as a Jewish home, dating back to 1921, from the Star of David at the entrance. The guard at the door told me that the lodge belonged to the Rubin Moses family. After a succession of telephone calls, I was able to trace my steps to Rubin House on Main Guard Road, where I met Deepa Moses. She promised to arrange for me to meet her mother-in-law, Seema Moses.

Meanwhile, many of my friends had joined in my earnest search for Jews in Bangalore. My friend Naveen told me of Sidney Moses, who worked at the Bangalore Turf Club. When I called him on his mobile phone, I found that he was married to Deepa Moses. Finally, I took my first steps into their home, where I came face to face with the grand old lady Seema Moses, who opened the world of Jewish Bangalore to me.

The history of the Rubin Moses family in Bangalore can be traced back almost a century. As I entered Rubin House on Main Guard Road, a short distance from Safina Plaza, I noticed a Mezuzah on the doorstep. A Mezuzah is a small case containing a piece of handwritten parchment, the Shema, a passage from the Bible, which expresses the fundamental tenet of the Jewish faith. The hundred-year-old building was still intact amidst the bustle of commercial complexes, where history crumbles every day to make way for modern malls.

*

FIVE JEWISH families lived in Bangalore in pre-Independence India —those of Rubin Moses, Isaac Cohen, Caduri, Noah and J. Moses. While the family of Rubin Moses has lived in Bangalore for over a century, the other four families migrated to other lands after the Second World War.

Among the many Jewish soldiers and officers who worked in the British Armed Forces during the war was one who served in the Royal Air Force in Bangalore, Ezer Weizmann. Weizmann later shot to fame as the President of Israel from 1993 to 2000!

In the early twentieth century, gold was being mined at Kolar. It was during this gold rush that the Rubin Moses family, originally from Iraq, came to Bangalore from America, where they had lived for a long time. It was after the San Francisco earthquake, remembered as one of the worst natural disasters in the history of the US, that Rubin Moses shifted here. Like thousands of other Jews who have taken root and flourished on alien soil, Rubin became a successful businessman in Bangalore. He married Rahma from Calcutta. His home, the huge Hazelmere House, still stands on Palace Road.

Rubin Moses was farsighted. His family once owned half of Commercial Street, though the property was later divided among their seven children. Only the Rubin Moses and Sons Shoe Shop remained with the Moses family. At the beginning of the twentieth century, the shoe shop was said to have been the largest in Asia!

Rubin built the family home on Cavalry Road in 1921 in the Iraqi Casbah style. The shoes were manufactured in Rubin House on Main Guard Road. Rahma Moses converted a huge hall within into a place for worship, placing a holy Torah from the Cochin synagogue there. The Torah, the holy book of the Jews, consists of five chapters of the Old Testament. Every Friday, the Sabbath night, Rahma Moses hosted an open house, where kosher food was served, and the Torah was read.

As I flipped through the visitors' book at Rubin House, it was like coming across pages from history. Jews from all over India, the US, England and Palestine had visited their home. An entry dated 26 September 1946 bears Weizmann's signature and his address: 4, Melchett Road, Haifa, Palestine. I smiled at the irony of seeing

'Palestine' in the address of Weizmann, who was to be the president of Israel, a country where most Jews deny the existence of Palestine.

The children of Rubin Moses carved out their own futures. In 1956, Margaret and Cathaline went to South Africa, later shifting to Israel. The oldest daughter, Sophie, was a fashion designer. She had a readymade garment shop on South Parade, located where the Barton Centre stands today. Sophie later settled in England. The second son Ezra Moses now lives in Canada. The youngest daughter Rosalind, who studied at the Mysore Medical College, has settled in America. Both the eldest son Aaron and the youngest son Maurice Moses stayed on in Bangalore.

Rubin Moses loved India and Indians. He passed away in Bangalore in 1939. Rahma Moses died in 1959.

The Rubin shoe company was later run by Aaron. It was on a trip to China that he met Seema Levi, a Chinese Jewish girl. Born in 1918 in Hong Kong, she had studied in China at a time when it had a large Jewish population. Seema arrived in Bangalore to marry Aaron at the Mythic Society in January 1941.

Aaron and Seema Moses had four children—three boys and a girl. Two of their other children died young. Tiny graves at the Jewish cemetery bear witness to these tragedies. The eldest son, named after his grandfather Rubin Moses, lives in Los Angeles. The second son is in Canada. But their last son, Sidney Moses, married a Punjabi lady, and remains a Bangalorean.

Aaron Moses died in 1984. The family shoe shop on Commercial Street closed the next year. The popular eatery, Woody's, now stands where the family business once ran.

The house of Moses today celebrates every Jewish festival—including Passover, Hanukkah, Rosh Hosanna, Yom Kippur and Purim—in addition to Hindu festivals and Christmas.

In 1997, when Israeli President Ezer Weizmann was in India, he visited Seema Moses in Bangalore. In her company, he recalled his happy days in the city.

To this day, the cemetery on Mysore Road tells the long-forgotten Jewish story of Bangalore. Three generations of the Moses family have been laid to rest there, in a space cared for by a local Muslim family.

But how was the cemetery created on Mysore Road? A century ago, Subedar Nowgaowkar, a Bene Israeli Jew, worked as an engineer with the Mysore maharaja. Pleased with his efficiency, a royal decree allotted him the plot adjacent to the Muslim burial ground, earmarking it for a Jewish cemetery.

An unusual grave at this cemetery is that of a Russian Jewish lady. Isaco, the wife of a travelling Russian circus owner, who happened to pass away in Bangalore before Indian Independence. Her funeral was led by white horses from the circus.

According to my investigations, Rubin Moses and his family were the only ones to live in Bangalore for almost a century. In 2001, Joshua M. Benjamin, an elderly Jewish writer, came to settle in Bangalore from Bombay. In 1947, he lived in Delhi for a few years. Joshua is the author of an intriguing book, titled *The Mystery of Israel's Ten Lost Tribes and the Legend of Jesus in India*.

By 2007, with the establishment of a large number of foreign companies in Bangalore, many Israeli citizens today work here. Our city also attracts a large number of Jewish tourists who visit India.

Against this backdrop, Hazelmere House on Palace Road, Eastern Lodge on Cavalry Road, and Rubin House on Main Guard Road still stand testimony to the Jewish heritage of Bangalore amidst the rapidly changing cityscape.

Notes from Another India

Jeremy Seabrook

A British journalist shares his impressions of a lesser-known face of the metropolis in the early 1990s.

❦

'YOU'LL LOVE Bangalore,' people said, often adding, 'it isn't like India at all.' Now there's a dubious recommendation, if ever there was one.

I didn't love Bangalore, especially in the beginning. As I came in from Hyderabad, the whole of central Karnataka seemed to be swimming in milk: the remains of a fierce winter cyclone that had struck Tamil Nadu had spread westwards and flooded the fields with a rose-coloured liquid that spilled over the boundaries of rivers and tanks. The sky was grey and swollen, the streets chilly and humid.

Bangalore looked pretentious, Westernized, with too many pubs and discos, full of cynical, knowing youngsters wearing the livery of nowhere, the uniform of transnationalia. Perhaps being ill with a high fever had something to do with my perceptions.

*

From Slum to Community

BANGALORE NOW has a population of about 4 million, and is one of India's fastest growing cities. About one-fifth of the people live in slums, and these comprise the largest element of the urban poor. Because of its reputation as a 'garden city', the corporation has had frequent bouts of 'beautification' which, in most cases, means

From *Notes from Another India*, Pluto Press, London, 1995.

demolishing the homes of the poor and exiling them to remote places beyond the city boundaries.

Ruth Manorama started work with slum women in 1979, and the organization Women's Voice has over 15,000 members now. In May 1993, almost 100,000 urban poor gathered for a rally in Cubbon Park. Over the years, Women's Voice has petitioned the high court and Supreme Court for stay orders against demolitions; and indeed, the Slum Clearance Office has now adopted a policy of providing amenities for the poor rather than evicting them from their homes.

Lakshmipuram was a slum on marshy ground opposite the Muslim and Christian burial ground on Ulsoor Road, originally an uninviting place where people squatted in the 1950s and 1960s on what was then worthless land on the periphery of the city. There were 127 families in the slum, a population of 600 or 700.

'Why did the people come here?' says Ruth Manorama. 'The truth is that all urban poor were once rural poor. They have fled drought, flood, deforestation, debt, development.'

The people of Lakshmipuram had been in the city for thirty years when, around 1980, the city authorities discovered that the land they were occupying was valuable. The slum dwellers had raised its value by reclaiming it from the marshes; their work and tenacity had transformed it into a desirable piece of real estate, the more so since the city had expanded, and what once appeared a distant settlement was increasingly part of the central area. There was a plan to turn it into a commercial area, and to banish the occupants to a site some 30 km away.

At that time the slum had no facilities, only one water tap. During the monsoon the huts were flooded, and all the vessels and belongings would float away on the water. The houses were *kachcha*, of rags, polythene, bamboo and palm leaves. 'We had a meeting of the people to decide their priorities for development,' says Mrs Swarnamohan, who has worked in the community for fourteen years. 'The poor have every right to stay in the city; the rich depend upon the services they provide. The women and the youth approached the Bangalore City Corporation to ask them to provide street lighting and paving for the road.'

'At that time,' says Glory, health worker for Women's Voice, 'infant mortality was very high. If a child had measles, for instance, the people thought that the disease was a god who was visiting them. Their way of making the measles go away was to neglect the child, not to feed it, to let the house get dirty. By doing this, they thought the god would cease to be drawn to the child, and would go away. The measles had come because of the love of the god for the child. That way, many children died from what appeared to be neglect; although there was an inner logic to the people's reaction.'

The slum was insanitary, unhealthy; its symbolic situation between the burial grounds showed how short was the journey from life to death. Most of the families are from Scheduled Castes; there are nine Christian families. The people's attempts at self-improvement were cut short when the corporation announced in 1984 that the community was to be relocated in specially built Bangalore City Corporation tenements outside the city.

Madhavi, a domestic worker, says, 'They were dumping us here. We could not leave this place, because our work was here, as domestic labour, construction workers, coolies, labourers, vegetable vendors.' In fact, 75 per cent of the women were working as domestic labour; it was, therefore, the women who led the resistance to relocation to a site where there were no opportunities for work.

According to Mrs Swarnamohan, 127 families were staying on a long triangular-shaped site, only 1.08 acres. The community had become strong over time, and wanted to remain together. If new housing was to be provided, they wanted to remain in the same place, close to the source of their livelihood. The corporation said it was impossible to accommodate so many people in pucca housing, concrete and tiles, in so congested a space.

Mrs Swarnamohan says, 'We approached the Ahmedabad Study Action Group to help us draw up plans that would keep everyone together. A number of plans were put forward, and the people chose the one they thought best. This was then submitted to the corporation. The design was such that there would be a number of tenement dwellings facing the main road, 20 feet by 20 feet, while the row of houses alongside, and in the narrow streets behind, would be 10 by

15 feet, with a small upper room, 9 feet by 6, and a terrace fronting the road.'

The Bangalore City Corporation agreed to provide the materials for construction, while the people—most of the men were in the building industry—would supply the labour. The venture was to be financed by the Housing Development Finance Corporation (HDFC). 'But HDFC had very strict rules. They demand minimum standards for width of roads and so on. That was impossible, given the size of our site. Their norm is 30 feet for main roads, and 5 feet for side roads. We had to reduce these to 12 and 9 feet respectively. At the apex of the triangle, the road narrows to a mere 3 feet. The estimated cost of the housing was Rs 16.13 lakh, about $50,000, for 127 houses (about $400 per house),' says Mrs Swarnamohan.

The people knew they would have to live elsewhere during the period of construction. The corporation refused to provide temporary accommodation: if they had done that, the site they gave would have become a permanent slum, with others coming to occupy it once the present inhabitants had moved into their new accommodation.

Mrs Swarnamohan says, 'They told us to occupy corporation land. There was some vacant space in the burial ground. We agreed to move there. But the residents of the area objected: they said the slum dwellers would disturb the bodies of the dead. If the people moved there, they threatened to attack the slum with kerosene and fire.'

'So we had to make our own arrangements. Some domestic workers would be able to stay in the compound where their employers lived. Others could go back to their native place. Half the site would be evacuated, and then, when that was finished, the other half would be evacuated,' she adds.

The people did as they had agreed. The houses were not demolished by municipal workers in a tangle of wood and metal, but were dismantled with dignity by the owners themselves, and the materials stored for when the new houses were completed.

Work began in 1988, a new form of community building. The construction workers here had also been unionized, and had done away with contractors, the exploitative *thekedars* and middlemen. They were used to negotiating directly with builders for contracts. Carpenters, masons, labourers, formed themselves into the Lakshmipuram Housing Construction Association, and operated for the first time as contractor to the corporation. The material was duly supplied, and the workers completed the first thirty-eight houses within the space of a few weeks, as high as the roof level.

It seemed too good to be true. Then work had to stop: the status quo on the site had to be maintained. A private person, falsely claiming the land was his, had filed a stay order.

Worked stopped. It was hard for the people, because they were all scattered. They had to stand by and watch while the rain damaged the half-finished structures. Women's Voice approached an advocate: the dispute was, technically, between the corporation and a private individual. But the people did not trust the corporation to fight with any particular vigour on their behalf. For one and a half years the lawyer fought for the people. Some women from Lakshmipuram went into the courtroom every single day. The decision came in their favour early in 1991.

Work began again. On the same day, another legal stay order came, from the same person. This time, he was challenging the notification of the slum, a legal technicality. Once again, work had to be stopped. This time, it lasted two years. 'We became very frustrated. We began to think we would never see our houses built. It looked as though the powerful had everything in their favour. All we had was our solidarity. We stuck together,' says Mrs Swarnamohan.

The case was again found in favour of the people. Work began in earnest once more, after a gap of three and a half years. It was finished very quickly. By the summer of 1993, the houses were ready for occupation.

The site had been transformed. Because they knew they were building for their own community, the work was carried out with great care and attention to detail. The row of houses on the long edge of the triangle fronting the main road looked like a street from industrial Britain in the early nineteenth century, except that it was better paved and drained. Each house had a small bathroom and toilet, and a front room opening on to the street.

Because the houses were of restricted size, many people sit on the doorstep to do their work. The atmosphere is convivial, open. Some women are sorting rice, picking out the bad grains and small stones; others are chopping vegetables. One man is stitching garments with a sewing machine on the threshold. Everywhere children are playing, with marbles, old cycle tyres, pieces of wood transformed in imagination into the chariot of Rama or a jet engine.

Kanakamma, a woman in a grey sari, with a silver stud in her nose, is a herbal medicine healer. She is removing the leaves from small twigs which, boiled, will serve as a cure for a neighbour's rheumatism. A creeper grows from a terracotta pot and climbs the wall of her house. This is good for both blood pressure and diarrhoea, she says. She will not tell the name of her plants, because she fears they will lose their potency. Kanakamma learned all she knows from her mother. Her family came to Bangalore from a small town about 100 km away, where a gold mine had been closed. Both her father and her husband worked there.

Madhavi is nursing her grandchild. She is a strong woman, a powerful figure who has been instrumental in keeping the community together during the period when it was scattered. She says it is tempting now for poor people to sell their property, to turn it into quick money to pay off debts, or to finance marriages or festivals. 'This must not happen. The community has to stay together. We have been through so many hardships, we cannot fall apart now,' she says.

Madhavi herself had five children; but her daughter will only have two, three at most. 'It is like this. Now people feel that their children will live, they do not need such big families. When our children died, we had to have some who could replace them, or who would take care of us when we are old, who could work for us when we become infirm,' she says.

Some of the houses have been decorated with bright colours, with patterns on the walls. There is a tulsi plant in a pot in front of some doors; a few chickens scratch among the roots. Most of the houses are colour-washed, yellow, blue, pale green. Clothes hang over the upper-storey balconies, drying in the mild winter sun. Some people are cooking outside the houses. Each house has a concrete window frame forming diamond or lozenge patterns. There are strings of seashells at some doors, over others, a thread of chillies and a green lime to ward off the evil eye. Vendors walk with difficulty through the narrow thoroughfares, some with carts and cycles—a scrap metal man with some Palmolein and vanaspati cans tied to his cycle, and a perilous roll of rusty barbed wire; a vendor of beans at Rs 6 a kilo, a seller of brushes with plumes of blonde grass tied around a bamboo handle.

The problems of the community have not all been solved; but the issue of security has. There is much youth unemployment. Illiteracy is still high. The economic straitjacket still remains. The corporation subsequently tripled the estimated cost of the housing. People had agreed to pay for the material at the rate of Rs 105 a month. The corporation has yet to fix the final rate. There will certainly be resistance to any rise in the original assessment. There is to be an official civic opening of the houses. Water has yet to come, but every house now has electricity.

'We have been building the people as well as houses,' says Mrs Swarnamohan. 'Women used to think this is fate, whatever happened to them. Now they know things can be changed. And once you have a victory like this, it is wonderfully empowering. We have achieved a far greater equality between men and women than ever existed before. One young woman, not far from here, was kidnapped, raped and murdered. The police came here, pulling in all our youths, beating them and asking them who the culprit was. Of course they didn't know; they were not involved. We wanted the culprit to be punished as much as anyone, but we don't want our youth abused. We sat on a dharna in front of the Police Commissioner's office, demanding that all police station committees should have women members, bold women, women who know their rights.'

In the pre-school class in the slum, there are now thirty-five children. Here, the women know through direct experience that when child mortality is high, families will have more children: what gives people the confidence to reduce the size of their family is the first glimmering of social security.

Self-help, self-reliance, self-restraint—this is the vision of India coming from the slums. Whether those obsessed with Western mirages of expansion, wealth and endless growth will have the wit to make use of the vast wisdom, the reservoir of human resources at hand in every such settlement in India, remains to be seen.

Do the Needful

Mahesh Dattani

This radio play was first broadcast on 14 August 1997, by BBC Radio Four.

🙏

Interior. Taxi.

Alpesh (*thought*). Bangalore. Quite charming. You can always tell a city by the number of good-looking cops on the road.

Pause.

Chandrakant Patel. It has changed so much. Look! That is the Vidhana Soudha. It was built by a Gowda.
Kusumben Patel. Why are you telling me that?
Chandrakant Patel. Arre, I said it just like that only. Since we are meeting a Gowda family . . .
Kusumben Patel. Will they give this Vidhana Sabha as dowry?
Chandrakant Patel. Are you mad?
Kusumben Patel. It doesn't belong to them, no?
Chandrakant Patel. No, but . . .
Kusumben Patel. Then don't talk.
Alpesh (*thought*). I must admit I was uneasy about the whole thing. I had no reason to be. It was just another mad window shopping spree. They couldn't at all be agreeable to the . . . venture. Somebody would say no, so it didn't have to be me. Yet . . .

'Do the Needful' was originally published in *Collected Plays*, Penguin Books India (2000).

The driver honks. An auto-rickshaw whizzes past. Car drives in and stops. Three car doors opening and shutting over the conversation.

Exterior. The Gowdas' portico.

Devraj Gowda. Hello. Good afternoon.
Prema Gowda *(overlap)*. Hello!
Alpesh. Hello.
Devraj Gowda. I hope the driver didn't have any difficulty in finding the place.
Chandrakant Patel. No. No. He followed your . . .
Devraj Gowda *(overlap)*. I am Devraj Gowda.
Chandrakant Patel . . . instructions very . . . Pleased to meet you. I am Chandrakant Patel.
Devraj Gowda/Chandrakant Patel *(together)*. This is my wife . . .
Devraj Gowda. Prema Gowda.
Prema Gowda. Hello!
Chandrakant Patel *(overlap)*. Kusumben Patel.
Prema Gowda. Come inside.
Chandrakant Patel *(overlap)*. My son . . . My son, Alpesh.
Alpesh. Hello.
Prema Gowda. Oh, do come in.
Chandrakant Patel. What a nice house!
Prema Gowda. Just a few years old.

Pause.

Chandrakant Patel. The rose garden is beautiful. No, Kusum?
Kusumben Patel. Yes. Very nice.
Devraj Gowda. Are you fond of gardening?
Chandrakant Patel. In Bombay? What is the point of being fond of gardening?
Kusumben Patel. Is it marble or marble finish?

Pause.

Prema Gowda. Please do come in.

Devraj Gowda. Yes, come into our humble abode.
Chandrakant Patel. Come, Alpesh.
Kusumben Patel. Hmmm. Teak wood?
Prema Gowda. I hope you had a pleasant flight. Yes, it is teak.
Chandrakant Patel (*overlap*). Yes. Yes. It was all fine.
Kusumben Patel. I don't like aeroplane.
Alpesh (*thought, while they move from exterior to interior*). Trilok, my face hurt from smiling . . . That woman looked liked she was sneering.

Interior.

Prema Gowda. Do sit down.

Pause.

Chandrakant Patel. Nice house.

Pause.

Devraj Gowda. Yes. It's just a couple . . .
Chandrakant Patel (*overlap*). Look, Kusum, a Krishna painting.
Kusumben Patel. Hmmm. South Indian style.
Prema Gowda. Yes, it's . . .
Kusumben Patel. My friend Manjulaben's daughter does this type of painting, very fine girl.

Pause.

Prema Gowda. It's an original Thanjavur . . .
Kusumben Patel. How much?
Prema Gowda. How much what? Oh, that . . . Let's see.
Devraj Gowda. It's insured for sixty thousand.
Chandrakant Patel. That much. Worth it. It is worth that much.
Alpesh. Maybe more.
Prema Gowda. Alpesh is right.
Devraj Gowda. What have you studied, Alkesh?
Prema Gowda/Chandrakant Patel (*together*). Alpesh.

Devraj Gowda *(a little loudly)*. Alpesh. Sorry.
Alpesh. Er . . . well. *(thought)* Here's where I scored *(clears his throat)*. Er . . . I haven't done much. You see . . . I dropped out of college.
Chandrakant Patel. He wanted to start an industry. After all, what is there in a B.Com. degree? Today, he is earning very well. He is the sole supporter of the family.
Prema Gowda. And which school did you go to?
Alpesh. Jamnabai Narsibai *(thought)*. Bingo!
Chandrakant Patel. It's a good school.
Prema Gowda. Yes, I am sure . . .
Devraj Gowda *(overlap)*. I have heard of it . . .
Kusumben Patel *(cutting both of them)*. All the film stars' children go to that school.

Pause.

Prema Gowda. I'm sure it is a good school. In spite of the film stars' children.
Kusumben Patel. Where is Lata?
Prema Gowda. She should be out any minute. She is in the kitchen.
Kusumben Patel. Oh. Helping your cook.
Prema Gowda. We don't have a cook.
Devraj Gowda. We have one on the farm. He looks after the farm, too.
Chandrakant Patel. How far is your farm?
Devraj Gowda. Hardly fifty kilometres. In fact, we were thinking about . . .
Prema Gowda. Would you like some tea now? It should be ready.
Chandrakant Patel *(laughs)*. We were ready to have some nice filtered south Indian coffee.
Prema Gowda. We usually have tea. Besides, I thought, since you are Gujarati . . .
Chandrakant Patel. Hanh. You were saying . . .
Devraj Gowda. Something about . . . Ah, yes. The farm.
Prema Gowda. Lata!
Devraj Gowda. Oh yes. We were thinking about . . .

Prema Gowda. Lata could easily make coffee for you.

Chandrakant Patel. No, no. Tea is fine.

Alpesh. Yes, yes. Tea is fine.

Prema Gowda. Since you have come all the way to the south, I feel we should . . . I know what. Why don't you play some Carnatic music for our guests?

Devraj Gowda. Do you like Carnatic music?

Alpesh. Do you have L. Subramaniam?

Chandrakant Patel (*chuckles*). Alpesh really knows a lot . . .

Devraj Gowda. L. Subramaniam? He is not really . . .

Alpesh. I like Carnatic–Western fusion.

Prema Gowda. Why don't you play M.S. Subbalakshmi? Meera bhajans! North-south fusion. That will be cute.

Pause.

Alpesh (*enthusiastically*). Yes!

Prema Gowda. Good. That's settled. Dev, do the needful. Excuse me.

We follow Prema. Prema sighs. Fade out voices.

*

Interior/Exterior. Car moving on highway.

A coconut vendor. Silence for a while.

Devraj Gowda. See that—all of that has been acquired by the government for the international airport.

Chandrakant Patel. All this land by its side must have appreciated.

Devraj Gowda. By 500 per cent in the last three years. All of it belongs to Gowdas.

Chandrakant Patel. Oh, I see.

Devraj Gowda. We, Marasu Vokkaliga Gowdas, have been landowners since the Vijaynagar empire.

Chandrakant Patel. Oh! That was two hundred years ago maybe?

Devraj Gowda. Eleventh century, sir! Eleventh century!

Chandrakant Patel. You must be very much together as a community.

Devraj Gowda. Yes. That is true. We have our own association. We have our pontiff in Chinchinagiri. A very educated man—went abroad for his studies.

Chandrakant Patel. Then why don't you find a nice boy for your Lata in your community?

Prema Gowda. Don't listen to Dev. We hardly ever move in the community. Bangalore is quite a cosmopolitan city.

Devraj Gowda. We Gowdas made it a cosmopolitan city. Our hospitality . . .

Prema Gowda. We want a suitable match. Period. What about Alpesh? Why don't you also . . . ?

Pause.

Kusumben Patel. Bombay is also a cosmopolitan city.

Alpesh. Mumbai, not Bombay.

They drive along in silence.

Sthala Puranagalu:

Place Legends

Pushpamala N.

An artist's interpretation of city stories old and new, based on an exhibition of installation art that she curated in 1999.

AT THE end of the millennium, Bangalore seemed to illustrate the Third World cliché of a small town breaking out with sudden violence into a metropolis. Piles of rubble, dug-up roads, real estate mafias, crime: an indescribable chaos, seemingly shapeless, with incessant destruction and never-ending construction—everything half-built, half-conceived, careering along with a ruthless brashness, but full of vitality.

I wondered if we, as artists, could intervene to break the mind-numbing exhaustion of negotiating this city: to somehow excavate its histories, its memories and its associations, to experience an exhilaration of the senses and to pin down images of the fragmented and amorphous quality of life here—not in a flaccid, sentimental way, but with critical thought and study, by talking about things in the strong sensual language of art, with all the rawness of the direct physical encounter.

The title of the show *Sthala Puranagalu*, which translates from the Kannada to mean 'Place Legends', usually refers to the tales woven around holy sites in a vivid and popular style. At the end of 1998, I thought of working on a project with three artists whose work interested me for their performative and interactive qualities, to make large public installations which would converse with three symbolic

From Pushpamala N.'s *Sthala Puranagalu*, catalogue for an art event held in Bangalore in May 1999.

places in the city. The sites we chose were the Ulsoor Lake in the Cantonment area, the statue of Queen Victoria at Mahatma Gandhi Road and the Samudaya House at Basavangudi, all important markers of different histories. The actual process of organizing the show, making the works and getting the funding would also be a way of understanding the working of the city.

We met every Friday evening at five o'clock over a period of six months at the Ravindra Kalakshetra canteen to discuss ideas over coffee. During that time the artists—Shamala, Ramesh Kalkur and Srinivasa Prasad—were making sketches, researching the history of each site, and trying to negotiate the labyrinthine bureaucracy for permissions.

The Kalakshetra canteen itself has been a legendary *adda* for Kannada writers, theatre people and intellectuals. In the early 1980s, theatre director Prasanna had introduced me to Dr U.R. Ananthamurthy, Ramachandra Sharma, B.V. Karanth, D.R. Nagaraj and Ki Ram Nagaraja, who used to meet there in the evenings before moving on for a drink or *gundu* at Mobo's around the corner or the Press Club at Cubbon Park. When J.C. Road was made one way in the 1990s, the adda somehow fell apart.

*

THE IDEA for the exhibition started off with my getting the Karnataka State Sculpture Akademi award in 1998. I wanted to use the award money of Rs10, 000 to investigate Bangalore itself as a site, stretching the meaning of sculpture into monumental public works. Bangalore, in fact, was already a place where artists had done large outdoor art like U.S. Umesh's four-acre *Earthwork* in a field outside the city. It was, in a way, to sort out my own confusions about sculpture, a form that I was leaving behind, and to try to find new meaning in a place I had just come back to after twenty years in Baroda and Bombay, a place quite different and much more complex than what I had left. The curating and organizing of Sthala Puranagalu, then, became my own art work.

We needed a lakh for expenses, and went in for an entirely alternate way of funding. Friends were asked for donations and donors ranged from artists, art lovers, galleries, collectors, writers, theatre people, environmentalists, architects, film-makers, academics and IT executives giving from Rs 1,000 to Rs 10,000 each. The artists' friends worked with them for free and many people contributed free materials for the work and collected small amounts of money for each artist. Towards the end there was a crisis when a building company, which was to fund Ramesh Kalkur's tableau, backed out at the last minute because they feared the work on Victoria might be too controversial.

I had some interesting experiences while fund raising. When I asked the writer P. Lankesh at the *Lankesh Patrike* office in Basavangudi for a donation, he said very irritably that he hates monuments, that he thought that the whole of Europe would look like an anthill from space because it was so choked up with monuments, and that the Veerashaiva poets had always said that the moving spirit is more important than the still object. I had to assure him that we were only putting up temporary structures that would be dismantled after a week!

The actual event took place at three locations in Bangalore between 7 and 15 May 1999. In the Chitra Gallery in the Kannada Bhavana, Ramesh Kalkur's tableau *The Royal Feast* occupied an entire wall like a giant mural. His fifteen painted photographs of the statue of Victoria were also exhibited there. Shamala had a large work table on which she displayed her preparatory work sketches and crayon drawings, photographs of work on site and several blue clothbound books containing her research notes about the history of the lakes in Bangalore, with material photocopied from different reports, books and newspapers. A thousand small glass perfume bottles with the screen-printed brand name 'Bihisti', filled with water taken from the Ulsoor Lake, were displayed on the table, along with posters she had designed, advertising 'free water samples' to be taken away by the visitors to the exhibition. Srinivasa Prasad had the two entrance walls full of black-and-white translites of himself performing at his work at the Samudaya House. Simultaneously, Shamala's floating sculpture at Ulsoor Lake and Srinivasa Prasad's labyrinth/fairground at Samudaya House were open for viewing.

Shamala

BANGALORE WAS once known as Kalyananagara, the city of lakes or *kalyanis*. The city has a ridge and valley topography; its lakes are basically irrigated tanks to catch rainwater. Like prehistoric towns, Bangalore grew around ponds and tanks which were then connected by channels or *karanjis*, which also watered the orchards and gardens of the city, even till the 1960s. The tank irrigation system itself is considered unique to south India.

The lakes were once among the most beautiful features of the city. The writer D.V. Gundappa, describing the visit of Prince Albert in 1889, wrote:

As the Royal Party got down at the Railway Station and proceeded by horse-drawn coaches toward the city, a grand sight greeted it at the Totadappa Choultry corner. The tank in front, the Dharmambudhi tank, was a broad sheet of cool clear water with a float (*theppa*) gently gliding upon it. The float carried a party of Bharatanatyam dancers in colourful attire. As the processions turned to the East and took the tank bund, there was another delight in the small park to the south of the tank bund, now called the Municipal Park (the Chik Lalbagh). With *theppa*, dancing and music to the left and Nagaswaram pipe music to the right, the Royal party should have felt as in a fairy land.

With the growth of the city, and the introduction of piped water from the Cauvery river, the tanks were no longer needed to supply water or support agriculture. The streams and channels have dried up. The tank beds, once seen as damp and mosquito-ridden sites for slums, now have office buildings like the Millers Tank or rich residential suburbs like Koramangala.

The Kempe Gowda family, which founded Bangalore, constructed the Ulsoor Lake, the temple and the village around it. The Survey of India of 1894 says that Ulsoor Lake, then known as Alasuru, extended over an area of 125 acres and was constructed during the second half of the sixteenth century. The tanks needed to be regularly desilted and dredged with considerable labour. Somerset Payne, writing in 1914, has testified to the trouble taken by the British to keep the Ulsoor tank clean. He says when 'weeds of a noxious character accumulated, it was drained and burnt . . .'

Shamala, who is interested in ecological and environmental issues and these in-between places of the city, wanted to reclaim the history of the lake, now toxic and dead, and create a sacred and contemplative space by using natural materials and the elements of earth, water and sky.

Her meditative, poetic sculpture made of bamboo, beeswax, rope and water hyacinth, floated in a pool of water in the middle of the large horseshoe-shaped island in the lake. The journey by boat from the clubhouse on the shore across the water and the walk around the island in the shade of its rain trees, through the rustling undergrowth of its ferns and plants, the sound of birdsong and the splashing of the water, became intermingled with the experience of her work . . .

Ramesh Kalkur

THE STATUES of Bangalore have historically been centres of violent controversies. When it was first installed in the 1980s, there was a hue and cry that the figure of the late Karnataka chief minister Kengal Hanumanthaiah did not resemble him at all and that it was a dishonour to his memory. It was finally replaced; so was the statue of another late chief minister, Devaraj Urs, in front of the Vidhana Soudha, for the same reasons. It appears that the government hastily commissions these portraits on populist grounds and they are made in a hurry. However, there seems to be no real outcry when the figure has no relevance to local communal and casteist power politics, like the ungainly statues of Nehru or Rajiv Gandhi, seen as distant national figures.

The most recurrent controversies seem to concern the statues of the fourteenth-century Veerashaiva saint Basavanna, who established the powerful Lingayat sect and the Dalit leader Ambedkar in Gulbarga in the far north of the state, where Lingayats routinely defile the Ambedkar statue, and Dalits routinely defile Basavanna. Some years ago, there was an incident near Bangalore when the statue of Dr Ambedkar at the medical college campus in K.G. Halli was allegedly vandalized in the night by the drunken son of a state minister, who happened to be a Dalit.

In Bangalore, the bronze painted fibre glass statue of the saint-poet Basavanna at Race Course Circle, shown as a martial figure on horseback, has been the centre of a bitter quarrel between the two factions of the Basava Samiti which commissioned the statue. The defeated faction felt it would have been more appropriate if he was shown as a Shivasharana or a devotee worshipping the linga, or as a poet reading from a palm-leaf manuscript.

Statues map the politics of a city. For many years now, the figure of Thiruvalluvar the Tamil poet, erected near Ulsoor Lake, a predominantly Tamil area, has been wrapped up in plastic sheets like a work by (Swiss installation artist) Christo because of protests from Kannada nationalists. They have been demanding that in return, a statue of Sarvagna, the Kannada poet, be put up in Tamil Nadu. And while there are a plethora of colonial statues still erect, there are no statues at all of Hyder Ali or Tipu Sultan in the city, not even in Lalbagh that Hyder created. Queen Victoria and Rani Kittur Chennamma, who fought against the British in the 1857 war, are the only figures of women.

The Victoria statue, 'erected by public subscription' and unveiled by Prince Albert in 1906, stands resplendently opposite the Mahatma Gandhi statue at the edge of Cubbon Park, which divides the Cantonment from the City. Strangely, the statue has not been put away in disgrace but instead occupies a prominent place in the centre, in the hub of the business district. It is at a spectacular location where three major roads of Bangalore meet.

Ramesh Kalkur, who saw the city as defined and mapped by its statues and hoardings, which he calls 'the urban screen', commissioned cinema hoarding painters to create a huge painted tableau around the figure of Victoria, in which twelve important statues of Bangalore dialogue with each other in a work he called *The Royal Feast*. The tableau, described as 'a homage to the leaders', is a tongue-in-cheek exploration of the political history of the state as revealed by its own monuments and visual culture . . .

Srinivasa Prasad

SAMUDAYA WAS started in 1975, just before the Emergency was declared in the country, when Prasanna, who had graduated from the National

School of Drama, and other intellectuals decided to form a broadly left theatre group based on the lines of the Indian Peoples' Theatre Association' (IPTA) and the Kerala People's Art Club. The name 'Samudaya', which means 'community', was suggested by the critic Ki Ram Nagaraja.

The Samudaya office was at member C.K. Gundanna's house in N.R. Colony, close to where Prasanna and others lived. The props and costumes were stored there, while the rehearsals took place at the National College, Basavangudi. Later, a house at Puttanna Road, which was soon going to be demolished, was given to them free of charge.

As extreme left Naxal movements spread in India, Samudaya had to contend with the theme of the 'rural' and the 'peasant'. In the Samudaya *jathas* started by Prasanna, urban youth travelled all over rural Karnataka for the first time, putting up agit-prop street plays while staying with the locals. On the other hand, thousands of farmers came to the city during major farmers' agitations and rallies. Badal Sircar's ideas of Third Theatre inspired the street play *Belchi*, written by C.G. Krishnaswamy, based on newspaper reports of atrocities against Dalits in a Bihar village. Progressive movements in Karnataka, like the Bandaya (rebel) and Dalit Awakening, and the People's Science and Literacy movements grew out of Samudaya.

Just before the historic Chikmagalur by-election of 1978, a poster workshop against fascism was organized by artist R.M. Hadpad in Bangalore, where 10,000 posters were made by the public, for which the Kannada newspaper *Prajavani* gave the newsprint and the students from the Ken School of Art helped to select the best posters.

Prasanna believes that Samudaya was able to hold highly political anti-fascist street plays at the Cubbon Park bandstand and all over Bangalore during the Emergency because the government was naïve and there seemed to be no censorship unlike the rest of India. In the play *Thaayi*, based on Maxim Gorky's *Mother*, directed by Prasanna in 1976, B. Jayashree as the mother walked on to the Ravindra Kalakshetra stage waving a red flag with the slogan 'Workers of the World Unite'.

While Samudaya's heyday was during the 'left moment' in the

1970s, it continues to be one of India's most important and widespread theatre movements.

Srinivasa Prasad's work used images and props from the company's plays to turn the Samudaya House, its ruined outhouse and garden, into an enormous theatre set, part labyrinth, part urban playground. Built like a large construction site, its fragile, eccentric pathways turn the rustic inside out, where the city dweller can wander about experiencing the smells and sights and sounds of a lost fantastical rural past.

Macbeth at Bangalore University

Paul William Roberts

'NOW,' I said to my students at the University of Bangalore, 'you've all read Shakespeare's wonderful tragedy, *Macbeth*—so, before we start examining why it's so wonderful, does anyone have any questions?'

A resonant silence descended upon the acoustically challenged room, broken only by a creaking of chairs, the gurgle of metabolic processes and the short-circuiting of brain synapses. Faces looked as if I'd caught them masturbating. Then a voice said, 'If the Macbett is believing these sadhu womens when they are telling him he will be the raja, why is he not also believing them when they are saying his children will not take the crown because the Banko's issues, *they* will be taking crown?'

It was the most intelligent question I had ever been asked about *Macbeth*. Students I'd taught at Oxford were always more interested in whether Lady Macbeth and the witches had a conspiracy going, or if Macbeth could be fairly described as a paranoid schizophrenic suffering from delusions of grandeur and hallucinations.

I looked at the list on my massive desk. There were five columns: *Sl. No . . . . Name of the Student . . . II Language . . . Caste . . .* and *Remarks*. I looked down at the list.

'Sundaresan C.N. isn't it?'

'No, sir, I am Bhagvanulu, sir.' He sounded hurt.

Sundaresan's second language, I noticed, was listed as Sanskrit. Where had he picked that up? I soon found the correct name. It spanned half the page, flowing into an adjacent column. Nunna Sathyanarayana Bhagvanulu. His second language was Telugu, and his caste was described as Kamma (B. Co.). There were no remarks in the entire Remarks column.

From *Empire of the Soul: Some Journeys in India*, HarperCollins Publishers, India (1999).

'Very good, Nunna,' I told him, wondering how far down the hierarchy Kammas were. Most of my students were listed as Brahmin. And hadn't the caste system been officially abolished, anyway?

It took me a while to discover that there was a quota system operating in Indian colleges, as well as a vestigial caste system. They were obliged to take a certain proportion of local students, whether these students were up to university standards or not. This meant that over half my class consisted of sophisticated, urbane rich kids from Delhi who spoke fluent English, and often nothing else, and poor kids from the surrounding villages whose second language, I soon learned, was often also their only language. For people who would have big problems reading Dr Seuss, it seemed rather cruel to be asking them what they thought of Shakespearean tragedy. Yet, as Bhagvanulu's question proved, *Macbeth*, with its tribal feuds and supernatural phenomena, was something south Indians in particular could relate to. Macbeth himself would probably have felt quite at home out in the more remote parts of Andhra Pradesh or Tamil Nadu. There were still tribal feuds and witches in 1977, and still are.

My teaching duties were hardly onerous. The job turned out to be a sinecure arranged by an Indian academic I'd met in England in order for me to study his country's literature and culture. My lectures on Shakespeare consisted of my explaining plots and leaping around, acting out scenes. Try summarizing Shakespeare's plots sometime; half of them don't make sense. I'd overlooked this aspect of his work when I was studying the plays myself. Staggering coincidences were often the only way he could come up with any sort of conclusion by the close of Act Five. I ended up playing all the parts myself to spare us the agony of Raghunandhan V.A. (Kannada, Balijiga B.Co.) or Vasudeva Murthy R. (Telugu, Neygi F.C.) stumbling through *wouldsts* or *perchances*. We spent an entire hour on 'Thrice the brinded cat had mew'd.' No one seemed to understand why the greatest writer in the English language did not appear to write in English at all. When I told them that many words no longer meant today what they meant in the late sixteenth century, I had the distinct impression that my students assumed this meant Shakespeare had been semi-literate. Adding that the Bard occasionally appeared to make up words, or adapt them, using nouns for verbs, for instance, and that the dictionary was devised after his death, confirmed their suspicions about the rudimentary state of English culture a mere four hundred years ago.

They'd been taught that Indian civilization had been going strong for over thirty thousand years now, and many believed Vedic sages possessed nuclear weapons, radar and magnetically powered aircraft equipped with cannons. Translations of the Vedas do in fact contain, in somewhat obscure stanzas, words that can be translated as 'airplane' and 'electricity'. But the translation of Sanskrit, like that of Egyptian hieroglyphics, seems to be a fairly personal business. One well-known Bengali scholar eschews the word *translation* altogether, his books stating that they have been 'transcreated' from the Sanskrit.

'Why is the Shakespeare making these play in five act only?' asked Subramanian R. (Sanskrit, Brahmin F.C.).

This, too, had never occurred to me before. I told him it was a legal thing—Elizabeth I insisted all plays have five acts, violators subject to execution by big axe. Subramanian R. found this an eminently reasonable answer.

They were so well behaved, these students, so polite, that they began to irritate me. This exemplary behaviour, I came to see, made up for their salient and prodigious laziness. The first essay I sat down to mark consisted of one single sentence: 'The Mabeth is play by english genius SHEIKH SPIRO he was knowing king and some bad peoples they are not wanting this man to be their king so forest is walking to kill him.'

Maybe teaching wasn't my forte?

The Sound of Two Hands Clapping

C.K. Meena

THE NIGHT queens are blooming on the green metal fence. They stand like bright synthetic flowers stuck in individual vases, each hijra dressed in the colour of her choice, with the sari *pallu* draped over the arm in the manner of a mannequin. At evenly spaced points they stand, almost pasted to the inside of the Cubbon Park fence, sprays of pink or lilac or lemon yellow silk with silver plastic *zari*. Men who pass by the busy road stop and whisper through the mesh. Some clamber over the fence and disappear into the long grass, plucking a flower as they wander into the darkness. In time, all the flowers will have been plucked. And the fence will turn dull and green once again.

*

'WE ARE like paper flowers.' Tamil lent poetry to the sentence. Plucked from the mouth of an eloquent transexual, it was trimmed and shaped into the name of a documentary film. *Paper Flowers*, conceptualized and produced by the late Deepa Krishnan, featured members of Mumbai's hijra community and involved them in its making. The community picked the title and decided the content.

Paper flowers. They are not what they seem. And they are always a little brighter, a little showier than the real.

When the film was screened here a few years ago, it made us re-examine femininity. As a spirited young viewer commented: Here we are, modern women trying to break the stereotype, and there they are, doing their best to conform to it! Transgender men yearning to be women—the 'third gender,' as some call them—cling to the superficial trappings that, in their eyes, represent the female of the species. Long hair, flowers, jewellery, make-up, coy speech, high-pitched voice, mincing gait, swaying hips, sideways movements of the neck, they adopt them all. Their gurus have schooled them in 'feminine' ways. Paradoxically, they have none of the self-consciousness of diffident middle-class women. They carry their female bodies with an enviable boldness.

Can you blame them for choosing the easy stereotype? They want to peel away the suffocating false skin, strip their bodies of every physical attribute that would suggest they are men. Exaggeration is their only resort.

That is why the colour of the paper flower is a little gaudier than the real.

*

I AM used to people mistaking me for a man. When I was a teenager I would regularly hear 'Boy or girl?' when I walked down the street. But that was because I used to tuck my shirt into my trousers, in a town where girls wore only salwars, saris or long skirts. I'm pushing 50 and I live in Bangalore, where women wear all sorts of clothes, and I still get mistaken for a man. Just the other day a bus driver at Shivajinagar bus stand called me *'yejamanru'*—sir—before realizing his error.

What is it about me that suggests masculinity? There are a lot of trouser-clad short-haired women in Bangalore, but they don't all get called 'sir'. Is it my gait? The way I swing my arms? No make-up or jewellery—is that it? Perhaps I don't fit the feminine stereotype. I am no flower.

There was a strange desire inside of me after puberty. I wanted to be a boy. At some moments, the desire grew unbearably strong. It lasted a couple of years. Inside Meena, was a Manu trying to emerge? But then, I was attracted to boys, so was it just hormones at play?

Mysterious are the ways of human sexuality. It radiates the splendorous colours of the divine rainbow. How dare we presume to imprison it within two blocks of black and white, male and female?

*

MANU WALKS beneath a yellow cassia in the park, hoping a night patrol jeep doesn't swoop down on him. The last thing he needs is a constable's rough stick up his arse. Stick or dick, it could be either.

He taps away the leaves and dirt that cling to the rear of his sari and puts the money into his white handbag. His head hurts. His customer had punched him in the face, a parting shot to efface the guilty pleasure of the hypocrite. His arse hurts. Torn again. Some are gentle, but most are not.

This hateful thing between his legs, he wants to get rid of it. Maybe he should take the Mumbai train next week, or search for a reliable local doctor. Get the 'operation' done, and begin to feel more like the woman he wants to be.

A Manu who wants to be Meena.

An expensive process, by any means. Crude surgery would cost him several thousand. Getting his male organs removed at a government hospital would set him back by nearly Rs 60,000. Nagging urinary problems and other post-operative complications will follow unless he opts for reconstructive surgery, but that costs Rs 4 lakh.

If Meena wants to be Manu she'll have to go abroad and spend Rs 40 lakh to get a penis fashioned. Much cheaper to pretend she has one.

*

BACK IN the late 1990s, a meeting at the Centre for Education and Documentation (CED) in Domlur. We were talking about harassment of male and female sex workers by the city police. A group of transexuals joined us. A whisper in my ear: 'They've just had their operation done.' They were dressed in shirts and trousers and looked male. One of them said his name was Ranjitha. He wanted to be known as her.

Three years later, I saw a photograph of a Bangalorean called Ranjitha who won a beauty contest at the annual hijra fair at Koovagam. Was it the same Ranjitha? I stared hard at her features, trying to match them with those I had seen at CED. She was unrecognizable. And gorgeous.

*

LOCAL PHOTOGRAPHER K. Venkatesh had wanted Ranjitha to inaugurate his exhibition in 2002 but she was unavailable—jailed on trivial charges. So Revathi did the honours, Revathi who got her book published later, documenting (in Tamil) the stories of members of her community.

Venkatesh's photographs were taken during the festival at Koovagam, near Villupuram in Tamil Nadu. The main ritual is at the Koothandavar temple there. The story goes that Aravanan was going to fight and face certain death in the Mahabharata war. Since he was a bachelor, his last wish was to be a bridegroom on the eve of his departure for battle. Krishna took on the form of Mohini and fulfilled his desire for just one night. At Koovagam, hijras, who identify with Krishna, dress up as brides and go to the temple. The priest ties *thalis* around their necks to signify their marriage. They spend the night in celebration. The very next day, to coincide with the death of Aravanan, the priest breaks the thalis, snaps them one by one, to signify their widowhood. The tears of the grief-struck 'widows' stain the temple grounds.

*

AH, THE craving, constant and undeniable. The most powerful expression I have seen of this yearning was in fact tragicomic. I haven't met this person, don't know her name, but the ripples of her words have stayed with me. It was in 2002 at Jagruti, the organization that Renu Appachu runs. She'd been working with the MSM (Men who have Sex with Men) programme. Kajol was answering a call on her mobile, grinning and saying in Kannada, 'Yes, yes, *kanditha bartheeni*, definitely I'll come.' After many reassurances, she turned to us and, in a half-mocking, half-affectionate tone, reported what the caller had said: 'She says she has got her period. She is inviting everyone to her house for tea today because she thinks she has started menstruating.'

After the sex change operation, she believed she had become a woman when she saw blood down below. The sight brought her hope, hope that sprang from ignorance, hope that was temporary and ridiculous—and moving.

*

KAJOL WAS someone you wouldn't forget in a hurry. That day, at Renu's office, she hadn't yet crossed over. Looked like a tomboy with the emphasis on 'boy'. Argued and joked with Renu. Amidst her banter, she told me that as a child she had wished to wear frocks and liked drawing *rangoli* patterns. She showed me a shiny brown salwar set she had bought at a bargain price, challenged me to guess what it cost her, and was mighty pleased that I had got it wrong.

Renu was telling her about condoms and safety. The topic turned to the inevitable AIDS. Kajol said in Tamil: 'Everyone is talking about AIDS. Everywhere you look, it's AIDS, AIDS, AIDS. AIDS has become a *periya* superstar now.'

The big superstar claimed her life in 2005.

*

AT A memorial for Famila at CED in 2004, Kajol reminisced about her best friend. Could she have known that she would join her a year later?

Famila and Kajol. With their deaths, the transgender community lost two leading lights. Famila was the pioneer, soft-spoken yet firm. Speaking in public forums whenever she could, organizing the Bangalore Hijra Habba two years in a row, working to spread awareness, inspiring confidence in her companions, she was someone you would never imagine committing suicide.

If Famila's energy was the quiet kind, Kajol's was noisy—and how! Flashy, exuberant and impulsive, she was a gregarious creature, but she brooked no nonsense. Encountering her was like coming up short against a sturdy branch of a rain tree. She could knock you over with her directness.

They were the best of friends. At the memorial meeting, Kajol's portrait of Famila was searingly intimate. She mourned Famila who gave her respect, who reunited her with her family, who stole the *Boys Don't Cry* CD from the Sangama office because she knew Kajol loved the movie. 'We used to lie beside one another, naked, not having sex, just talking, *sumne*, asking one another how the day was, what happened at the office . . .'

I saw their ghosts at a multiplex in early 2006. Santosh Sivan's film *Navarasa* was about a girl who goes in search of her uncle; he is kicked out of the house by her father for displaying his sexual preference. Her search ends in Koovagam. In the movie, I caught a fleeting glimpse of Kajol and Famila joining the multitudes at Koovagam.

*

IN 2005, local film-maker T. Jayshree's award-winning documentary on the transgender community, *Many Voices, Many Desires*, was being screened at the Nayana auditorium attached to Ravindra Kalakshetra. A contingent of hijras had turned up in their colourful best. There was Rex, head of the sexuality minorities organization Sangama, who had decided to come in *satla* (cross-dress) for the occasion. He was formidably statuesque in a silk sari, the *pallu* occasionally slipping to expose his smooth and graceful back. 'Rex the king,' I thought to myself. 'Or is it queen?'

Speaking to Rex recently at the bustling Sangama office in Shivajinagar, I got an overview of just how far the cause had progressed in Bangalore. Rex was optimistic. The media no longer uses derogatory terms like 'khoja' or 'eunuch', he said. Hijras travel by city buses during the day. Revathi and Chandini have passports stating that their sex is female. Christy and Sonu took part in a half-hour discussion session on national television. Self-esteem has grown: of Sangama's 120 employees, 22 are active and confident workers. Hijras have emerged from the traditional *hamams*, the bathhouses where they used to live as clans, and almost 300 of them have taken up houses on rent in places such as Amrutahalli and Dasarahalli. On 31 March 2006, at Malleswaram grounds, about 5000 people, of whom 1200 were transgender, gathered to celebrate a cultural festival of sexuality minorities. It was open to the public. During the four-and-a-half-hour programme, there was not a single disturbance. Just the sound of clapping.

*

THE HIJRA claps with a sharp and ringing sound. She claps to say, 'You can't ignore me. I exist.' She claps to give the impression of confidence although, inside, she might be fearful of rebuff and contempt.

You cannot clap with one hand, goes the saying. Society must lend a hand, welcome them, employ them, befriend them. And then, we might begin to hear the joyous sound of two hands clapping.

Temples of Food

Achal Prabhala

FIRST, I set out to write an essay on vegetarian food in Bangalore. I was interested in food that might be, in some way, representative of Karnataka. Then, I fretted that I was equating regional vegetarian with Hindu, and further, with Hindu Brahmin. No getting away from this: though luckily for us, words like 'natural', 'fresh' and 'vegetarian' have not yet been hijacked by new-age spirituality. Vegetables are cheaper than animals. I felt better.

Unluckily, whether they like it or not, vegetarians are deeply in debt to the Brahmins. K.T. Achaya, a somewhat legendary Bangalorean and author of definitive books on the history of food, said that when he enters a vegetarian restaurant, he subconsciously assumes it is clean. Of course—so confoundedly, do a whole lot of people. The obvious Sanskritization made me queasy. I'm fairly sure about why I'm vegetarian, but not so clear on vegetarianism's nefarious links. Yet I prepared myself to write about Brahmin food, imagining that something like that exists.

Then I found out it didn't. Not in a city like Bangalore anyway: outside, perhaps. But it seems that the Brahmin restaurant is itself a bit of an oxymoron, as the concept of a restaurant would run counter to the ideal career trajectory of the Brahmin male. Brahmin-run restaurants in urban areas like Bangalore, for the most part, have been secularized; the only remaining exclusion being economic. Except perhaps for the south Canarese Brahmin (from Udupi and Mangalore), the food business ranks too low in the hierarchy of professions to be a significant marker of caste.

Which probably explains why, when Kadambam opened its doors in Bangalore many years ago, it shot right into the A-list. Kadambam

A version of this essay originally appeared in *Outlook Traveller*, February 2002.

serves 'authentic Iyengar cuisine' which, though Tamilian in some sense, is really the cuisine of Karnataka Iyengars, from Mysore and Bangalore. For a while, it was an empire—its three restaurants, neatly covering three important parts of the city, flourished madly. Kadambam's puliyogare, bisi bele bath, curd rice, pineapple sajjige, avarekai pallya, sakkere pongal, and even their meals, are undoubtedly among the best in town. Given the community's prominence in Karnataka's history, it is surprising that no one thought of an Iyengar restaurant before. But perhaps the reason is precisely this prominence. The community was too busy churning out India's most important sociologists, writers, administrators and scientists to notice a business opportunity, least of all one to do with food.

Kadambam has recently downsized, though the Rajajinagar branch stays put. Here, the aesthetic is domestic, the aspirational motif a middle-class south Indian home. This is the puja room, the drawing room and the kitchen all combined. Gilt-framed religious posters line the walls, the floors are polished marble, the table-tops spotlessly clean, and the chairs, though comfortable, plain and austere. The kitchen is open for all to see (a hallmark of other, less glamorous, *darshinis* as well). As befits a restaurant with a loyal, steady clientele, Kadambam is permitted some eccentricities: like deciding what can be served when, or on what day, or more irritatingly, what dish has just arbitrarily run out of supply.

My parents live in Ulsoor, and one of the pleasures of visiting them was that Kadambam had a branch on Dickenson Road. When they decided to close shop I was glum. But then I discovered Adiga's right next door. Like a crazy scene from a Chaplin film, about forty employees cook in a kitchen of alarmingly small dimensions, miraculously never bumping into each other or missing a step. The result of this superbly orchestrated, continuously performed opera is cheap, fast and high-quality south Canara food. Adiga's is a flourishing darshini with outlets mushrooming in the city even as I write—but what sets it apart from others is the attention to detail. In season, the uppittu will contain avarekai and cashew nuts, and you'll simply never go wrong with the sambhar. Like the best of them, Adiga's has all three signs of an exceptional darshini: long lines that move fast, high-class patrons and working-class customers.

Kadambam and Adiga's are relaxed places, though they have the hustle of a bus stop during lunchtime. What is distinctly un-festive, and austere to the point of rudeness, is the legendary Mavali Tiffin Rooms, otherwise known as MTR. For seventy-five years, this nondescript little building in Jayanagar has served as a steady symbol of austerity, purity and exclusivity. I remember being woken up on Sunday mornings at six (much against my will), and bundled off for the sheer joy of standing in a line, in the freezing cold, for many hours until MTR deemed it fit to serve me breakfast. But it mattered little. The food is excellent. And its intimidating sense of hospitality is almost endearing.

MTR's staff can effortlessly reduce their customers to feeling like gauche American tourists gatecrashing a Michelin-star restaurant in Paris. Understandably, many would rather avoid that experience altogether. Everyone else apparently has the Stockholm Syndrome— for it remains consistently crowded and feted. It is run by a Brahmin family, and a trademark practice is to parade you through the kitchen, where you can observe gleaming steel machines and equally gleaming Brahmin cooks doing their job. MTR has complex and irritating rules, where the menu is divided into breakfast, lunch, tiffin and dinner. If you like your dosa and rava idli drenched in ghee, and your badam halwa rich enough to induce immediate cardiac arrest, then this is the place. Coffee is served in stern little silver tumblers, and extra ghee is grudgingly doled out by the thimble. MTR's secret weapon is its pallya, a potato curry made consistently well, with the potato cut into impossibly little pieces and flavoured perfectly. Dinner (a special occasion, which needs advance booking) starts off with chandrahara, which is khova baked in a sweet crust, floating in a thick, creamy liquid; while this is passed off as tradition, it's a good way to ensure that there isn't much appetite left for anything else.

MTR's alter ego is the instant-food business. A shrewd move in brand extension, the name now endorses everything from sweets to instant mixes, and pickles to ice cream. Consumed by the millions of software engineers who will eat nothing else (even, and especially, in the other Silicon Valley), it is now perhaps the resurgent Hindutva interest in the NRI that keeps the flag for MTR flying, adding a wholly unsavoury dimension to the notion of Brahmin food.

Unfortunately, the politics of MTR food are mainly in my idle head: everything they make, they make very well. If you can put up with the casual weirdness of it all—or better still, not even see it—then it is simply a very good place to eat.

MTR and Kadambam are temples of food which are quite self-consciously so. Thankfully, Bangalore has other places to eat, where the atmosphere isn't cloaked in the same aura of ritual purity, and where good food isn't confused with haute cuisine. At the top of that list is Kamat Yatri Nivas, an unpretentious hotel in Gandhinagar. Part of a state-wide chain (and not to be confused with the ubiquitous Kamat restaurant), the speciality here is the north Karnataka thali. The jolada rotti, made from jowar, is quite unique; as is the brinjal curry, the salad and the sambhar. What the Gandhinagar restaurant lacks in ambience is made up for at their outlet in Ramanagaram, an hour outside Bangalore, on the Mysore road. Here, thatched roofs, cowsheds and pleasant wooden tables create the perfect ambience; the place stays remarkably unmarred by an overdose of the ethnic touch.

Easiness, of course, is a quality more frequently found in the City, which is roughly the area that is not the Cantonment. The Cantonment is continental cuisine, café culture and occasional exotica (Thai, Burmese, Keralite); the City is everything else. One place in the Cantonment that remains a sort of hidden treasure is Ibrahim Koil Street, which runs parallel to Commercial Street, a major shopping Mecca. The difference in style is spectacular: Commercial Street has Barista, Allen Solly and Hidesign. Right next door, Ibrahim Koil has brandless clothes, roadside coffee, fruit chaat, and a range of street food, from the traditional south Indian, to Punjabi and Chinese. A key node of this locality is Sasta, a two-room tenement serving up idlis, dosas and parothas. The idlis are hot, fluffy and incredibly light —they fly up, fly in, and spontaneously dissolve. The dosas are great, but what is really special here are the parothas. Like a lot of business establishments in this area, Sasta is Tamil-run, and imports, among other things from across the border, the smashed parotha. This is like egg bhujiya, only made with flour, and delicious. Other than this, one also finds all the usual suspects: Kerala Parotha and Ceylon Parotha (which we have affectionately and efficiently renamed KP and CP).

The kitchen is open, the turnover is high, and it is impossible to spend more than about Rs 25, even if one tries really, really hard.

KP and CP are widely available in Bangalore, but the places they are really good at are the very non-vegetarian, Malayalee-Muslim restaurants in Shivajinagar. The Grand Taj and Empire are two famous city landmarks, where the egg curry and parotha are consistently good (and also, about the only vegetarian things on the menu). These two restaurants run a thriving business in brain fry, which is reputedly excellent. However, that is dead animal territory, and another story altogether.

A true city gem is embedded within the shops of Old Market Road in V.V. Puram, near Basavangudi and Jayanagar. The area itself is a pleasant reminder of what the city looked like before real estate crashed the party. Across from a large circle, which encloses a leafy park, is a road filled with a variety of food establishments. At night, they come alive like firecrackers. Apart from the regular fare (dosas, idlis and chaat), which is expectedly good, you can get Gulkand and Masala Soda. Gulkand is a sweet made from rose petals crushed in a sticky base. It is served with bananas and apples, or with vanilla ice cream; and while not everyone's favourite, it is the sort of thing that must be tried once. The Masala Soda is a regular carbonated drink, with a dash of masala; the ideal after-dinner aperitif, and probably quite good for your digestion as well. Though cheap, it is more the ambience —the crowds, the smell of food, the burning lamps and appreciative noises all around—that make it such fun.

Street food is cheap. But there's another reason to like it: it tastes better. Avenue Road is a busy commercial area during the day. Come nightfall, and dosas with spicy irulli chutney are served from mobile carts that take over the street. Extremely cheap and extremely good, the irulli chutney is worth the trip alone. Yet the queen of dosas, undisputedly, sits in the busy lanes of Gandhibazar, near Basavangudi. Here, at Vidyarthi Bhavan, the dosa is elevated to an art form. Hundreds queue up every day for the obligatory ticket to paradise. If you can take the wait, then this is the place to sample what is definitely the last word in masala dosas.

Privately though, I am obsessed with Gobi Manchurian (GM). You will never see a recipe for it in traditional south Indian cookbooks, but if Butter Chicken is the national bird of Khalistan, then GM is the national vegetable of the Republic of Bangalore. This, not Blair's Britain, is the ultimate multicultural fantasy: a south Indian version of a north Indian dish that is a version of an Indian Chinese chicken dish that is itself a vague version of something that might never have been eaten in Manchuria. Fantastic!

I think people eat it because it has a vaguely non-vegetarian feel— both from the spices and the texture of the fried cauliflower. While it is a staple of darshini menus everywhere, the best GM is usually found at a seedy hotel. And there's the trick: to find that place, which is not too dirty or roadside (that GM tends to be a little overfried and crisp), but is neither too clean nor posh (this GM would be pointlessly soggy and bland). Somewhere in between is a hotel with harsh lighting, slightly stained tablecloths and rexine couches, where shady-looking people are 'taking drinks'. And this is where you will get the best GM because, as everyone knows, drinks go with meat, and if not, with something as close as possible.

Meat for the meek: in these challenging times, surely the Brahmins would approve.

A Dream of a Theatre

Aditi De

IN 2000, Arundhati Nag joined the ranks of visionaries who dare to make the near-impossible their destination. That's when this multilingual stage and screen actress set out on a quest—for a Bengaluru theatre venue as perfect as Mumbai's Prithvi Theatre.

Arundhati's dream came true when Ranga Shankara opened with a 35-day global festival from 28 October to 1 December 2004. The city's theatre lovers were dazzled by the 12,500 square feet, three-storey complex, with its air-conditioned 300-seat state-of-the art auditorium, in the southern suburb of J.P. Nagar.

Ranga Shankara's distinctive qualities were apparent even at its opening performance in 2004—of *Maya Sita Prasanga*, a stylized, Kudiyattam-influenced exploration of reality and illusion through the Ramayana, by Mysore's Rangayana repertory. A hush preceded it. A theatre aficionado settled into her shoulder-to-shoulder cushioned seat, examined the coir matting under her toes, gazed at the overhead ventilator pipes. Her friend studied the minimal settings, made of bamboo and board.

Four musicians took their places onstage. Two actors entered, holding a banner with a picture of a golden deer on it. The stage was set. The play began. The acoustics were perfect. The spell it cast rippled through Bengaluru, and beyond since then.

'I wanted our first festival to be a tribute to the greats of Indian theatre today—Habib Tanvir and Ratan Thiyam—who have transformed the essence of it all,' Arundhati said in 2004. 'This theatre will strive to bring Karnataka to the centre stage of world theatre, as well as bring world-class theatre to the common man in Karnataka.'

As if wishes were plays, so it came to be. Vital cues to the heartbeat of Ranga Shankara emerged from the brilliant staging of Tanvir's

A version of this article appeared in *Simplifly* magazine in March 2008.

Charan Das Chor in Chhattisgarhi and *Agra Bazar* in Urdu, the latter revived after over a decade, both performed by his famed Naya Theatre troupe. Each proved why the charismatic theatreperson's experiments since 1958 with language, form and an urban–rural mix are still celebrated. Just as potently, Thiyam's Imphal-based Chorus Repertory Theatre stunned viewers with its visually poetic *Ritusamharam,* performed over a hundred times globally. The staging was proof enough of why Thiyam is often spoken of in the same breath as avant-garde theatre giants like Peter Brooke or Jerzy Grotowski.

In January 2005, the travelling French Footsbarn theatre company performed a Shakespearean mosaic, *Perchance to Dream,* juggling song, dance, mime, masks and storytelling, into memorable total theatre. That November, the breakaway Euro-British ensemble Complicite interpreted *Measure for Measure* as a take on the Bard for our time. Led by director-actor Simon McBurney, they chose to introduce cinema-like staging, visual clues that ran counter to speeches without blurring the foci, yoking the plot to sexual politics and contemporary social commentary.

Charmed by this perfect theatre, McBurney decided against performing at larger, central Bengaluru spaces like H.N. Kalakshetra (the hub of Kannada theatre) or Chowdiah Memorial Hall (favoured by amateur English groups). Instead, he adapted the production, which premiered at the British National Theatre in 2004, for five back-to-back performances on the intimate Ranga Shankara stage. In an indelible moment, the rear screen beyond the performing area went up, allowing us to glimpse a shadowy tree backstage as the action played out in the foreground, melding the real with the surreal for magical moments. McBurney, a veteran of the European theatre circuit, cited this dramatic innovation as his personal 'tribute to Ranga Shankara'.

Gauging Ranga Shankara on par with the Prithvi Theatre, McBurney said in an interview, 'We felt a true exchange with the audience, who participated through their concentrated listening, their sophisticated understanding of the language. It wasn't the false exchange of coming to India on a holiday and supplying money to an economy. We take back a deep sense of meaning, a sense of hope that is rare in our world. If is a gift of such preciousness that it is almost indescribable.'

Has the venue been as responsive to Kannada theatre? Ranga Shankara has been true to this promise, too. Playwright-actor Girish Karnad's *Odakalu Bimba* in Kannada premiered on its thrust stage with Arundhati in its challenging solo role in February 2005 (she was equally at ease in Hindi in *Bikhre Bimb*), while the English version of the same play cast Arundhati Raja of the local Artists' Repertory Theatre in *A Heap of Broken Images*. The play, which straddles theatre and technology, explores the Indian literary establishment with a scathing gaze. It was the first that Jnanpith awardee Karnad had directed in forty years, along with K.M. Chaitanya this time. It doubled as the first independent Ranga Shankara production.

For three hundred days each year since October 2004 (with Mondays closed for maintenance), Ranga Shankara has cast a theatrical spell. It has since completed over a thousand shows.

Rekindling the spirit of theatre as a complete entity, Ranga Shankara heralds many firsts in south India. It has a revolving thrust stage with a trapdoor for stage experiments. A unique computer-based script and sound bank, besides a video archive, bolster research into theatre history, while signalling future trends.

At its breezy candlelit cafeteria, theatre buffs discuss performances, characters and issues threadbare over crisp akki roti and kokum juice or coffee. Quieter spirits browse through play scripts or novels at Sankar's, the bookstore. Others giggle over cartoons of eminent Bangalore thespians in the lobby. Or even take in theatre photographs in the sweeping gallery leading to the stage door.

Over time, Ranga Shankara has lent itself to excursions beyond theatre. Such as dreadlocked, charismatic British performance poet Benjamin Zephaniah reading to an entranced audience in March 2007. Or an electrifying contemporary dance performance, *Hell's Bells and Furtive Folly*, by Zurich-based Compagnie Drift, in January 2007.

Each moment of wonder at the theatre has impelled a question. For an actress equally fluent in Hindi, English, Marathi, Kannada and Tamil, who was doing forty-two shows a month for about twenty-eight years, what sparked Arundhati's journey to Ranga Shankara?

She recalls that her late husband, the Kannada thespian Shankar Nag, saw the role of theatre 'as a unifying language, a forum for creating sensitive experiences'.

Her dream was backed by the Sanket Trust, headed by Karnad, which included Bangalore Little Theatre (BLT) founder-member Vijay Padaki, National School of Drama graduate S. Surendranath, and theatre enthusiast S. Parameshwarappa. President of the Indian Peoples' Theatre Association (IPTA), M.S. Sathyu, was its consultant. They collectively decided to name the theatre Ranga Shankara, which combines the Sanskrit word for theatre—*ranga*—with that of the deity who presides over the art, Shankara.

All the trust had at the outset was a foundation stone laid by former Karnataka chief minister S.M. Krishna on 9 November 2000, at a government-donated site at J.P. Nagar, and an initial corpus of Rs 20 lakh.

How did this translate into a theatre complex worth about Rs 4 crore? As Arundhati's infectious spirit communicated itself, other enthusiasts joined the enterprise, often as volunteers. Some stalwarts have been invisible to the public eye. A chartered accountant has taken care of its inflow and expenditure since 2004. A lighting expert with twenty-eight years of specialization has lit productions, whether homegrown or international, right through. A software specialist still assists with the everyday details of Ranga Shankara, including its website. A journalist often coordinates the annual festival's seminars, workshops and screenings. Mumbai-based director Atul Kumar pieced together the brilliant inaugural 2004 festival. En route, local theatre groups staged plays by Moliere, Douglas Huff, Badal Sircar and Mahasweta Devi as a fund-raiser for Ranga Shankara.

Against a backdrop where every paisa counted, granite for the flooring and the dramatic staircase was donated by a quarry, while another concern cut it for free. Manufacturers of sanitaryware and bathroom fittings offered their products. While none of the city's IT majors pitched in to round out the big picture, industries like MSIL, Biocon, L&T, Himatsingka Seide Ltd., and Volkart contributed to the corpus. A woman labourer from rural Karnataka gave Arundhati Rs 5.

By its fourth festival in 2007, Ranga Shankara had established itself as a premier theatre space. At the festival, out-of-towners rubbed shoulders with locals, performances by local colleges and poetry recitals were held on the ground floor, even as stilt-walkers conjured up festive vibes in the foyer.

For that eagerly anticipated week in 2007, theatre overwhelmed Bengaluru's days and nights. Naseeruddin Shah, Ratna Pathak Shah and Benjamin Gilani starred in director Satyadev Dubey's searing, resonant production of Jean Anouilh's *Antigone*. Chorus staged its impressionistic Manipuri evocation of Dharamvir Bharati's *Andha Yug*, proving definitively that theatre soars beyond language. Jaimini Pathak, feted for his Gandhi-inspired *Mahadevbhai*, experimented with a folksy, exuberant staging of Kannada literary giant Chandrasekhar Kambar's *Tukra's Dream*.

Ranga Shankara has now become a meeting ground. As Arundhati pointed out in 2004, 'We have the riches of Kannada theatre. There's always been English theatre in Bangalore. But the two have not met. In Ranga Shankara, both will happen.' They have. It is as easy to access B. Jayashree's brilliant Spandana theatre or the Ninasam troupe from Heggodu, as to take in *Commedia dell'Arte Galore* by Italy's Luoghi dell Arte.

Occasionally, history comes alive on the boards. As it did when Lahore-based Ajoka's *Ek Thi Nani* was staged in 2004 with theatre veterans, sisters Zohra Sehgal and Uzra Butt, matching moves and nuances in a plot parallel to their real lives. The former, recovering from a fever at ninety-two, improvised a line as she coughed, went offstage for a pill, then continued like a true trooper.

Next to us sat a young collegian with her boyfriend, intending to slip away during the interval before the gates to her hostel slammed shut. 'How can you walk out on Zohra Sehgal?' gasped my friend, horrified. 'If you stay till the end, you can always sleep over at my flat in Frazer Town. Can you?' Abashed, the young woman called an aunt, and arranged to stay out for the evening. Her companion, an IT employee, was delighted. Both of them, moved to tears, joined the standing ovation to the thespian sisters.

What makes Ranga Shankara special? M.S. Sathyu says, 'It's the only theatre built entirely by theatrepeople. It's the best in India today, completely responsive to our needs.'

'The community has embraced us totally, both the theatre groups and the audience alike,' Arundhati reflects. Shouldn't they, when the theatre facilities—including thirty lights and fifty tonnes of air conditioning—can be hired for just Rs 2500 a day? Or when tickets to certain shows are pegged at Rs 49?

Today Arundhati, who sees herself merely as the public face of the theatre, lauds the inputs of sponsors like Vodaphone and Hivos, who have made the experiment possible.

'Theatre has landed in a chicken-and-egg situation in Bangalore, where all the actors in search of a livelihood are working in television or films. Once this space is ready, theatrepeople will have no excuse. They have to get the audiences back,' she had observed in early 2004. 'This theatre was born with the foundation stone. That's when I relinquished my power over this project.'

Her team is keen to support more positive dreams in the future. Such as enhancement workshops in improvisation, speech or lighting. Or a novel one-hour enactment of the journey of Indian theatre, against the backdrop of, say, Greek and Noh theatre, which is still at the research stage.

Theatre, to both the connoisseur and layman, is about the here and the now. The moment rendered live, when immediacy and illusion meld to create an unforgettable experience. That is the very essence of Ranga Shankara, the theatre that transformed Bengaluru.

On the Street, Everybody Watches

Nisha Susan

Standing at protests makes me laugh, Kostub. You say it's because my heart is in it (the cause, that is) but my mind is not and that is why I'm laughing. Of late, I'm inclined to think that you don't think I've much of a mind, anyway. Worse, I'm beginning to believe it myself.

Someone showed me the picture of two girls he'd met in Madhya Pradesh. The photo was awash with their smiles and the mauve, purple and blue of their dupattas. The same guy then told me how (two days after the photograph) they had been arrested for leading protests against a dam that was going to drown their village. They were dragged off to jail. In the prison compound, they climbed a tree and stood on the highest bough, dancing and singing for hours on end. The police was totally *popat*.

And then, there is me. My bile-ridden hatred for cops is equal to my fear of getting arrested. When I see a cop talking to a kid, I automatically glare, and think: 'Rapist.' Yet at protests, as soon as the cops appear, fatly, grandly, I sidle away with the others who are rolling up the placards and removing the black gags. I think 'Coward! Coward!' to myself, but that's about it.

I think I'm worried about getting beaten up. I can *feel* my cheekbones shattering and my teeth being loosened, appearing as a tortured, wide-angle vision in next week's *Outlook:* an innocent victim of police brutality. Of course, what is really frightening is that having shattered cheekbones scares me more than the shattering itself. Much good reading *The Beauty Myth* has done.

Perhaps it is some nervous, hysterical reaction of my deep middle-class roots. The giggling and laughing, I mean. 'Stands around in street corners,' in my kind of household is an insult meant to shake you to the core. It is a contemptuous smirk at the lack of honour in the family, with the unspoken addendum that not only does the subject have no job, she is probably having illicit sex when not standing at street corners. One morning, Kostub, your friends on their afternoon shift saw me standing at Gandhi Statue on M.G. Road. There I was, with a placard in the rain, protesting the razing of three slums for yet another mall. Seeing me, the boys' eyeballs fell out of their air-conditioned cab. They quickly put their shades back on and pulled out their cellphones, probably to SMS you and tell you about your girlfriend's eccentric behaviour. A week later, one of the idiots mailed and told me that he had uploaded a picture of me on his blog with some choice rude comments.

It comforts me to see Anu ducking behind a placard whenever red Marutis pass by. She has never gotten over the time she aggressively stuffed a thin, yellow leaflet against Section 377 into the gap of a tinted window of a red Maruti. The gap widened slowly to reveal a scandalized neighbour from Malleswaram, a neighbour who had once changed her diapers: 'Does your mother know you are here?'

The one time we were all arrested, Anu's mother *was* the one who got us out. She laughed at us for the next six weeks because she saw one of my colleagues from the English department reading *The Tin Drum* in the cell and avoiding the advances of a pickpocket who, poor man, was only trying to OC a cigarette.

There is something to be said for embarrassing middle-class origins. I know most people on M.G. Road would not take the leaflets from me if I were not standing there in an expensively shabby bought-from-Gujarat Emporium shawl over my jeans. *What's the chick doing standing in a public place?*

People are different in Banappa Park and Mysore Bank Circle. There, at least the *kadlekai* guys take the leaflets, read them thoroughly and then wrap the next sale of nuts in 'the dichotomy of globalization'. But my favourites are the auto-drivers, who are the most politically aware human beings. They lecture their passengers on the need for dissent and give us cocky grins that say that we are on the same side. *Right! I'm a fraud and you don't know it. If you asked me for ten rupees extra, I would screech at you.*

Chap with placard standing next to me at one protest asked me why people were coming across the street to pick up leaflets from me. I thought, 'Political sensitization has affected your hormones if you can't see *this* cleavage,' but I smiled sweetly and told him that it was only because I was barefoot. Since he was from out of town, I let him think that the barefootedness was because of my radical politics and not because of my broken shoe strap.

You attended two protests, Kostub, and then began to say that they were utterly useless. However, if someone is less unhappy because there are people who will stand with them at a street corner and bitch about globalization, that's good, I think. Otherwise, people might forget what standing in public places mean. Rush from your cubicle to your house and back to the cubicle, with a short stop at the supermarket. Spend no time anywhere where you don't have to pay to park.

Because only 'those' kind of people stand around at street corners, kanna.

Not that laughing at protests is cool. Sometimes, at the reviews of our 'actions', kind hints are dropped about a need for less frivolity, only to be met by catty rejoinders about old fogies who can't bear to see anyone else having fun. I was shaken up when I read a Doris Lessing novel in which a bunch of people keep returning triumphantly to their squat after futile protests and even more futile close brushes with the police, flushed with laughing excitement, the kind you get from winning a cricket match. I was supposed to be reviewing it for the new MA syllabus for Bangalore University and all I could think was: 'Oh God, that's us!'

Yes, I get very troubled but . . . I don't know. There are always intense discussions about violence and how Gandhi was shrewd and how he was not and how satyagraha can't work for us. No one is saying what *will* work, though.

You know, Kostub, I don't see the point, anyway, in looking for the Grand Unified Theory, the One Answer to Life, The Universe and Everything. It is just as bad as the wistful, charming copy for branded-MNC packaged-happiness. I want! I want!

You call me a Gandhi-Statue-Candle-Holder, your happy variation on Wagah-Border-Candle-Holder. I mumble that we stand at Mysore Bank Circle, too. (In Bangalore there are three popular protest spots: Gandhi Statue on M.G. Road, Mysore Bank Circle and the always benevolent Banappa Park.) You get your cheap thrills by telling innocent people about Gandhi-Statue-Candle-Holders. You love describing our jholas, our black saris, our large bindis, our thin fashionable cotton clothes, our earnest, perpetually outraged faces. I laugh along with you. It is not as if the comedy of protest protocol is not obvious to us. I swear, when a newcomer, a virgin protester turns up, it always rains and the old hands put on an extra bit of drama to show them how only the bourgeoisie are afraid of the elements. I know how careful we are about making cries of '*Awaaz Do! Hum Ek Hain!*' alternate with suffix-laden Kannada slogans, so that we are not slain dead by the Kannada abhimanis. I know how strange it seems to you that after protests, we go for coffee and sometimes do post-mortems of the protest with the rude relish of actors from a theatre company on their hundredth performance.

But Kostub, why do you refuse to concede that the affiliations formed by Gandhi-Statue-Candle-Holders can be as embarrassingly heart-warming? How can I convince you that I would never otherwise have known anyone from a slum in Koramangala or a village in north Karnataka? Ponni and I were at the *kaka* shop the other day, buying milk, when it occurred to me that I am an outsider. Ponni and I and you and all of us are actually outsiders. Ponni and I, with our super-short hair and our loose red pants, buying milk just for our outsized mugs of coffee are bloody freaks, and I never noticed before. The shopkeeper knows, and so does the lady sitting outside with a basket of yellow lemons. I didn't know, because we are indulged and protected from glimpses of our true identity. Everything in the television and on the billboards and in the right-hand bottom corner of newspaper front pages is created to indulge Ponni and me. Everything in this country exists, Kostub, so that Ponni and I can go home to our muted lighting and read Ondaatje over coffee and not know that we are freaks.

There be dragons that post-modernism and your sardonic face have bred. I take revenge by having conspicuously flirtatious encounters with butter-smooth good-lookers from the slum associations. Never mind the clichés that are strewn *there*.

Shit, why am I apologizing about laughing? Protests are funny. (Last year I read a Nadine Gordimer story about half a dozen people in a one-horse town, who form a secret Marxist society and how, when their social life improves, their political life ends. There! Corroboration from an award-winning author!)

Protests make me laugh. But I see in the eyes of your friends, those smiling financial analysts, kindly collection strategists and software engineers, the knowledge of what outsiders we are in Bangalore. That is when I want to say to you, 'I love you, da, but don't make fun of my people.' That is when I want the reassuring insider-ness of the protest.

Here we are at Gandhi Statue. Here we are at Mysore Bank Circle. Here we are—we who need not be careful about saying anti-America things. Here we are—we who don't have to explain why we wear khadi every day and why that is neither 'ethnic' nor 'radical'. Here we are—thin, fat, dark, fair, razor-sharp, not-very-clever, tired, worried people —holding sheets of K.G. cardboard against a world that has picked our city to be its fall guy.

You have accused us of liking the weather up here in our moral high ground. That is far from the truth. How can we, when we envy and are shamed by the presence of those among us who pick up their cheap luggage after coffee to go back to their village in Raichur or Gulbarga or Orissa, where they have been living without running water for the last six months and where they say that they feel that they are *beginning* to establish a rapport with the people. When there are amongst us those who smile and wave and hop back into a bus back to L.R. Nagar slum because that is where they live.

Now you want us to consider leaving because Bangalore is not comfortable enough any more. You can't deal with the commuting, the traffic, the pollution. You want to live in a country that is 'more disciplined'. You think that when I'm a few years older all of this will stop being so important to me. At least you are not as dense as that friend of yours who told you that he wants to 'do social service like your girlfriend' when he is retired. Of course, even among us there are the ones who have done this entire route of rainy-street-corners-with-coffee-after half a lifetime ago. They tell me to Transcend the Question. What can I say to that, except to point out that they'd get along rather well with you, Kostub? And that standing at protests makes me laugh.

Veena Tapaswi Doreswamy Iyengar

K.N. Raghavendra Rao

Though Bangalore was never quite considered the heartland of classical music in the sense that Mysore or Dharwad were, it did nurture the glorious voice of R.K. Srikantan, besides the gentle maestro evoked here.

IT WAS an evening in 2006 at the M.E.S. College 'Kalavedi' in Malleswaram. Old times were being recalled. The time belonged to legendary maestro Veena Sheshanna, the strings echoed the master's unique rendering of a *tillana* in Raga Darbari to the slow tempo of a *vilamba kala*. Bringing alive the memories was veena *vidwan* or maestro Balakrishna. His grasp of the composition and movement had sincerity, a lyrical quality. His fingers moved through time, carrying the music and melody passed on to him by his father Veena Doreswamy Iyengar—one of the greatest exponents of the veena.

The evening left an indelible imprint on me. It rekindled memories of enchanting moments spent in the company of Doreswamy Iyengar in early 1991. Though I was based in Chennai then, thanks to the late B.V.K. Shastri, a great writer and critic of Carnatic music, I had the good fortune to meet many a master of music during my short stay in Bangalore. I was, at that time, trying to create a visual essay on the great exponents of Carnatic music and Bharatanatyam.

Naturally, I was slightly nervous, almost anxious, before meeting the great veena vidwan. But I need not have worried. Doreswamy Iyengar proved to be a simple man, imbued with modesty and grace. He was keen to know about my work and plans. I was deeply moved when he blessed me.

With Shastri as my guide, I sat before the master and his veena at his home on Fourth Main, near 17th Cross, in Malleswaram. As his fingers caressed the strings, I felt his music still held traces of the innocence of a child. He quietly answered many a question of mine regarding the veena and the unique Mysore style. It was a rare experience of listening and learning. After two hours with the master, I was filled with a sense of fulfilment and sheer happiness.

I have another fond recollection of Veena Doreswamy Iyengar, dating back to 1992. 'Laya', an exhibition of my photographs of these masters of the classical arts, was to open at Sakshi Gallery in Bangalore. I had gone to him with just Rs 1000, to request him to bless the occasion with a lecture-demonstration. It was an unforgettable event, listening to him that evening. With the veena keeping him company, he detailed the history and the great *parampara* or heritage that Mysore (now Karnataka) is blessed with.

The master told us: 'To the lay listener, all veena recitals may sound alike. But like the various schools or *gharanas* in Hindustani music, Carnatic music has its schools, too. Especially so while playing the veena. In the south, there are three major styles or *banis*, from Thanjavur, Andhra and Mysore. The Mysore style is unique for its *meetu* or special way of plucking the strings, its distinctive embellishing *gamakas* or tonal curvature, besides its *chittetaanas* or phrases. These enhance the melody, grace and aesthetics of the instrument. Let us not forget our epics. We should remember that the veena was the constant companion of Sage Narada (known as a divine messenger, a counsellor to royalty, a celestial musician, and a holy mischief-maker)!'

The maestro's knowledge that evening cast a magic spell on all those who had assembled there. The notes wafting off his strings had a story to tell. It is impossible to forget his goodwill, his generosity when he came to the gallery with his accompanying artistes that evening. That moment made me feel that people who have music in them lead a truly qualitative life.

From Chennai, I moved to Bangalore in 2004. Ananya, a home for music, beckoned us to Malleswaram. As a youth, this had been home to me. Yet, close to where the goddess Saraswati sits with her veena, I sensed a void. For her disciple Doreswamy Iyengar left our midst in 1997. But today, Balakrishna seeks her guidance and blessings to continue the tradition. He is grateful for the legacy left to him by his father, and his grandfather Veena Venkatesh Iyengar.

Keen to trace the history of generations of such genius, I seek the help of Balakrishna. For hours, I listen to him, spellbound.

I am taken back to the early twentieth century. To Madihalli, near Belur, in Hassan district. Janardhan Iyengar owned a small piece of land there, not quite enough to maintain a family. Yet, as he tilled his fields, he brought home contentment and happiness. He had lost his wife early, and so had to take care of their three sons. The eldest, who bore his own name of Janardhan, helped him with the land, but the second—Venkatesh—was much keener to listen to the devotional songs his father sang at home or in the field. The latter wanted to drop out of school. He dreamt of learning music. The youngest, Varadachar, was happy with his slate and chalk.

How was Iyengar to make Ventakesh's impossible dream come true? Who could teach him music in the village? Yet, he was determined not to disappoint the boy. One day, he entrusted the fields to his eldest son, and set off on foot for faraway Mysore with the two younger children. Impelled by his trust in God and his own willpower, he and the boys began to walk the distance with a few rupees in his pocket and some packed food.

When they were tired, they slept wherever they could. When they were hungry, they shared the small amount of food among themselves. Sometimes Iyengar would go hungry, so that the boys could eat. It was a difficult journey. The children were often in tears. Iyengar would comfort them, or even carry them on his shoulders by turns. After what seemed like an eternity, they laid their eyes on Mysore for the first time.

A long search resulted in temporary shelter at the Parakala Math, a religious centre. The hot meal there meant so much to them.

Mysore state was then ruled by the gracious monarch Krishna Raja Wodeyar IV, who reigned from 1884 to 1940. Krishna Raja's rule was based on the right ethical values, besides great recognition for art, literature and music. His court was home to luminaries like Veena Sheshanna, Veena Subbanna, Veena Venkatagiriyappa, Shri Vasudevacharya, Bidaram Krishnappa and others.

Janardhan Iyengar sought the right guru for Ventakesh at this confluence of music. But whom should he approach? What could he offer as a guru dakshina or tutor's fee? Someone suggested veena vidwan Chikka Subbaraya: 'He is kind, even generous. Do go to him.'

Father and son stood in front of the vidwan's house, with fear welling up within them. It was noon. The guru was resting. When he emerged, both of them fell at his feet. The guru was taken aback. With tears rolling down his cheeks, Iyengar pleaded with him to take Venkatesh on as a *sishya* or pupil. He narrated the tale of their journey from Madihalli. He added, 'Please give my son *vidya daan*, the gift of knowledge. We are poor, but Venkatesh is well mannered, honest and willing to do any task you give him. That is the only guru dakshina we can offer. Please accept him.'

Touched by the family's plea, veena guru Subbaraya accepted Venkatesh Iyengar as a disciple. The father and son, so fond of music, now found it their everyday companion in the form of the veena.

Food and shelter were initially a problem. But, in the early twentieth century, many families volunteered to take care of poor students. Much to his relief, Janardhan Iyengar got a job as a priest in a Brahmin's family. His youngest son, Varadachar, was admitted to a school. Their food came from many homes.

Venkatesh proved to be a very good pupil. He took to music easily. Learning vocal music proved essential, so that the same touch or nuances could emerge as his fingers moved on the veena. Years rolled by. Venkatesh mastered many *kritis* to the satisfaction of his guru. Veena Venkatagiriappa, who listened to him once, told Guru Subbaraya that he was keen to take this boy on as his own disciple too. That was a stroke of good fortune. There were, thus, two masters to train Venkatesh. At a young age, he even became an *asthana vidwan* or court musician, an honour bestowed by royalty.

His was an unusual saga of a child who realized his dream—from Madihalli to Mysore, then to the palace as a court musician.

Years rolled by. Vidwan Venkatesh Iyengar was now married. His first son, Doreswamy Iyengar, was born in 1920 at Doddagaddavana Halli, close to their ancestral home in Hassan district.

Venkatesh Iyengar was very keen that his first born should inherit the majesty, the magic and the grandeur of the veena. In response to his plea, his own Guru Venkatagiriappa took Doreswamy—then just seven—as a disciple. Typically of a boy that age, he was more keen to play marbles, spin a top, play *chinnidandu* or climb any tree in the lane!

But he took heed of a well-meaning warning from his guru: 'Remember, you were born for the veena.' By the time he was twelve, a passion for music had gripped Doreswamy Iyengar. His guru told him that the veena should sound as if it was singing on its own, not as if notes were being cajoled out of it. He quoted Veena Sheshanna's words to his disciple: 'Hold the veena as the mother tigress holds its young cub—firmly, but with loving tenderness.'

Doreswamy practised constantly. He adhered to the teachings of his guru. He listened to the music of celebrated vidwans. Unusually knowledgeable for someone so young, he soon came to be noticed by the leading lights of the day. One day, the Maharaja invited him to his chamber, along with other young talents. Pleased by the youth's confidence and promise, the king rewarded Doreswamy Iyengar with a gift of fruits and flowers, in addition to fifty silver rupees! Soon, despite his youth, the palace invited him to be one of its asthana vidwans. It was unusual for both the father and the son to be so honoured.

Apart from his music lessons, Doreswamy had to attend regular school, too. A rather different reception awaited him there. He would later note, 'My effort was to just get pass marks, not to excel. I took my own time to get to my BA, spending a year extra at every exam!'

Decades later, Mysore University honoured Veena Doreswamy Iyengar with a D.Litt.

The highlight of his life in Mysore was the privilege of playing at the palace, besides attending music concerts with his guru at the then well-known music hall, Lakshmi Theatre. Many musicians—including Mysore Vasudevacharya, Thitte Krishna Iyengar, Bidaram Krishnappa, and T. Chowdiah—cast a spell on him. He even listened to concerts by musicians from outside the state, such as Ariyakudi Ramanuja Iyengar, who once sang a Kannada *devaranama* or devotional song, '*Yaake bande jeeva*' ('Why this life') by the saint Vijayadasa. The song left a deep impression on the young vidwan.

More moments to treasure followed. He would now accompany Guru Venkatagiriappa who, recognizing his disciple's talent, once said, 'You make the veena sing . . . ' This compliment delighted everyone, but more intensely his father Venkatesh Iyengar, and even more so his grandfather Janardhan Iyengar.

Doreswamy Iyengar was often invited to perform at the palace. The maharaja would ask him to elaborate on a raga. Thus, the palace became a site of learning for him. The maharaja loved Carnatic music, but he was equally fond of Hindustani and Western classical music. The veena vidwan loved this opportunity to expand his own musical horizons. Later in life, he became a close friend of musicians like Vilayat Khan, Ravi Shankar, Nandalal Ghosh and Ali Akbar Khan. The great Hindustani vocalist Mallikarjun Mansoor loved to sing to the accompaniment of his veena. Balakrishna recalls that he often saw his father enjoying the music of Beethoven and Mozart.

Over time, Doreswamy Iyengar had opportunities to render small solo concerts. And then came a chance to play on All India Radio (AIR), facilitated by a well-wisher, the violin maestro T. Chowdiah.

In 1954, he was asked to join AIR at Bangalore as a producer, shortly after he had played on its national programme. He was faced with a dilemma. Mysore was his home. The palace and the great musicians there were his life. Would this be a wise decision? He finally took the advice of the then maharaja, Jayachamaraja Wodeyar, who said, 'Mysore . . . yes. But Bangalore is the state capital now. I want your music to spread far and wide.'

At the outset, Doreswamy Iyengar seemed reluctant, even rebellious about the prevailing bureaucracy at AIR, but he soon made friends who brought joy to his working life. They included veteran Kannada poet P.T. Narasimhachar, well-known literary figure Maasti Venkatesh Iyengar and the great philosopher-writer D.V. Gundappa. The revered Carnatic vocalist Semmangudi Srinivasa Iyer had high regard for his music. Doreswamy Iyengar brought brilliant musicians like Carnatic vocalist Balamuralikrishna to AIR, and set Gundappa's poems to music for him. Pandit Ravi Shankar described Doreswamy Iyengar's music as 'fantastic mastery'. He even created the masterly composition, Geetha Bharathi, based on Rabindranath Tagore's songs with tunes from Carnatic kritis.

Doreswamy Iyengar's music won him much acclaim. His was an unusual journey, studded with success and concerts abroad, yet few men were more modest than him. Devoid of flamboyance, this simple man just surrendered to music. Even a national honour like the Padma Bhushan sat lightly on his shoulders.

He was instrumental in establishing a strong bond between Carnatic and Hindustani music. This came to the fore in an unforgettable *jugalbandi* he had with sarod maestro Ali Akbar Khan in 1964 at Lalitha and Shivaram Ubhayakar's home at Malleswaram. Those who were present that evening still recall their impeccable togetherness—and how the music flowed!

A *kala tapaswi* or a sage of music. That is how the poet Narasimhachar described Veena Doreswamy Iyengar, who once said, 'The veena is the god I believe in. But he has witheld so many secrets from me. There have been moments when it looked as though the mystery might be revealed to me at last, but the next moment it was gone. But I shall continue my *tapas* or the search.'

The veena vidwan had dreams for his son, Balakrishna. The father watched the child on his wife's lap, as the boy listened intently to the veena late at night, a time for *sadhana* or spiritual practice. The boy once said to his mother, 'Amma, before I go to sleep at night, you give me milk and sugar, while Anna plays the veena. How lovely both are . . .'

The great *parampara* or uninterrupted succession of the veena has to continue. For, as Balakrishna says, 'My sadhana or effort is already there. I hear my father saying that creating music, being one with music, makes one belong to the sublime, perhaps even the divine. I need my father's blessings . . .'

Finger-lickin' Bad

William Dalrymple

QUITE HOW far the new Bangalore had moved from its immediate hinterland was made horribly clear in mid-October 1996, when it was announced that the 1997 Miss World contest was to be held there.

The state government and the city's hotels immediately welcomed the move, but no one else did. Within weeks, an unlikely coalition had formed in protest against what was seen as the ultimate foreign cultural invasion. Feminist suicide squads formed, promising to immolate themselves if the 'degrading' pageant went ahead. Hindu fundamentalist organizations such as the RSS and Vishwa Hindu Parishad (which masterminded the destruction of the mosque at Ayodhya in 1992) joined hands with their sworn enemies, the Muslim Jamaat-i-Islami, to decry what they saw as an assault on traditional Indian morality. Closing ranks to defend the chastity of Mother India, the right-wing Hindu BJP stood on the same platform as the (supposedly) left-wing and secular Congress party.

The Karnataka farmers and Kannada language chauvinists, not to be outdone, continued their agitations, unloading a trailer-load of cow dung outside the showroom of one of the Indian sponsors of Miss World, the consumer electrical goods company, Godrej, coating the interior, the exhibits and even some of the staff with dollops of slurry. Soon afterwards a small homemade bomb, 'about the size of an orange', was thrown at the electrical transformer controlling the lighting of the stadium where the pageant was due to be held. The transformer was undamaged, but a large crater was left in the asphalt nearby. By the end of October, strikes, marches and demonstrations were taking place in Bangalore on an almost daily basis.

From *The Age of Kali: Travels and Encounters in India*, Penguin Books India (2002).

The day I flew in, the south Indian newspapers contained little news that was not in some way linked to their rapidly escalating protests. The *Deccan Herald* announced on its front page that a thousand commandos of the élite Indian Rapid Action Force were to be drafted in to guard the Miss World contest after 'the leader of a rural populist activist group had threatened to torch the venue of the show, which he described as an example of "cultural imperialism".' In another part of town, 'a group of noted women artistes have expressed their support for the beauty contest. The artistes feel that the protests are nothing but silly and ridiculous exercises. "These protestors are an insecure lot who cannot face the world," remarked Arundhati Nag, the noted theatre artiste.'

On its op-ed page, *The Hindu* ran a full-page feature linked to the Kentucky Fried Chicken protests. It was entitled, 'Vegetarianism—Ideal Choice': 'Scientific investigations have firmly established that vegetarian diet is far better and ideal for one's health and environment protection,' claimed the writer, V. Vaidyanath. 'South American forests have been cut down to grow cattle for hamburgers. Some outstanding personalities such as George Bernard Shaw, William Shakespeare, Percy Shelley and Isaac Newton were vegetarians. To preserve health and environment, the people should prefer vegetarian diet.'

All this seemed, at first, to be quite a spectacular overreaction. Miss World may be tacky and tasteless, but surely only in India would anyone threaten to commit suicide over such an issue. Kentucky Fried Chicken may not be gourmet cuisine, but it surely takes cultural insensitivity to a new extreme to regard fast food as an insult to the national honour. Yet when you begin to talk to people in Bangalore, you come to realize that beneath the xenophobia and the nationalism lies a very reasonable fear of progress, a genuine disorientation in the face of massive change.

Until the early 1990s, Bangalore had been a sleepy, well-to-do city, remarkable only for its botanical gardens, cool climate and excellent race track. Everything changed overnight when the city gained the reputation of being the cradle of India's hi-tech revolution. Foreign investment and personnel poured in at a quite extravagant rate. Unemployed migrant workers followed quickly on their heels, and what had been known as the Garden City suddenly found itself ringed with stinking shanty towns. Because of this unparalleled immigration, between 1971 and 1996 Bangalore's population jumped from 1.7 million to over 6 million, making it one of the fastest growing cities in the world. The pressure on land grew, causing house prices to rise stratospherically, increasing by 50 per cent per annum throughout the early 1990s. As pollution grew worse and the city's green spaces began to disappear, the average temperature rose by several degrees every year.

Such hyper-development obviously leads to massive strains. The Government of Karnataka, which had proved adept at attracting foreign investment, soon showed itself to be wholly unable to cope with the massive expansion it had helped to generate. Suddenly, there was never enough electricity; during some weeks power was totally absent. It was the same with water, which was usually available in the taps for less than an hour a day. In summer, it often disappeared completely for whole weeks at a time.

Everywhere, the old colonial bungalows began to be pulled down and replaced by towering office blocks. In a feeble attempt to keep the roads from clogging, the city's glorious green roundabouts were all bulldozed. Bangaloreans were horrified by what was happening to their once-beautiful city. The writer and historian T.P. Issar, who published a book on the city's architecture at the end of the 1980s, told me that his book is now of only archival value: 95 per cent of the buildings he described and illustrated less then ten years ago have been pulled down.

'These demonstrations are simply expressions of people's alarm at what is happening to Bangalore,' he said. 'Some people have certainly made a lot of money, but most have found that their life has got worse: think of the volume of traffic, the noise, the pollution. The people here have good reason to fear the future. In a few years, everything that is familiar in this city has been destroyed. The opening of these restaurants and the fuss about Miss World, these are just flashpoints.'

The growing discontent in the city was perhaps best articulated by the youthful general secretary of the BJP, Ananth Kumar, who has recently thrown his weight behind the protests. 'What I am objecting to is not any individual restaurant or beauty contest, but the mindset they both represent,' he told me as he sat in Gandhian homespun beneath a framed and garlanded picture of Shivaji. 'The entry of multinationals into Bangalore over the last few years has initiated a spiral of prices. The rich have flooded in, the poor can no longer afford housing, education, transport, and even the most basic amenities. In this country half the population—460 million people —has a daily income of not more than ten rupees (twenty pence). A situation where millions are kept in poverty, without education, while a microscopic minority enjoys all the facilities available to the élite classes of Britain and America, cannot continue indefinitely.'

I asked why Pizza Hut or Kentucky Fried Chicken should be the target, rather than the government or the houses of the rich.

'These foreign restaurants are symbols of the disparity between rich and poor,' replied Kumar. 'Only the tiny westernized élite want to eat there, or indeed can afford to eat there. There is a burning discontent which has begun to be directed against these outlets. A popular upsurge is growing that wants to hit out at those symbols.

'Take my word for it,' he said ominously. 'It won't be long before this becomes an explosive situation.'

*

ON MY last day in Bangalore, I woke up to find that every wall was posted with flyers announcing 'A MAMMOTH PROCESSION AND PROTEST MEETING: PROTEST INVASION OF WESTERN LIFESTYLE AND SAVE NATIONAL HONOUR.' Changing my plans, I asked the auto-rickshaw driver to take me straight to the venue.

This, significantly enough, was Chikkalalbagh, an old Moghul garden built by Tipu Sultan, who in the late eighteenth century had led attempts to stop a rather more aggressive invasion of Western multinationals in the shape of the East India Company.

As we neared Chikkalalbagh, our pace sank to a crawl. Well over two thousand people had gathered with their placards: *'Beware: Western Dogs Are Here!' 'Stop Kentucky!' 'Save Indian Culture!'* A cheerleader was standing by a rickshaw to which two huge loudspeakers had been attached. Fist raised, he led the crowd in a chant of *'Down down, Miss World! Up up, Mother India!'*

Abandoning my rickshaw, I pushed through to the front of the crowd, where I found Professor M.D. Nanjundaswamy, President of the Karnataka State Farmers' Association, standing around in a woolly tea-cosy hat and holding a huge picture of the Mahatma with his spinning wheel. It was Professor Nanjundaswamy who had organized the first wave of attacks, and he had spent several weeks in prison for his pains.

'Actually, we farmers believe in true Gandhian non-violent protests,' said the Professor, when I asked him about his protests.

'But that didn't stop you smashing up the Kentucky Fried Chicken restaurant.'

'Ah, you see, hurting living beings—such as killing cows and chickens: that is violence,' replied the Professor. 'But damaging inanimate objects: what violence is there? These actions are necessary if we are to save Indian culture.'

'But what harm is there in a single chicken restaurant?' I asked. 'Three thousand tandoori restaurants in London don't seem to have destroyed British culture.'

'Actually, our case is very different,' said the Professor. 'We have evidence that the entire livestock of Karnataka could be wiped out in two years. When the Government of India fails to protect the interests of its people and its cows, direct action is becoming inevitable. We are undergoing a cultural invasion worse than the Moghul invasion! Worse even than the invasion of our India by the Britishers!'

Professor Nanjundaswamy's ideas may be a little eccentric, but they are the very picture of calm moderation when compared to those of his ally, Ms Pramilla Nesargi, the BJP MP for Bangalore South. Ms Nesargi was standing beside the Professor, scowling at the police cordon in front of her.

'The Miss World organizers are definitely in league with this Kentooky,' she said. 'It is a conspiracy hatched by all these people to destroy our ancient Hindu culture. Kentooky is the same as East India Company. In that case one company was sufficient to occupy all India. But this government has let in many multinationals.'

By now the protesters had formed a crocodile and begun to march. As they passed through the bazaars, handing out flyers in English and Kannada, their numbers swelled with curious passers-by: a pair of *sadhus,* a party of schoolgirls, a man with an ice-cream trolley. While we walked, Pramilla Nesargi painted a grim picture of Colonel Sanders and the Miss World organization as sinister Riders of the Apocalypse, one of them descending on Bangalore bearing carcinogenic chicken nuggets to poison the unsuspecting Hindu youth, while the other perverted the morals of any left alive by the Kentucky plague.

'What is the impact of this Miss World?' she said. 'I will tell you. When children see Miss World they will always be wanting to see all women in swimwear only. There will be 100 per cent increase in sex crime. Since the government allowed MTV into India, sex crime has already increased by 100 per cent. Men are seeing these things and then committing rapes, committing murders. No woman is safe in our India any more. Eve-teasing (sexual harassment) is happening every day.'

No less damaging, according to Pramilla Nesargi, will be the effects on the contestants, each of whom, according to her, has to undergo a makeover on the sort of scale received by Robocop.

'These world beauties are coming,' Nesargi said. 'But I don't call them beauties. Not at all. These are artificial . . . all silicon. Excess fats are removed from body: this lipo . . . Then all the body hair is removed by electrolysis. Silicon injection is given. The face will be lifted. The eyebrows are taken. Bleaching is there. Then artificial eyes are given: green or blue are put in. You call this beauty? Beauty lies in nature. Not in this artificially made . . . thing.'

The arguments of the Bangalore protesters are shot through with a myriad of such myths and inconsistencies. Hinduism has celebrated the erotic for millennia, and it seems most unlikely that the religion which produced the *Kama Sutra* and the sculptures of Khajuraho will be fatally wounded by a selection of beauty queens strutting around in swimsuits. Indeed, modern Indian modesty seems to reflect imported Victorian notions of decorum more closely than anything home-grown: after all, the women of Bangalore, as elsewhere in southern India, went about bare-breasted until the British encouraged them to cover up in the nineteenth century.

More importantly, economic liberalization and the entry of foreign competition has enormously strengthened India's outdated industrial base. The seed industry is a case in point. Fifty years of economic protectionism allowed Indian seed producers to get away with selling substandard seeds, which in turn led to Indian farmers growing substandard crops. When Cargill Seeds opened an operation in India, they immediately seized half the market, leading to the bankruptcy of many Indian seed companies. But those who learned to compete are now producing excellent seed strains at highly competitive prices. Ten years later, India now looks likely to become a major seed exporter, able to undercut and outperform almost all its Western rivals.

Yet to concentrate on such glaring holes in the protesters' arguments is to miss the point of a case that is more emotional than logical. They are firing warning shots across the bows of those who seek to turn India into a distant satrapie of Western capitalism. In their more xenophobic manifestations, the Bangalore protests can seem a ludicrous attempt at shutting out the twentieth century. Yet you cannot help feeling that there is something rather admirable in trying to preserve one corner of the globe free from McDonald's yellow parabolas, a last piece of territory where masala dosas will forever rule supreme over Colonel Sanders' finger-lickin' good Kentucky Combo Meals.

As the Moghul emperor Babur noted in his diary soon after he conquered the subcontinent in the early sixteenth century, 'In India everything is done differently from the rest of the world. Nothing will ever change this.' India will choose what it wants from the rest of the world; but its own unique and deeply conservative culture is not going to go down without a struggle.

Back to the Future

Ammu Joseph

LAST NIGHT, I had a dream.

I was dutifully polishing brassware, affectionately gifted by friends and relatives over the years, which have sadly turned into millstones thanks to the effusion of unidentified gases emanating from unmentionable effluents flowing through the storm water drain behind our house. I was, of course, thinking dark thoughts and muttering under my breath about the BDA, the BMP, the BWSSB and other benighted 'planners', 'administrators' and 'service providers' of Bangalore, whose accumulated sins of omission and commission were now being visited upon us, hapless and increasingly hopeless citizens for whose benefit they exist and on whose paid-up taxes they run.

Suddenly the *paandaan* at the receiving end of my grudging ministrations flew open and out poured a large vaporous being bearing an uncanny resemblance to an ex-chief minister turned prime minister turned no minister, who claimed to be a genie. And, as is the wont of such freshly freed spirits, he promptly offered to grant me three wishes to turn Bengaluru back into a land of *haalu* and honey.

When I had recovered from the shock and excitement, I panicked: three wishes? How could three wishes possibly restore this brutalized city, battered and bruised from two decades of unbridled and bungled growth? If wishes were horses, I grumbled to my not-so-genial genie, then Bangaloreans would ride the Metro or Mono or whatever his lookalike would condescend to consent to. But I might as well have saved my breath: my new-found benefactor was lost to the world, catching his forty winks where he was, while he could.

I had to think quickly in case the wish fulfilment offer had an expiry date. The trick was, clearly, to come up with multi-tasking wishes that could begin to bring back at least some of the charm of the Bangalore I moved to in 1988, when it was still possible to imagine why Joseph Machaud described it as 'the most beautiful habitation that nature has to offer to mankind upon earth . . . ' It was easy then to understand why Winston Churchill, too, waxed so eloquent about the quaint little town fondly known to Cantonment-wallahs as 'a spot of England in an alien land'.

Even in the early 1990s, the Garden City-turned-Pensioners' Paradise-turning-Silicon Plateau still retained much of its small-town atmosphere, although it was already on the verge of entering the big league as a city. Those were the days when there was a hill station feel to Bangalore, with the blazers that were part of the uniform of local 'public schools' making sense because mornings were chilly enough for children to need a sweater or jacket almost throughout the year.

In 1991, celebrated as Visit India Tourism Year, I was a relatively recent convert to the Bangalore way of life. In an article written then, I recorded its many attractions, among them its famous climate— described by an expatriate resident in a local guidebook at the time as 'one of the most liveable climates in India and, for that matter, most of the world'.

On the weather front, Bangalore continues to score above most other Indian cities most of the time. But in several other respects it has lost some of its sheen. Over the years, much of its environmental and architectural heritage has been sacrificed at the altar of 'development', while its infrastructure has been completely overwhelmed by unplanned industrial growth and the attendant population influx and geographical expansion.

So today, even as an Incredible India tourism campaign is under way, here I was desperately seeking solace, if not solutions, from a genie! That reminded me: it was time to switch from wistful to wishful thinking before the sleeping giant awoke and decided that I, together with Bangalore, was a lost cause.

If infrastructure, architecture and the environment are among the most conspicuous casualties of the long-standing and continuing mismanagement of the city, I thought, they clearly had to figure on my would-be wish-list. It didn't take me long to decide that my first wish would relate to traffic congestion, which has not only become a major bane of life in Bangalore but, to me, symbolizes its infrastructural crisis, closely linked as the problem is to the scarcity of public

transport, paucity and poor quality of roads and, of course, the
ineffectuality of zoning.

My second wish had to be about restoring the greenery and water
bodies that accounted for Bangalore's fast-fading reputation as a
garden city. This, to me, is not simply about 'beautification'—a term
favoured by city authorities, although their concept of civic beauty
generally does not involve nature. It has as much to do with natural
resources and climatic conditions as with the quality of life, as well
as the physical and mental health experienced by citizens.

I figured my third wish should be about refashioning the cityscape,
which has completely altered the look and feel of Bangalore over the
past decade: its traditional houses and colonial bungalows giving
way to multi-storey buildings, its unique and eclectic mix of
architectural styles replaced by bland but brassy structures, and
ubiquitous hoardings and haphazard banners adding to the visual
cacophony. To me, this is not only about urban aesthetics or about
the stress resulting from the lack thereof. It is also about relieving
the unsustainable strain on public utilities such as power occasioned,
for instance, by widespread, permanent artificial cooling in what is
still a naturally air-conditioned city through much of the year.

Now that I knew what I wanted, I was not sure how to proceed.
Having never dealt with a genie before I had no idea what the self-
appointed grantor of wishes expected from the would-be grantee: a
simple list of requests or a full-fledged project proposal—mission
statement, conceptual framework, target group, projected outcomes,
budget, monitoring mechanism, et al.? Since our friend was still out
for the count, I banished such vexing thoughts from my head and
took off on a flight of fancy instead. And here's a glimpse of life in
my little middle-class, semi-suburban corner of the city of my
imagination:

I wake up in the morning to the sound of birds twittering on the
trees that line all the beautifully asphalted streets in my neighbourhood.
I look out of the window and see that some senior citizens are already
walking along the wide, even footpaths towards one of the many
parks in the area where residents can congregate to enjoy fresh air,
socialize, exercise, have a round of chess or Scrabble at specially
designed tables, supervise toddlers playing in the kiddies' corner or

keep an eye on pets frolicking in the dog-run.

A few youngsters, too, are heading towards the local playground to enjoy a quick game before going to college or work. In the early evening, children home from school will occupy the space for a refreshing round of sport. Of course, they also have a choice of indoor games like table tennis, a modest gym in the area's community centre, which boasts a library and a room for playing cards and board games. The centre offers multi-purpose spaces for cultural activities, yoga, lectures and discussions and, of course, the monthly residents' meeting at which civic issues are aired and sorted out, with municipal officials or political representatives in attendance, when necessary.

I set out for a brisk morning walk in our own little version of Lalbagh, created out of the grassland at the far end of our colony (blessed with a small, recently resuscitated lake), thanks to the efforts of the environmentalists among fellow residents, who successfully lobbied against the conversion of the open land into a commercial-cum-residential complex.

On my way back home, I pick up some fresh bread from the bakery in the local shopping centre which houses a variety of shops and establishments that meet most regular needs of the neighbourhood and provides small businesses with legitimate space in which to operate. I note with satisfaction that the public toilets in the shopping area and next to the water-pump serving the village engulfed by our layout are clean and smell-free, despite their evident popularity. And that the secure waste-bins strategically placed near the toilets, as well as the community centre and the parks, show signs of being regularly used and emptied, with the area around them also litter-free.

After breakfast, I put my segregated garbage out for collection in the pilfer-proof covered bins provided by a consortium set up by residents of the nearby village: the local raddi-walla collects the paper and plastic while a group of once-unemployed youth have built a thriving business out of recycling the biodegradable waste, using a corner of our mini Lalbagh for vermiculture and supplying organic manure for use in private gardens as well as public parks in the neighbourhood and beyond.

Setting out for work, I wait at the end of our street for the van that conveniently connects our area to the nearest station of the railway that encircles the city. The frequent shuttle service, which follows a circular route within the suburb, picks up and drops residents at various points along the way, including the education hub where local schools and colleges are located, the commercial hub where banks and other businesses including larger shops and restaurants are concentrated, and the civic amenities hub where the offices of the postal services, public utilities and local administration, as well as the community health centre, are based.

I wave to my neighbour, who is heading towards the Inner Ring Road in her car, which she needs to go to a concert at the other end of town in the evening. On such occasions, she parks in one of the large parking lots placed at regular intervals along both the ring roads around the city and then takes a share-taxi from there to her workplace. It is not worth driving directly to her boutique in the city centre since the tax on private vehicles with just a single occupant entering the core business district is quite high.

My other neighbour does not have that problem because he belongs to a car pool. He is all praise for the mid-town underground parking facilities, which not only preserve the look of the city while freeing up space on the roads but also enable people to comfortably walk to their destinations. My family, too, now loves weekend browsing in the pedestrian plazas that Bangalore's famous shopping boulevards, Commercial Street and Brigade Road, have become. We particularly enjoy the outdoor cafés that have livened up the place and contributed to making even idle window shopping an enjoyable pastime.

From the railway station closest to my office I take another shuttle bus which lets me off just a five-minute walk away from my building. I really like my office, which is in a renovated old mill where the distinctive old exterior has been left intact and the interior has been converted into airy offices that take full advantage of Bangalore's nine months of cool weather. For extra comfort during the short, if intense summer, we use compact, movable, easy-to-store coolers.

In the evening I take a taxi to the main railway station, where the monorail from the airport located some distance from the city connects with the multi-faceted urban transport system. I had arranged to meet an out-of-town friend who had arrived on a late afternoon flight there, so that we could ride the commuter train back to my part of town together. In deference to her luggage and possible travel fatigue, we use an auto from the orderly stand outside the station to get back home even though we could just as well have opted for the shuttle van that I generally prefer.

As we cross the familiar bridge over the storm water drain, my friend looks around, puzzled: 'Hey, where is your infamous *nallah*?' I am pleased to point to the jogging track to the left of us and the sculpture garden to the right of us, both sitting atop the cleaned-up trench through which only rain water now flows. Further upstream is a food court showcasing the cuisines of Karnataka and at a distance downstream there is a *santhe* featuring crafts and handlooms from different parts of the state. The erstwhile public nuisance had metamorphosed into public assets, thanks to citizen action supported by official ingenuity and corporate sponsorship.

Getting out of the auto outside the house, I look around and see a group of elders walking home from the park, couples setting out for their evening run, children cycling back from music or dance classes at the community centre, young people waiting for the shuttle to take them to their favourite hang-outs in the suburb's commercial hub, the few vehicles on the road stopping for pedestrians waiting at the zebra crossing . . .

And I think: 'Into this heaven, oh genie, let my city awake!'

I guess that was the thought that woke me up.

PART VI

COFFEE BREAK 3

The Morphing of Bangalore: Drawings by Paul Fernandes

The Garden City

Pensioner

Pubcity

Boomtown

Silicon Valley

Bangluroo

PART VII

THE 24/7 CITY

nanolore

S.S. Prasad

I LIVE on the outskirts of nanolore
where builders promise gigaspace,
past Intel, Pulsecore, Freescale.
My roads transform overnight into one-ways;
the traffic jams form a constellation
of headlights along the national highway.
I go to my hometown for Christmas,
have learnt to thank God for Fridays.
I live in a silicon valley that is remote controlled:
when it burns elsewhere, here it smokes.
I'm part of a game of ladders and snakes—
I'm not sure I'll have my job tomorrow,
but for today, a six-digit gross is no joke.
The receptionist in my office panics at ISD calls,
and laughter fizzes in the cubicles like Coke.
I have upgraded my car to Mercedes
from Maruti, my family is proud of me. But
my neck hurts from Repetitive Stress Injury,
my evenings are masked and nights enlarged
by the company that patents circuits, basmati,
turmeric and neem. Will another Alavandan*
challenge this Akki Alvan, mon ami?
I wear my tag, lest I forget who I am.

---

*   Akki Alvan, a court poet under the Cholas, collected tax for
knowledge from his fellow pandits, whom he subdued during
debates. He imprisoned those who failed to pay him the tax.
The Vaishnavite saint Alavandan challenged Akki Alvan to a
debate, and defeated him, thus setting free the imprisoned pandits
and abolishing the tax.

Brand Bangalore:

Emblem of Globalizing India

A.R. Vasavi

Bangalored: verb; losing one's information technology job to someone in Bangalore. Bangalored is a neologism and used as a verb. Bangalored is used to indicate a layoff, often systemic, and usually due to corporate outsourcing of the business function to lower wage economies. The word is derived from Bangalore, India, which houses many outsourcing centers for Western economies. — Wikipedia, 2006

IN LENDING itself to becoming a verb, Bangalore's rise to global visibility is complete. From what in the 1980s seemed a false ambition to become the Silicon Valley of the East, the city and its name are now emblematic of the new globalizing India.

If 'Bangalored' signalled the rise of a threat perceived by the West of losing IT jobs to India, then additional prefixes associated with the industry cue us in to the arrival of the city as an international hotspot. In emerging as a global city, Bangalore has been subjected to dual processes—of emitting its own specificity to herald its rise as a city representing the new global India, and of lending itself to the designs and orientations of global capitalism.

Subject to international scrutiny, the city has generated new idioms and images that highlight its identity within the context of flexible capitalism, new technical workers, and the spread of élitist global lifestyles. Observing the increase in the numbers of returning technical and trained personnel, entrepreneurs and managers to Bangalore and to other metropolises in India, the term 'Bangalore Boomerang' has been coined to refer to the reversal of the brain drain, long associated with the loss of trained manpower from the nation. Interviewing Azim Premji of Wipro in the US, one newspaper refers to him as 'Bangalore's Bill', an IT billionaire whose entrepreneurial drive and acumen have made him one of the world's richest men. Devoting a whole book to the rise of Wipro, American author Steve Hamm labels the company as the 'Bangalore Tiger'. He lauds its business acumen, upholding it as a wake-up call to complacent Americans. Business journalist Thomas Friedman writes of the new 'flat' organizational structures of IT companies that make for an imminently new global capitalism, citing Bangalore's leading IT company Infosys. And *Forbes Asia* magazine nominates the CEO of Infosys Nandan Nilekani as the 'businessman' of the year 2006. Even as the popular media celebrate the rise of the city and its economy, academic assessments ponder potential future problems. As IT salaries rise with the stiff competition to retain personnel, the possibility of such increased salaries overcoming the cost advantage is assessed and the term 'Bangalore Bug' becomes a part of management jargon.

The city is now on the global watch list. The *New York Times* writes about a bandh called by either regional chauvinists or by mourning fans of cinestar Rajkumar. The *Washington Post* discusses the wealth of the rising IT czars from Bangalore. The *Guardian* comments on the city that serves as the world's back office. Heads of successful IT and biotechnology (BT) companies have become the stars of the media; they articulate worldviews that call for the making of a new India. Coming together to showcase the industry, the IT companies call for the recognition and strengthening of 'Brand Bangalore', and therefore the city's contributions to the new economy and life.

Integrated into the circuit of global capitalism, the city and its landscape, identity, orientation, and its key actors have been appropriated and altered to suit the needs and regime of the new flexible capitalism. Not only are the spectral buildings of IT companies the sites of new production; they are also closely matched with the attendant new sites of consumption—gated residential communities, malls that house global brands of consumer goods, international food chains, and upmarket branded cars that ride the roads.

In eclipsing Delhi and Mumbai, Bangalore, with its salubrious climate a far cry from the unbearable tropical heat of the rest of the country, has flagged its rise as the unexpected upstart—a city of high technology, the 'IT hub of India' with a large pool of trained and skilled personnel who would help India 'leapfrog' from an underdeveloped and predominantly agricultural economy to a global service economy. In its drive towards a global identity, it has sought a makeover in the image of other cities and regions: a potential Singapore, Asia's Silicon Valley. In place of its cultural economy of Bangalore silks, Mysore sandal, Bangalore agarbattis, jasmine, and even the 'Bangalore Torpedo', comes the economy of information technology and information technology-enabled services (ITES) which, in their visibility and dominance, have eclipsed attention to the other economies. The garment industry that draws on the labour of several thousand, whose own urban geography of factories is linked to semi-slum housing, fed by an increasing tide of urban migrants, is largely ignored. Transformed into a 24/7 city, the IT and BPO companies proclaim their triumphant presence and success. Hoardings exhort the youth to become part of the new ITES brigade, and invitations for walk-in interviews are posted at all junctions. At night, the BPO economy is visibly in full swing, linked to the working and daylight hours of the West, as jeeps, vans and cars ferry youth workers to and fro from their residences to work sites.

But Bangalore's circuit of international economy and lifestyle bears an uneasy link with the larger social and economic realities. The construction boom draws on the labour of the many displaced agriculturists: north Karnataka migrants seeking relief from recurrent droughts and non-remunerative crop prices, find new livelihoods; Rajasthani carpenters reproduce international designs in high-rise homes; Tamil workers move easily across the borders, fitting into the expanding service economy; Malayalee entrepreneurs set up neighbourhood stores with arrays of local and international goods; men from Bihar and Orissa respond to the demand for new security services and guard the homes and offices of the economic élite; pan-Indian domestic workers arrive to assist yuppie and young working couples. As multi-regional labour colonies emerge, one hears a cacophony of tongues as migrant workers wait in lines at STD booths to call their home. On a parallel track, new-age spiritual gurus make Bangalore their home, and their devotees, from various parts of India and abroad, throng the ashrams that are blends of resorts, therapeutic centres and spiritual abodes.

The grandeur of Brand Bangalore is occasionally threatened by regional and local claims. Voices arise from the increasingly invisibilized and the marginalized to claim Bangalore, not as a site of the international economy but as the capital of a regional state, the home of political aspirations and the centrifuge of Kannada culture. At actor Rajkumar's kidnapping in 2001 and years later at his death in 2006, the city is held to ransom by rampaging mobs, who ensure a total shutdown. Their targets are the symbols of non-Kannada/ Karnataka enterprises—the glass buildings of IT companies, buses that ferry the software engineers, the plush apartment complexes of the new rich. Similarly, farmers agitating for fair prices and policies converge on the city and lay claim to it, sending the traffic into snarls that last for hours. Political parties hold rallies, asserting their presence in a city that is otherwise largely oblivious to their existence. And in what must be the best expression of the city's global ambition are a range of new 'blade companies' that offer jobs to the numerous inadequately qualified persons seeking a piece of the global pie and a share in its glimmering new lifestyle and opportunities. In the spirit of robber capitalism, these fly-by-night enterprises shut down after raking in the recruitment money paid by aspiring employees.

Like the dissident voices, the infrastructure of the city, long neglected, is unable to bear the weight of the now voluminous population and traffic, and collapses. Stagnant drains, unpaved sidewalks, pitted roads and crowded streets become the bane of an aspiring international city. Even as the enclaves of the city are landscaped to resemble California, Venice or England, the region's natural topography seeks to assert itself. During the monsoons, water rushes into low-lying areas, as apartments, houses and streets are flooded.

In emerging as an emblem of the nation's drive towards globalization, the city is torn between the claims and counter-claims of the global and the local. Even as the reference and mention of the city in international circuits increases, the city is renamed Bengaluru, derived from its founding myth of a place where the hunting chieftain Kempe Gowda was fed with beans. What sums up the contradictory orientations and voices in and for the city most succinctly is a slogan painted at the rear of an autorickshaw: 'Let there be IT, let there be BT, but let there also be Kannada.'

The World Is Flat

Thomas L. Friedman

I SET out for India by going due east, via Frankfurt. I had Lufthansa business class. I knew exactly which direction I was going thanks to the GPS map displayed on the screen that popped out of the armrest of my airline seat. I landed safely and on schedule. I too encountered people called Indians. I too was searching for India's riches. Columbus was searching for hardware—precious metals, silk and spices—the sources of wealth in his day. I was searching for software, brainpower, complex algorithms, knowledge workers, call centres, transmission protocols, breakthroughs in optical engineering—the sources of wealth in our day.

Columbus was happy to make the Indians he met his slaves, a pool of free manual labour. I just wanted to understand why the Indians I met were taking our work, why they had become such an important pool for the outsourcing of service and information technology work from America and other industrialized countries. Columbus had more than one hundred men on his three ships; I had a small crew from the Discovery Times channel that fit comfortably into two banged-up vans, with Indian drivers who drove barefoot. When I set sail, so to speak, I too assumed that the world was round, but what I encountered in the real India profoundly shocked my faith in that notion. Columbus accidentally ran into America but thought he had discovered part of India. I actually found India and thought many of the people I met there were Americans. Some had actually taken American names, and others were doing great imitations of American accents at call centres and American business techniques at software labs.

Columbus reported to his king and queen that the world was round, and he went down in history as the man who first made this discovery.

From *The World Is Flat: The Globalized World in the 21st Century*, Penguin Books Ltd, 2005.

I returned home and shared my discovery with only my wife, and only in a whisper.

'Honey,' I confided, 'I think the world is flat.'

*

HOW DID I come to this conclusion? I guess you could say it all started in Nandan Nilekani's conference room at Infosys Technologies Limited. Infosys is one of the jewels of the Indian information technology world, and Nilekani, the company's CEO, is one of the most thoughtful and respected captains of Indian industry. I drove with the Discovery Times crew out to the Infosys campus, about forty minutes from the heart of Bangalore, to tour the facility and interview Nilekani. The Infosys campus is reached by a pockmarked road, with sacred cows, horse-drawn carts, and motorized rickshaws all jostling alongside our vans. Once you enter the gates of Infosys, though, you are in a different world. A massive resort-size swimming pool nestles amidst boulders and manicured lawns, adjacent to a huge putting green. There are multiple restaurants and a fabulous health club. Glass-and-steel buildings seem to sprout up like weeds each week. In some of those buildings, Infosys employees are writing specific software programmes for American or European companies; in others, they are running the back rooms of major American and European-based multinationals—everything from computer maintenance to specific research projects to answering customer calls routed there from all over the world. Security is tight, cameras monitor the doors, and if you are working for American Express, you cannot get into the building that is managing services and research for General Electric. Young Indian engineers, men and women, walk briskly from building to building, dangling ID badges. One looked like he could do my taxes. Another looked like she could take my computer apart. And a third looked like she designed it!

After sitting for an interview, Nilekani gave our television crew a tour of Infosys's global conferencing centre—ground zero of the Indian outsourcing industry. It was a cavernous wood-panelled room that looked like a tiered classroom from an Ivy League law school. On one end was a massive wall-size screen and overhead there were cameras in the ceiling for teleconferencing. 'So, this is our conference room, probably the largest screen in Asia—this is forty digital screens put together,' Nilekani explained proudly, pointing to the biggest flat-screen television I had ever seen. Infosys, he said, can hold a virtual meeting of the key players from its entire global supply chain for any project at any time on that supersize screen. So their American designers could be on the screen speaking with their Indian software writers and their Asian manufacturers all at once. 'We could be sitting here, somebody from New York, London, Boston, San Francisco, all live. And maybe the implementation is in Singapore, so the Singapore person could also be live there . . . That's globalization,' said Nilekani. Above the screen there were eight clocks that pretty well summed up the Infosys workday: 24/7/365. The clocks were labelled US West, US East, GMT, India, Singapore, Hong Kong, Japan, Australia.

'Outsourcing is just one dimension of a much more fundamental thing happening today in the world,' Nilekani explained. 'What happened over the last (few) years is that there was a massive investment in technology, especially in the bubble era, when hundreds of millions of dollars were invested in putting broadband connectivity around the world, undersea cables, all those things.' At the same time, he added, computers became cheaper and dispersed all over the world, and there was an explosion of software—email, search engines like Google, and proprietary software that can chop up any piece of work and send one part to Boston, one part to Bangalore and one part to Beijing, making it easy for anyone to do remote development. When all of these things suddenly came together around 2000, added Nilekani, they 'created a platform where intellectual work, intellectual capital, could be delivered from anywhere. It could be disaggregated, delivered, distributed, produced and put back together again—and this gave a whole new degree of freedom to the way we do work, especially work of an intellectual nature . . . And what you are seeing in Bangalore today is really the culmination of all these things coming together.'

We were sitting on the couch outside Nilekani's office, waiting for the television crew to set up its cameras. At one point, summing up the implications of all this, Nilekani uttered a phrase that rang in my ear. He said to me, 'Tom, the playing field is being levelled.' He meant that countries like India were now able to compete for global knowledge work as never before—and that America had better get ready for this. America was going to be challenged, but, he insisted, the challenge would be good for America because we are always at our best when we are being challenged. As I left the Infosys campus that evening and bounced along the road back to Bangalore, I kept chewing on that phrase: 'The playing field is being levelled.'

What Nandan is saying, I thought to myself, is that the playing field is being flattened . . . Flattened? Flattened? I rolled that word around in my head for a while and then, in the chemical way that these things happen, it just popped out: My God, he's telling me the world is flat!

Here I was in Bangalore—more than five hundred years after Columbus sailed over the horizon, using the rudimentary navigational technologies of his day, and returned safely to prove definitively that the world was round—and one of India's smartest engineers, trained at his country's top technical institute and backed by the most modern technologies of his day, was essentially telling me that the world was *flat*—as flat as that screen on which he can host a meeting of his whole global supply chain. Even more interesting, he was citing this development as a good thing, as a new milestone in human progress and a great opportunity for India and the world—the fact that we had made our world flat!

In the back of that van, I scribbled down four words in my notebook: 'The world is flat'. As soon as I wrote them, I realized that this was the underlying message of everything I had seen and heard in Bangalore in two weeks of filming. The global competitive playing field was being levelled. The world was being flattened.

Dancing on Glass

Ram Ganesh Kamatham

About the play

Megha works nights at a call centre. Shankar is a software engineer.
When Pradeep, Megha's boyfriend and Shankar's roommate, dies, there is suddenly a void in both their lives. They come together, braving the torture of their professional lives, struggling to connect, reaching out for each other in the darkness . . . An extract.

Characters

    Megha, 22, *a customer care consultant*
    Shankar, 24, *a software engineer*

The action takes place in Bangalore, India.
The play unfolds in a claustrophobic non-realistic space that both characters share.
This single space conflates the multiple spaces both characters inhabit and traverse.
    We watch, as if gazing upon two lab rats slowly dying.

02:54

Megha's office, a call centre. She fields a call from a drunken American.

Megha. Hi! You've reached I-soft Customer Care. How may I help you?
VO (Voice-over). Uh . . . Hi. Yeah . . . I'm having problems with my Internet.
Megha. I'm so sorry to hear that, but I'm glad I'm the one that got your call. I'm going to do everything I possibly can to help you today. Is that all right?
VO. Yeah.
Megha. My name is Megan. May I know your name, please?
VO. Uh. Dan . . . my name's Dan.

Megha. Thank you, Dan. In order to help you, I'll need to pull up your account and ask you a few questions to protect your privacy and security. Is that ok?

VO. Uh . . . yeah.

Megha. We'll get right to it. Dan, do you have your I-soft account card with you?

VO. Yeah. That's the one with all the numbers on it, right?

Megha. That's right. Could you read out the last four numbers of your customer identification number for me?

VO. Uhh . . . I don't know what that is.

Megha. It's the third number on the I-soft account card. The one labelled Customer Identification Number. It has sixteen digits. Could you read out the last four numbers of that number for me?

VO. Four . . . seven . . . nine . . . oh.

Megha. Thank you, Dan. I'll just check that number. *(Pause)* Dan, I'm having some problems with your account. Could you repeat that number for me?

VO. Four . . . seven . . . nine . . . eight.

Megha. Four seven nine eight?

VO. Yeah . . . that's what I said, didn't I?

Megha. Yes, you did say that, Dan. I'm sorry I didn't hear you the first time. I'll just check your account.

VO. What did you say your name was?

Megha. Megan. Right, Dan, I've just verified your account information. What seems to be the problem?

VO. When I try to connect to the Internet, it won't let me.

Megha. I apologize for the inconvenience, Dan. I'm sure I'll be able to help you out. Before we get started, I'll need to ask you a few questions. What operating system are you using on your computer?

VO. Windows.

Megha. Thank you. How are you connecting to the Internet—a modem, DSL?

VO. Modem.

Megha. Thank you. Are you sure your modem is operational?

VO. What?

Megha. Is your modem working?

VO. Now, how the hell am I supposed to know that?

Megha. Dan, when you switch on your modem, do you see lights flashing? Or do you hear some sort of dial-up noise? Like the noise a fax machine makes?

VO. Megan . . . right. You said you're Megan.

Megha. Yes, Dan?

VO. I don't think you're an American. I can tell a Pakistani cunt when I hear one. You're a Pakistani cunt, aren't you? In like fuckin' Afghanistan or something.

Megha *(pause).* Dan, I'm located at Bangalore, India. At the I-soft Customer Care Centre.

VO. And you're not Megan. You're Jamilla or Sushma or something, right?

Megha. Dan, I'm here to help you with any problems you have with your account. I'm just doing my job. And I'm here to ...

VO. Naw, bitch. You're doing my job. Sitting in front of a computer, and takin' calls. That's my job. That's what I feed my family with, yeah? And you took it away. Yeah?

Megha. Dan, is there a problem with your account that I can help you with?

VO. Your job, your job is to spread yer fuckin' legs and let the fuckin' marines teach ya a lesson. Yeah? That's your fuckin' job. Takin' calls is my job, ok? Not yours. You got that? That's my job.

Megha. Dan, once again, I'm afraid I can only help you with problems related to your account.

VO. The problem with my account is that it doesn't work and the other problem is . . . I mean, how the hell are you going to solve my problem when you're in fuckin' Afghanistan. Yeah? Do you understand what I'm trying to tell ya?

Megha. Yes Dan, I completely understand. But as a valued customer, I must ask you to focus on the problem at hand.

VO. I'm goin' to get another drink and when I come back, I'll tell you about the problem. Yeah ... and ... *(muffled thump, dial tone)*

Megha. Dan? Hello? Have a great day and thank you for calling Customer Support.

Megha takes off her headset. Moves away from the computer, stretches.

Megha. Fucking Yankee *chooth!*

'I can't connect to the Internet.'

'My modem's not working.'

Three o' clock in the morning. Give me a break!

When I joined, everyone told me about the Yank who called up and said his coffee cup holder was not working properly.

I'm sure you've heard this one.

Consultant says, 'Sir, could you explain the problem a little more clearly?'

'Uh yeah. The free coffee cup holder that came with my computer is not working. The one that has Sony 52X written on it.'

I didn't believe it then, but now who knows.

Fuck off, Megan. *(pause)* Hi. My name is Megha.

Lights change.

10:43

Shankar's office, a software company. He tries to work. Phone rings.

Shankar. Hello, Shankar here.

VO. Hello, I'm calling from Standard Chartered.

Shankar. Not interested. Thank you very much.

VO. Ok madam.

Shankar. Madam? *(hangs up, phone rings immediately)* Hello.

VO. Hello, is this Suresh?

Shankar. No. Wrong number.

VO. May I know who I am speaking to?

Shankar. I'm Shankar.

VO. Hello Mr Shankar, I'm calling from . . .

Shankar. Not interested; no, thank you. Bye.

Shankar hangs up. Expects it to ring again. It doesn't. He gets back to work.
Phone rings.

Shankar. Hello.

VO. Shankar, Krishna here. Can you give me an update?

Shankar. Oh, hi Krishna. Of course. I've finished 90 per cent of the third module. Moment I'm done, I'll send it out for testing. Should be done with this module by close of business today.

VO. Ok. We've decided to skip testing for this module. I'll be giving you another two or three modules, you'll need to test those. Moment you are done, let me know.

Shankar. Ok. I was wondering ...

The phone has already been hung up. Shankar returns to work, annoyed at the extra load. The phone rings again. Shankar answers.

Shankar. Hello, Shankar here.

VO. Hello Mr Shankar, this is Shruti calling from ICICI Bank. We are offering you a credit card absolutely free.

Shankar. Not interested; thank you.

VO. We are not charging anything. And you have a credit limit up to rupees three lakhs.

Shankar. Three lakhs! What am I going to buy worth three lakhs?

VO. Anything you want, Sir. Up to three lakhs.

Shankar *(pause)*. What's the catch?

VO. No catch sir. This is a 'special offer' for employees of your company. If you are interested, I will send my person. All I need is your payslip and a visiting card.

Shankar. Listen, I have no money. So, if I have to pay anything, I won't.

VO. How can you say that, sir! You are working in MNC.

Shankar. And that's the other thing. I'm a contractor here. So, is that special offer still valid?

VO *(pause)*. Certainly, sir. So, when shall I send my person, sir?

Shankar. I'll need to think about it.

VO. What's there to think about, sir? Tell me a time.

Shankar. Give me a call tomorrow. Same time, just before lunch.

VO. Definitely, sir. What's your number?

Shankar *(blinks)*. Didn't you call me?

VO *(laughs)*. Yes, sir, I did. But can you give me this extension number, sir? I've made quite a few calls today.

Shankar. 4002.

VO. Thank you.

Shankar. And listen. The seats next to me are 4003, 4005 through to 4010. No one sits here, alright. So, if you are calling in sequence skip these, because no one will pick up the phone and you'll just end up irritating me.

VO *(laughs)*. Ok, sir. Thank you, sir. Have a nice day.
Shankar. You, too. *(hangs up)* I don't believe this!

He tries to regain the coding rhythm. Smiles as he feels it kicking in. Phone rings.
Shankar lets out an anguished moan.
Lights change.

08.13
Megha's bedroom. The moan becomes Megha's as she tries to sleep. It is a wretched
desperate attempt, involving a lot of tossing and turning. The noises of the morning
plague her. Her cellphone rings.

Megha. Hello.
VO. Hi.
Megha. Hi baby.
VO. You sleeping?
Megha. I think so.
VO *(laughs)*. Which means what?
Megha. Day-night-sleep-wake—god knows. Bloody sun on my face.
Where are you?
VO. At work. I'm running another shift.
Megha. Are you mental? Take a break, for god's sake.
VO. Ok, listen. We have a small problem.
Megha. Oh shit.
VO. Roopa is ill.
Megha. No man. What's wrong with that stupid girl? Is she ever
well? I can't keep cleaning up her mess. And tomorrow's Saturday.
What about our weekend? We were supposed to go out.
VO. She's got that same throat infection again.
Megha. Can't she amputate it?
VO *(laughs)*. Ok. Pick up happening at 7.30. I'll tell the van guy.
Megha. I'm tired. Can't you give it to someone else? And what about
lunch tomorrow?
VO. I know, I know. I'll make it up to you. Promise.
Megha. Same shit you're telling me.
VO. I know, I know.
Megha. What 'I know'.

VO. Sorry. Promise I'll make it up to you. Promise. I have to go. Ok, see you at work.

Megha. I hate you.

VO. I love you.

Megha. Love you too. Bye.

VO. Bye.

Megha hangs up and tries to get back to sleep.

Megha. How the HELL am I supposed to sleep!

Lights change.

Call Centres Call On

Sahana Udupa

'I NEVER felt it was India. I could not see India there. If 10 per cent, or even 25 per cent was Indian, 75 per cent was American,' recalls Srinivasa Murthy, sixty-plus, of his first impressions of a multinational Bangalore call centre. 'People were moving around frantically! Oh, the way ladies were behaving! The party mood was far from the festival mood in Karnataka. What dancing! What jumping! What cigarette smoking! *Abbabba!*'

Seated on a worn-out wooden sofa in his home, he evokes with horror his first tryst with the 'globalized' Bangalore. He had accompanied his son Nithin to the plush office, responding to an open invitation from the company to the parents of all its employees.

After resigning his secure government job and testing his luck with twenty-odd private companies, Murthy now leads a retired, though not entirely peaceful, life. He is worried about call centres and other similar new industries. 'Their business is all for America. They are doing nothing for our country, our Kannada *nadu* or Bharata *desha*. Their business has no relationship with our land. I feel sad that my son is not being of any help to our country. As a patriot, I feel strongly about it. Even NRIs or non-resident Indians are of some value. Though they settle abroad and work, they get money to India and do some service here. My son does none. If there is some problem in America, its effects will be seen here,' he muses.

Nithin, Murthy's call centre son, smiles at his father's concerns as he moves from one room to another. He lacks the time to respond to his father's allegations point by point. The pick-up vehicle will be at his door in less than half an hour. These accusations are not new to him. He has heard them several times—that he is not patriot enough, that he is not 'secure' enough, that he is slipping away to the American mode of living. To Nithin, these are not real issues. The real issue is livelihood. As a failed civil engineer, he didn't have much to hope for.

The call centre has given him a job and a future to look forward to. 'I was promoted to the quality department one and a half months ago, after a long wait. I was always interested in quality. I don't have to take calls any longer. The quality department is more organized. This (being a quality analyst) is considered a higher position. This is second-level support. It certainly is growth,' says Nithin enthusiastically, almost as a counterattack to his father's observations.

Like Nithin, the call centre industry has rescued many other careers from an impasse. It has given them wads of currency to splurge, loads of cigarettes to smoke, and well-toned young company to elevate them in body and spirit.

About 300,000 people, mostly in the twenty to twenty-eight age bracket, work at call centres across India. They provide voice-based solutions to people calling from North American and European countries. Simply put, they attend to callers' grievances and enquiries over the telephone. Call centres in Bangalore cropped up around 2000, capitalizing on the city's successful IT industry. According to NASSCOM, the Indian apex body for IT industries, the software services industry in India has grown rapidly from small beginnings in the 1980s to generate total earnings worth $13.5 billion in 2004–05. In the wake of an annual growth rate of 50 per cent during the 1990s, it has grown at about 28 per cent per annum since 1999–2000. Riding on the software industry's success, ITES entered India more recently. As the new high growth industry at 50 per cent per annum in recent years, it generated export revenues of $4.6 billion in 2004–05.

Although the domestic market for IT services and ITES is expanding, IT–ITES remains primarily an export-oriented industry, with export earnings accounting for about 64 per cent of the total IT sector earnings of $28.4 billion. In 2001, software services exports constituted 14 per cent of India's total export earnings. By 2005, gross revenues from IT services accounted for 3.3 per cent of the Indian gross domestic product. According to a NASSCOM–McKinsey report, India now accounts for 65 per cent of the global market for offshore IT services and 46 per cent of global business process offshoring.

Bangalore's $47.2 billion economy makes it a major economic

centre in India. Indeed, the city is India's fourth largest and fastest growing market. Bangalore's per capita income of $6,460 is the highest for any Indian city. As of 2001, Bangalore's share of $3.7 billion in foreign direct investment was the third highest for an Indian city.

Bangalore, as the greatest beneficiary of the IT revolution, could be regarded as the cradle of India's tryst with global capitalism. Approximately 1200 IT companies operate out of Bangalore. According to the state-owned Software Technologies Park of India, IT and ITES companies in Bangalore directly employ over 250,000 people.

The might of manpower

THE DEMAND for manpower within industries of the new economy has been staggering. Innovative forms of recruitment have been floated to cope with the situation. Mega job fairs with attractive stalls on sprawling public grounds call on the youth at fever-pitch. Walk-in interviews are held on all weekdays inside the luxurious premises of huge companies. Thus, potential contenders can walk in, be interviewed, and recruited within a single day.

Call centre companies are often content with modest English speaking skills. As one HR manager put it succinctly, 'We are scraping/ scratching the bottom of the barrel.' The challenge before call centre companies is enormous. To meet their insatiable need for manpower, they have to overcome the ubiquitous mother tongue influence (MTI). Candidates familiar with call centre expectations are anxious to hide their MTI, for fear of losing a golden opportunity to join a mega multinational company. 'I don't want to learn too much Arabic because it might affect my English accent. I will be kicked out of the call centre if I allow that to happen,' says Abbas, a call centre aspirant, who flew in from Dubai to get a job in a Bangalore-based call centre.

MTI is an irritating obstacle to many Indian candidates. Their English accent supposedly bears the 'pungent odour' of their native languages. In the voice-based BPO industry, the MTI virus is of major concern because it might deter the ability of Indian call centre workers to effectively converse with American callers. Their accent, diction, pace and intonation should resemble, if not completely match, that of their American clients. Since the available manpower pool is limited, companies do not look for completely MTI-free English. They are content with curable accents. While some companies design elaborate training programmes to do away with MTI, others employ neurologists to tackle the 'MTI menace'.

'People in India unconsciously translate everything from their genetic language to their mother tongue to English. This creates a neurological block that is often a problem at call centres. This may be in terms of how the employee talks or how he deals with the customer. I know of a Malayalam speaker who thinks in his genetic language. The muscle control for each language is different. The movements that control speech patterns, from the lungs to the tongue and mouth, are determined by your genetic language,' explains Dr D. Topaz, consultant neurologist and psychiatrist at a multinational call centre. 'Language ability is genetically influenced,' he asserts. At his company, he remedies this deficiency by 'restoring' neural connectivity to make the muscles (for speech) respond to the brain. Apart from speaking and listening skills, newcomers are also given a crash course on American people, their values, ethnicities and festivals.

24/7

DESPITE THESE challenges, IT and ITES are successful industries. The key to their success is their round-the-clock servicing. 'We are a 24/7 industry. While the world sleeps, India wakes up,' says Sriharsha Achar with pride. He is a top HR manager at a multinational call centre. However, the round-the-clock servicing comes with its own set of challenges. The foremost one is employee retention. Many call centre workers succumb to health hazards very early in their lives. Hypertension, backaches, asthma, throat infections and sleep disorders are common. Retaining employees and keeping them in good spirits is a perpetual HR worry. Losing an employee costs the company dearly, albeit only up to a certain point.

Call centre companies in India spend huge sums of money to train new recruits and finally assimilate them into the process mode. 'It is an immense responsibility. The company takes care of its employees from recruitment to retirement, from the cradle to the grave,' states

Achar. On an average, companies spend nearly $2000 on every employee for hiring, induction and training. If an employee stays with the company for 270 days, they recover that outlay. If the stay is shorter than nine months, the company fails to achieve its return on investment. 'The industry is facing a lot of flux. It is a challenge for every organization to increase the longevity of its employees,' explains Achar. Attrition at some call centres has reached 100 per cent, often referred to as 'revolving-door attrition'.

Call centres sometimes try to arrest attrition by creating a bubbly, hyperactive social atmosphere within the office or doling out freebies at regular intervals. Most companies have a 'Rewards and Recognition' department, which designs contests and incentive systems. One large company has spent $200,000 on rewards alone. Often, awards are given to the firm's 'best coach', 'best leader', 'best manager', or even 'consultant of the year'. Others hand out grandiose titles, such as 'Roaring Tiger'. Colour television sets, DVD players, caps, T-shirts, cellphones, washing machines and numerous other consumer goods are handed out to workers who have fielded the maximum number of calls or have the highest sales in a month. One company sends its top 2 per cent performers on a Mediterranean cruise. Some even appoint a CFO or Chief Fun Officer. 'As [the psychologist] Abraham Maslow recognizes a hierarchy of needs, in reality people are driven by different motives at different points of time. The primary drives for any employee would be respect, opportunity, development and money,' explains Achar.

Panoptical control

BANGALORE's National Institute of Advanced Studies (NIAS) did a study of the city's call centre workers from December 2003 to March 2006, with Dr Carol Upadhya as its principal researcher. Professor A.R. Vasavi and Professor Peter Van der Veer of Utrecht University in the Netherlands were its project directors.

What were its findings? That companies deliberately create a fun atmosphere and institute rewards as strategies to divert the attention of its workers from the monotony of work and to arrest high attrition levels. In order to deflect attention from the extremely rigid and structured techniques of direct control, and the stress caused by working night shifts, BPO companies offer comfortable, 'fun', or even 'hip' working environments. They come up with days when all employees come to work wearing a certain colour or a style of clothing. Many holidays, both Indian and foreign, are celebrated with elaborate decorations, rituals and parties. On Halloween, the 'Grim Reaper' came through each floor to entertain the workers at one call centre.

These efforts are designed to combat the ordeal of incessant call-taking, round-the-clock monitoring, and nerve-wracking pressure to sell goods or services to callers. Critical organizational researchers point out that these companies employ panoptical modes of control. There are automated complex tracking tools that continually monitor and time each call, including how effectively it delivers the company message. Managers and team leaders constantly keep an eye on the workers on their teams. Apart from quantitative measures, the quality of their work is also evaluated, and later fed into the performance appraisal process. Remote monitoring, performed by a separate department, involves plugging into the call of an agent without his/her knowledge. Competition is constant, triggered by various technologies. All these make the call centre floor as hot as a furnace.

Lifestyle shifts gear

CALL CENTRE workers are also considered to be equally 'hot'. 'Look at that girl. She is so sober. Let her join a call centre and work for some time. She will explode! She will begin to sport snazzy clothes and long earrings. They enter like Gandhis, and come out like Hitlers!' says the youth from Dubai, pointing to a young lady, a potential recruit at a call centre.

Is this true? Widely held notions assume that because call centre workers talk to Americans for hours, they tend to adopt their culture. They are said to drink, smoke, take drugs, date, and even have numerous sexual flings. These service workers can pursue the new consumerist urban youth lifestyle to a greater extent than others in their age group due to their higher incomes. Call centre agents often sport emblems of the new global youth culture such as body piercings, tattoos and coloured hair. The Bangalore media run regular stories on call centre lifestyles, including lurid details about how office toilets were clogged by condoms. Some companies now enforce an official ban on drugs and sexual activities. Their conference rooms are locked at night, while common aisles and work stations are monitored by hidden cameras.

The NIAS study found that the emergence of a westernized youth subculture within BPO companies has earned the industry a rather negative reputation among many middle-class Indians. 'Many countries attacked Indian culture several times in the past. But our culture didn't change. But if the entire generation undergoes a cultural change, what will happen to our culture? Their way of life is leaning more towards foreign culture. Even the music they listen to is Western. If this goes on, won't our culture be washed away?' asks an infuriated parent.

However, it might be premature to conclude that all call centre workers embrace Western culture with open arms. To some, regular interaction with foreign clients highlights the strengths of Indian roots. 'I have begun to respect Indian culture much more. Many American callers talk about Indian culture. They respect our culture. I learnt a lot about India, even began to like the Indian social system of rearing children. I respect the fact that Indians are more tolerant than Americans. Compared to Americans, we are very mild. India means a lot to me now. I never want to leave India. I see India from a totally different perspective. We have lots of ethics. We need to show them what India is,' observes an emotional Anu Blackham. She has worked at a Bangalore call centre for over three years. By call centre standards, she is a veteran.

I Dream of Bangalore

Kevin Maney

She came on the setting sun
She made me come undone
She's hot like fresh-baked *naan*
She's got what was my job
She learned everything I know
She said, Now home I must go
She left me wanting more
I dream of Bangalore

When the tide turns round
And the balance falls away
Leaving you unbound
For a brand new day
She left me with my debts
She made me have regrets
She's who I so adore
I dream of Bangalore

Author's note: *I'd been reading stories about tech workers whose jobs were getting outsourced to India, and who were forced to train their Indian replacements to get their severance packages. So, I got thinking: what if some guy was in that position and his Indian replacement was a woman he falls in love with as he's training her? That's the genesis of the song which I wrote in 2005.*

Bit by Byte

Sham Banerji

I HAVE heard it said that living in India is like living in different centuries—all at the same time. As observations go, this captures most accurately, for me, the contrasting experiences of the past, the present and the future that India excites in some indelible way. This apparent proximity with what has been, what is, and what is yet to be, I think, is braided somewhat uniquely through the streets of Indian cities. From the first encounter Bangalore, more so than any other city, evokes this contrast with little regard for the time axis. In writing about Bangalore, I found myself unravelling this *triveni* and trying to pick up strands of connections from disparate starting points.

Starting with one unlikely connection, I discover that Bengaluru was founded during the Italian Renaissance. About the same time as Michelangelo was putting the finishing touches to *The Last Judgment* in the Sistine Chapel in the Vatican, Kempe Gowda I was struggling with a different project for a future capital where people of all trades and professions could coexist. Several centuries later, the Renaissance-like dream of the founder has perhaps come true in some respects. Over the past twenty years, at least from the standpoint of technology, Bangalore has become a preferred destination for professionals from all around the world. The assayed connection with Italy may be of chronological interest only but, as I was to discover, the link with Italian art and Bangalore is in fact much more direct. Recently, much has been written about Bangalore, leaving little room for fresh narratives, especially from my familiar domain of the IT industry. Bangalore has been usurped by concrete and steel monuments to information technology. Ironically, midnight's children now have the option of beginning their day at midnight in the countless BPOs spread around the city. Once the city of retirement, Bangalore no longer retires.

My encounter with Bangalore began on Gandhi Jayanti, 1995, when

I landed at Bangalore airport along with my family, after over thirty years in England and America. With non-resident or NR-eyed vision, it is not difficult to start noticing things with a different perspective. I struggled to inflict a new order and understanding on familiar settings distanced through time. The rectilinear, logical reasoning skills that my Indian brain had acquired in the West caused a level of discomfort at first. You tend to notice all that is wrong and dysfunctional. The insistent beggar tapping on your car window, no older than your own child, touches a deeper nerve. You notice the young boy hawking his precious handmade toys, weaving his way through dense traffic. You want to buy all his wares at once, because you can afford to. But you don't. In India, you soon learn how much more difficult it is to act than to react, how much harder it is to be judged than be judgemental. Then you begin to feel the welcoming arms of India fold around you, and you become totally enveloped by the embrace. I succumbed and realized that I had never left and, as an Indian, perhaps I never could. Our roots bury deep sometimes, clinging possessively on to shared beginnings in familiar settings to provide nutrients for our emotions and give us the confidence to reach out and touch a wider world. Hence, unravelling the Bangalore connections with reference points that were familiar to me was crucial for a more tactile relationship with a place that I experienced as morphing and forming at the same time.

I had come with the mission to start a new Integrated Circuit (IC) or chip design operation for Texas Instruments in India. My intent was to recruit a team of world-class engineers who understood digital signal processing (DSP)—the science of converting real-world signals like sound and images into zeroes and ones, and then back into real-world signals again. This seemingly futile exercise of manipulating ones and zeroes is the technology behind many critical modern-day applications like mobile phone communications, medical imaging, internet surfing, and numerous others. What I discovered in Bangalore was a lot more.

Cowboys and Indians

I HAVE often thought that India has always been a knowledge-based economy. An innate propensity to wrestle with the complex and over-complicate the apparent so that it sits more naturally in our understanding of the universe is a strand that led me to more new connections. Circa AD 620, the great Hindu mathematician Brahmagupta and head of the astronomical observatory at Ujjain (only an hour's flight from India's IT capital) was pondering the intricacies of zeroes and ones—*When zero is added to a number or subtracted from a number, the number remains unchanged; and a number multiplied by zero becomes zero.* He invented several other fundamental rules of arithmetic, negative numbers, quadratic equations and geometry. As is often customary among great thinkers, he left behind some unresolved problems for future generations of mathematicians—for example, the solution to *zero divided by zero,* he asserted, was itself zero ($0/0=0$). Others disagreed. The following excerpt from a report from the American Public Broadcasting Service (PBS) captures the historical trajectory of ones and zeroes thereafter, most succinctly:

> The Indian numbers were a smash hit across the Islamic world before they were finally brought to Europe, where they met fierce resistance. It took 500 years for the battle between Roman and Indian numbers to play out, but by the 16th century, the Indian figures, now commonly called Arabic numerals, finally triumphed—perhaps because Florentine mathematician Fibonacci showed Christian merchants how useful Indian numerals could be, for instance, for calculating profits.
>
> But the story doesn't end there. Within a hundred years, German mathematician Gottfried Leibniz invented a binary system, using the Adam and Eve of mathematics, One and Zero. Since then, as the language of computers, this two-digit binary system has come to dominate every part of modern life.

Given a brilliant idea, it is amazing what a few geeks and a skilled sales and marketing team can create in the way of useful products. Nearly 2000 years later, India's struggle with ones and zeroes continues, now more in the design of hardware and software, as do the challenges of Brahmagupta's digital divide. Inexorably, the present is digitally linked with India's past and Bangalore since the mid-

1980s, more so than any other city in India, has been uploading India's future bit by byte. Some of these packetized digits carve unlikely connections between Bangalore and the rest of the world but the past, present and future line up in familiar chronological order.

I unravel another connection. In Texas, USA, around the same period as Brahmagupta, a different group of Indians were struggling towards their own future until, of course, the cowboys came along. That opened up some new possibilities, at least for the Indians in India, albeit 1200 or so years later. In 1958, Jack Kilby, deep in the heart of Texas, invented the IC, perhaps the perfect vehicle for Brahmagupta's zeroes and ones.

I was fortunate enough to become a part of Bangalore's struggle with ones and zeroes. The Texans, however, had arrived here before me, in the early 1980s, when Texas Instruments first started the export of zeroes and ones from Bangalore. They had arrived with their private supply of drinking water, granola bars and toilet paper, well prepared for the challenges of local cuisine and personal hygiene. Happily, such measures are no longer necessary thanks to the adequate supply of bottled water, even for brushing teeth, and an excessive spread of five-star luxury hotels. Indian germs are no longer able to infect foreigners and NRIs with such tacit abandon.

Mission control, Houston, had launched me here to start a first-of-its-kind product to be designed by Brahmagupta's descendants entirely in India. Ten thousand miles from headquarters, I had the enviable opportunity of naming this product anything I liked! Something definitely Indian, I thought, and lasting. I named it 'Ankoor'. The team loved it. I did not let it be known, at the time, that my choice was driven more by my undying love for actress Shabana Azmi and her first movie of the same name, than by any metaphor for a new beginning. Little did I know at the time that some schoolchildren a few years later would have to rack their brains in quiz contests to recall the name of the first DSP to be designed in India. If I had, I would have indeed thought of a grander name. Something more durable beyond a few quiz contests.

After Ankoor was launched as a product, *Business Today* affectionately referred to it as Hamara Pentium, clearly missing out on the real scoop of connecting Bollywood with DSP, and the enduring technology connections between Cowboys and Indians.

Fish and Chips

WIND TUNNEL Road, Murugeshpalya. Were it not for a chance sighting of one of India's national heroes on this road, the name would not have raised such curiosity in my mind. The road is a typical Indian side street, busy, chaotic, and full of pedestrians, teeming with life and a fascinating assortment of vehicles from different centuries. The modern shops, restaurants and the ubiquitous Pizza Hut outlet that now line this road were not there a decade ago. Nonetheless, there was commerce and comparable structural neglect on a more basic scale even then.

I discovered that the road gets its name from one of India's finest scientific achievements of the 1970s—a wind tunnel, which has been the critical simulation and model test centre for the country's aviation and space research industries. Most, if not all, of India's aircraft and satellites are model-tested in the Wind Tunnel. Only a few hundred metres long, the road links the Indian Space Research Organisation (ISRO) at one end with a pond at the other, beyond which lies the famous Wind Tunnel. Coincidentally, or perhaps as per Kempe Gowda's wishes, no less than four of the most well-known high technology companies in the world—Hewlett Packard, Lucent, LG and, of course, Texas Instruments—found their operations sharing the Wind Tunnel Road address. This technology connection clearly had to be preordained by a greater plan dating back centuries, I am sure.

One evening, staring out of my car window at the unique Bangalore collage of past, present and future I spotted an astronaut. Dressed in casuals and sandals, unnoticed other than by me, was the only living Indian to have circled our planet, Rakesh Sharma. He walked right past my Tata Estate as it threaded its way through the traffic. Where else on this planet, I thought, could one find an astronaut, a space research centre, Fortune 500 companies, an assortment of animals, and street hawkers in such inconspicuous harmony?

Later, when I had the opportunity to become friends with Rakesh, I shared a proud moment of introducing my son, who was just seven, to him. Little did my son realize that he had to travel 10,000 miles, all the way from his birthplace near NASA, to shake hands with an astronaut who curiously would be introduced to him as 'Uncle Rakesh'. I do not think he was particularly impressed with the encounter at the time. He may have been expecting someone more familiar to him from outer space settings—Luke Skywalker or perhaps Darth Vader. After all, he was only a sparkle in my eye when Rakesh circled over India in a Soyuz spacecraft, and three-quarter of a billion Indians missed a heartbeat when he declared from outer space, '*Sare jahan se achhaa ...*'

At the top of the road and right opposite Pizza Hut, a small family of fishermen used to do brisk business with the nascent Bengali community of Bangalore of ten years ago. Whenever my mum and dad were in town in those days, they would stock up on fish from Wind Tunnel Road, fresh *rui* and *katla* every Sunday morning, ever so proud that their son designed chips just down the road.

Om's law and the golden ratio

I KNOW a man in Bangalore, tall, dark and erect with large hands that can shape iron and steel. He has been running a Sunday art school for children for the past thirty years. Kids love him. The only fee he insists on is a creative mind and a love for art. His sculptures can be seen all around Bangalore and in exhibitions around the country. His enamel paintings, an art form he learnt from his famous Italian artist father-in-law in Padua, Paolo de Poli, are a rare treasure. To the best of my knowledge, Balan Nambiar is the only living Indian artist who picked up the mastery of this unique art form directly under the tutelage of de Poli, considered the greatest Italian enamellist of the twentieth century.

It was my destiny to meet this man, with a Pythagorean fascination for numbers and shapes, in the late twentieth century. He spoke to me of the chambered nautilus and the golden ratio, of Leonardo da Vinci and Lord Shiva. His sculptures at the Jawaharlal Nehru Centre for Advanced Scientific Research at Jakkur are some of the best that I had seen. I wondered: Could he be inspired also into entering our world of zeroes and ones, and the mathematics of DSP?

I was fascinated by his connections with Italian art and his roots in the ritual performing arts of the Indian west coast. I took the liberty of walking him through our labs at Texas Instruments, perhaps not the most inspiring of places for artists. I spoke to him of how chips are three-dimensional structures, like the pyramids built on sand. I had grossly underestimated Balan's ability to connect science with art. Once commissioned, Balan created one of the most exquisite pieces of sculpture in stainless steel, the Valampiri Shankha that is now housed at the Indian Institute of Science (IISc), perhaps the only one in the world inspired by DSP. Curiously, it made its way into the *Limca Book of Records* under the category of the largest steel sculpture of a *shankha* or conch by an Indian. In Balan's words,

> The sound of the Valampiri Shankha, when blown, has been equated to the perfect pronunciation of 'OM' or Omkara. OM consists of three root sounds—*a, u* and *am*. When pronounced together properly, these make up the Omkara or OM, which is used to initiate the chanting of every mantra . . . At one point, I began to visualize the inherent mathematical effect of the sound of Omkara produced by the Valampiri Shankha in terms of digital power, and considered the viability of converting this digital power in myriad ways. The possible end result still tantalizes me. The sculpture is 2.25 metres high, inclusive of its 15 cm high granite pedestal. The size of the conch is 80 cm wide and 129.44 cm high, which is the proportion of a golden section (or golden ratio), that is, 1:1.618. Incidentally, this proportion was widely applied by painters, sculptors and architects of the classical Greek and Renaissance period of Europe.

Years later, I had the opportunity of showing the Valampiri Shankha to none other than Al Oppenheim, one of the founding fathers of DSP technology, during his visit to Bangalore. We talked of how the piece resembled the regular sampling of natural sound waves, a technique basic to DSP. Mathematics, art and religion, coming from disparate directions like Ganga, Yamuna and Saraswati, locked in permanent embrace, forever entangled in stainless steel in Bangalore.

The golden mean means a lot more to me now after my lessons from Balan, a dear friend and Bangalore's direct connection with Italian art.

Hand of God

'The Hand of God', one of my favourite sculptures, is at the Musée Rodin in Paris. In unfinished marble, it captures the birth and unfolding of form in the process of creation. A skilled and powerful hand, moulding humans into beings. Preservation of life would surely need the strength and the compassion of such a hand, I thought.

Threading my way through the blocked arteries of Bangalore, I arrived at Narayana Hrudayalaya (NH) which now provides world-class cardiac care for the poor, performing 5000 surgeries a year, with over half of them on children. The paediatric intensive care unit is one of the largest in the world. Over 10 million poor in the surrounding villages have been on a health scheme run by the hospital for a premium of just ten rupees a month. The statistics are baffling.

I had gone there to meet India's heartthrob surgeon, Dr Devi Shetty, personal cardiac surgeon to Mother Teresa. He wrote,

One day, Mother Teresa, who at that point of time was convalescing in the intensive care unit of the hospital, saw me examining a 'blue baby' (baby with heart disease). After a few minutes of thought, she turned towards me and said, 'Now I know why you are here. To relieve the agony of children with heart disease. God sent you to this world to fix it.' To my mind, this is the best definition ever given of a paediatric cardiac surgeon, and perhaps the best compliment that I have ever received.

NH is his passion. Through technology, he wants to convert 'atoms into bytes', he says, 'so chips can make medical care affordable for those who desperately need it'. Like the man in the picture he shows me, who cleans the underground drains of the famous IT capital of India, and has a life expectancy of forty-five years. Health care, he emphasizes, only reaches a very small and lucky minority of people in the world. He wants it to reach everyone.

Recently, I had checked the world population dashboard on the Internet. On 30 March 2006 at 14:19 GMT (EST+5), the US Bureau of Census estimated a count of the total population of the world at 6,506,644,443. The odds are clearly against the doctor.

Entering the hallway leading to the elevators, my eyes were drawn to an unusual sight. An almost empty hospital bed was being wheeled hurriedly towards the elevator by a couple of attendants. On the bed, towards the centre, was a cluster of medical equipment—monitors, beeping displays and laboratory instruments. Curiously, two nurses were cautiously escorting these appliances into the elevator. I was impressed by the care with which NH handled capital equipment, until I was able to take a closer look. Cradled in the midst of all the gadgets, in a small island of space, attached to the instruments through an assortment of cables and tubes, lay the tiniest of babies, seemingly sedated, no more than a few months old, possibly on its way to surgery—totally helpless, like me staring at him. So much hardware for so little 'soft' ware, I thought, suitably calibrated on how fragile life can be and how critical technology has become to its preservation.

As I got to know Dr Devi Shetty, I became more informed and more involved emotionally. Fifty thousand dollars for a digital X-ray machine—he needs one for under a thousand or less, and he needs to be able to transmit the images digitally from distant locations to save on the cost of reusables. This is what he means by converting atoms into bytes (ones and zeroes). Then, he wants to be able to do the same with angiograms, ultra-scans and MRIs. He has a telemedicine unit that connects him to his heart centre in Kolkata, 800 km away, through a satellite link donated for his use by ISRO. Via this link, he is able to diagnose and then treat patients, some of the poorest in the world (they call him Dr God), through his unique insurance scheme and business model of sharing costs with paying patients and an obsessive focus on reducing costs. Dr God wants to do the same for villagers around the country, and he needs technology to help him. What strikes me about Dr Shetty is not just his obvious compassion for the poor and the needy (he did have a great mentor), but the apparent success of his service model that is able to provide high-quality, state-of-the-art open heart surgery (OHS) at a fraction of the cost. His requirements are challenging, to put it mildly, his belief in being able to treat patients in thousands of remote villages defies logic. I am both inspired and intrigued to take a closer look at the enabling technologies that could support such a vision.

Like Balan Nambiar, Dr God has expressive, assertive hands. Only, he uses steel to mend bleeding hearts. I feel proud to have shaken the hands of the only living surgeon, perhaps the only surgeon ever, to have operated on a saint.

Back to the future

FOR ME, coming to Bangalore has been like a journey back to the future, where it seems technology, art and the most fundamental battles of human survival compete for attention on an equal footing. In years to come, it is not yet clear what will survive and what will perish. Silicon chips, like roaches, will have crept into our bedrooms, kitchens and even into our pockets with each new electronic gadget that we allow to enter our lives, by far outnumbering human beings on this planet. Bangalore is one of the prime breeding grounds and it's not all bad. But it is an infiltration of our more natural carbon-based existence.

What will Bangalore be like twenty years on? An intricate network of hi-tech parks and shopping malls of glass and steel, and hive-like high-rise shelters for humans connected by highways and flyovers? Based on current trends, it is hard to imagine any future state of a modern city as anything different. It is perhaps a blessing in disguise that in India we are encumbered by a democracy that constantly gets in the way of the future becoming just a quick and obvious extrapolation of the present.

As Indians we know that creation, preservation and destruction come in a divine pack of three. I am somewhat relieved that my more mortal Bangalore connections—Rakesh, Balan and Devi—the astronaut, the artist and the mender of ailing hearts, will challenge such an obvious and predictable future. However, to me, the past, the present and the future has never felt so adjacent and as tactile as it has in Bangalore.

Metroblogging

Anita Bora

In this tech-savvy city, blogs are a popular means of expression and communication for a cross-section of those who are computer enabled. This sample from a prolific blogger focusses largely on the metropolis at Just A Little Something (http://www.anitabora.com/blog).

City No. 45, Bangalore is now live!

Posted: Monday, April 3rd, 2006 @ 7.37 p.m.

So after going back and forth for about a month, **Bangalore** joins the metroblogging network as of today!

BarCamp Bangalore is on!

Filed under: <u>Living</u>—April 22, 2006 @ 9.37 a.m.

So <u>BarCamp</u> is officially on here in Bangalore. <u>I walked in</u> at about 8.30 a.m. and found a few people hard at work already. Quite a few people walked in around 9ish and I'd estimate around 50–60 people have arrived and I guess many more will be coming through different stages of the morning ...

There are five spaces for the sessions and <u>Jace</u> has innovatively named them Toddy, Arack, Narangi, Santra and Feni. I guess that should get folks started in high spirits!

More as the sessions start ...

10 a.m.: Atul Chitnis on Mobile Computing and Pete Deeemer on the Art of Scrum

The Art of Scrum is a project management methodology applied to software projects and has been used at Yahoo for the last one year. All teams around the world are implementing it and surveys of the team revealed that two-thirds of teams feel they are more productive with this system. The methodology uses what is called Sprint (cycles anywhere between 1–4 weeks) and also conducts regular reviews (including daily stand-up sessions with team members) in the product cycle.

*

11.30 a.m.: <u>Sathish</u> & Jayanth

What do you do when you miss a class in school or college?

Copy someone else's notes and try and catch up! Or fall behind in your class. Well, this new concept that has been suggested by Sathish and Jayanth is about podcasting in schools to create a student–teacher community.

So whenever you miss a class, all you need to do is log in to a website and view a podcast of the session you missed! This could be a mix of audio/video podcasts.

There are, of course, many challenges to this concept, including the fact that teachers today don't have access to computer resources. There is also the bandwidth issue that comes into play when you talk about multi-casts or streaming audio/video. An interactive session with the audience is going on and throwing up more perspectives on the idea.

More on: <u>Podshaala</u>

*

12.45 p.m.: Chris, <u>Tara</u>, Alex, <u>Jay</u>

Chris talks about how BarCamp started . . .

How BarCamp started, a little about the history. Why pay thousands of dollars to attend a conference, they asked? They had no money and no venue and came up with the first BarCamp in 6 days! Everything was then documented in a Wiki for everyone to share and learn from. From there it has spread and today BarCamps have proliferated all over the world. In India, Delhi, Chennai and Hyderabad have had BarCamps with Bangalore following and Mumbai in the pipeline. Amit Ranjan talks about his Delhi BarCamp experience.

There is a discussion about the spirit of the BarCamp, the diverse backgrounds of people attending, local flavours depending on cities (Delhi had people of entrepreneur backgrounds, while Bangalore has a large developer community as participants.)

One day, we might even have roads in the city!

Filed under: Living—November 14, 2005 @ 8.53 p.m.

I know you're probably really tired of traffic woes, but can I really help it?

Bangalore's roads now resemble the moon's surface—craters and all. Especially with the recent rain episode, whatever little we had in terms of roads has now become a figment of our imaginations. We will soon need moon buggies to get from one place to another. And we might even have to start from home the prior day to get to office on time, is what I am thinking.

My dad who was in town (and who I have earlier extolled Bangalore's virtues to very profusely, I might add) pointed out to me the lack of pavements.

(Have you noticed that in many parts the pavements are so bad that you are forced to walk on the road, and that is really not a choice at all, because you'd get the Nobel Prize for new discoveries if you actually find anything that resembles a road).

Getting back to my dad, he was talking about pavements and I said, 'How can there be a pavement when there is hardly a road?!'

So here we are, threatening to become a world superpower, but we haven't figured out how to make a road that can survive the rains.

Amazing. I would think that all the engineering brains in India (and the world) haven't been able to work out that equation. So anyway, here we are going over about 50 million potholed roads. It is of course, a wonderful state to arrive in office. Shaken and stirred. They should soon have doctors at all destinations making sure all our bones are intact, when (and if) we ever arrive.

Case in point. There are two approaches to my house. One of these has been under construction for the last one year, I kid you not! One year. How it can take one year to dig up a road, put cables under it and patch it up again is beyond every stretch of my imagination.

The other approach was also dug up and hastily reopened. At one point of time, I thought we'd have to actually get swings or large catapults to get across the large drain if they closed both the roads at the same time.

Once they were done with the extensive digging and whatever it is they do when they have nothing to do, they decided to be kind to us and put in some form of a road. In the process, they put in some rough stones (with really sharp edges) and patched it up with mud.

So what do we have now? A joke for a road and craters the size of the Sahara desert and many sharp edges to navigate through each time we drive through. It's surprising they haven't opened a puncture shop there yet.

Hey, I know that we need some excitement in our life, but getting jolted and shaken up every time I cross that path is something I had not bargained for. After all, I get enough excitement during the one-hour journey to work on Hosur Road, one of Bangalore's most notorious stretches now in terms of traffic, I would say.

If you've been on this stretch recently, I think you'd tend to agree that excitement is something you will not lack. Cars, huge (and I mean huge) trucks, cement mixers, two-wheelers, tempos, autos, call centre vans (and I think you'd know why they deserve their own category) and the nightmare of all drivers—cyclists and cows. If there's something you can't find on this stretch, please inform us immediately.

Last week, I read an encouraging news report of a group touring Bangalore to find out which roads have been affected. Isn't that amazing news? So, by next month, they should have a committee ready to discuss these roads. By early next year, they will have their plan in place. By April/May, they will set up a committee to discuss and review it again. Then they will reconvene in about two or three months' time. By this time, there would be additional bad roads to be considered, so the process will have to be repeated.

Anyway, by this calculation I would estimate that at least by 2050 they will have decided whether they are going to be kind enough to us citizens and give us roads.

After all we only pay 30+ plus per cent of what we earn to the government to give us a semblance of a road.

I'm not sure where all our money is going (and I have a suspicion that I won't *like* where it's going either), but it obviously doesn't seem to be enough to give us decent roads.

On the subject of potholes, you have to check out this link: Bangalore Potholes

Insider or Outsider?

Filed under: India, Personal, Living—November 21, 2005 @ 6:45 p.m.

This is inspired by the responses I got to the post about roads, which somehow got into a discussion about insiders and outsiders.

First, let me say that I really think that I reserve the right to 'crib' in my own space. I think that as far as Bangalore goes, I have been a great champion of the city and have taken to it like a fish takes to water.

My friends in Mumbai are amazed that I turned 'Bangalorean' faster than I ever turned a Mumbaiite (even after five years there, I didn't really feel like one). So when Shub writes about 'her city' and how she cannot take a word against it, I must say that I gave this some thought.

Why can't we take the facts? Just because it is 'our' city, should we be oblivious to the realities that exist? Should we as concerned citizens remain mute bystanders and just take anything that comes our way? I think without people who protest, raise dharnas, fight for their rights as a citizen, we would be still in the dark ages.

I think if you've been following my blog, I've been a champion of living in the city and the opportunities that exist here and harped quite a lot on the positive side. But I have to call a spade a spade once in a while. It is a known fact that infrastructure is crumbling and that the city is no longer able to cope with it. I am sure solutions will emerge in a few years. But are we to keep totally silent till then? And the sad part is that the government saw this development coming and still has not been able to do much about it. An editorial in *The Hindu* said that it's not a problem of money, but of poor governance.

Maybe things will improve over the years, but we all have our limits of patience and I think Bangaloreans are being tested to their limits already.

I object even more about being called an 'outsider'. Not only have I settled into my life in this city, I am proud of it and what it offers.

And what is 'my city' anyway? I have never lived in one city for more than five years in my adult life. If I decide that this is the city I want to live in, earn a living and settle down, why should I be called an outsider and asked to leave? It is but a city in my own country, isn't it? Why should I then be discriminated against? Just because I was not born here?

I live here, pay my taxes to this government, what else should I do to qualify as an insider? I strongly object to this and I think that only narrow-minded people can still stick to the ideology that their state is for them alone. What happens to Mumbai, Delhi, Calcutta if they decide to throw out all the so-called 'outsiders'?

Some truly narrow minds still exist as displayed through <u>anonymous comments</u> and it's rather shameful that they exist in today's times, when what we should be thinking about is how to progress as a nation and not as individuals stuck in some prehistoric time zone clinging to concepts of 'my state, and my city', where everyone else qualifies as 'outsiders'.

And what if all the countries filled with Indian immigrants like the UK and the US decide to do this one day? We will cry out loud, saying its racism and discrimination and yet it is as insidious in our own country, as is apparent by this particularly offensive comment, 'The Kannadiga anger is near the brim and one day when it would explode all of you would know.' What a crying shame!

I am a huge supporter of being a global citizen. People should be able to live and work anywhere in their country and the world, without being called outsiders and being told to 'go back'. And go back where, I ask? I, for one, wouldn't know where. I have lived all over — in Shillong, Guwahati, Pune, Sydney, Mumbai, and now in Bangalore. So where do I really belong and where do I go 'back' to?

Notes on Contributors

U.R. Ananthamurthy, a well-known Kannada writer, is among the most eminent of contemporary Indian literary figures. He is a recipient of both the Padma Bhushan and the Jnanpith award, the highest Indian literary recognition. He was vice-chancellor of the Mahatma Gandhi University at Kottayam, president of the Sahitya Akademi and chairman of the National Book Trust. His novels, including *Samskara* and *Bharathipura*, have been translated into several Indian and European languages.

Clare Arni is a British architectural and travel photographer, who has lived most of her life in India. Her solo books include volumes on the Cauvery river, Banaras and Hampi for Marg Publications. She has been published in the UK by Thames and Hudson, Phaidon, Dorling Kindersley and The Blue Guides. In India, she has contributed to books on the works of architects Charles Correa, B.V. Doshi and Geoffrey Bawa, as well as to magazines like *Man's World, Outlook Traveller, Architecture+Design* and *Inside Outside*. She is an inveterate traveller, who has been to Peru, Afghanistan, Russia and Burma. She is currently documenting the vernacular architecture of south India, in addition to writing a book on the beauty traditions of Asia.

Bageshree S. lives in Bangalore and is a correspondent with *The Hindu*. Translation is her special area of interest. Some of her translations are included in *Gulabi Talkies and Other Stories* by Vaidehi (Penguin, 2006).

Sham Banerji is director, corporate business, at Texas Instruments (TI). He earlier headed TI's systems and embedded software development operations in India. In 1996, Sham led the team that developed the first commercial digital signal processor (DSP) to be designed entirely in India. Under his leadership, over five hundred advanced DSP labs and numerous industry/university joint projects are operational throughout India as part of TI's worldwide university programme.

Anita Bora began blogging in 2001, and was the brain behind the first Indian bloggers list. You can catch Anita on Just A Little Something (http://www.anitabora.com/blog). She shifted to Bangalore from Mumbai, and is busy discovering arts, music, theatre, films, bird-watching, photography and French in and around the Karnataka capital. She earns a living as a communications professional for an IT company.

Winston S. Churchill, one of the most important leaders in modern British and world history, the former prime minister of Great Britain, known as an orator and strategist, also won the 1953 Nobel Prize for Literature for his books on history. Voted the greatest-ever Briton in a 2002 BBC poll, Churchill was a soldier in the British army when his regiment was posted in Bangalore in 1897.

Dilip da Cunha is an architect and city planner, on the faculty at Parsons School of Design, New York, and University of Pennsylvania. He has co-authored *Mississippi Floods: Designing a Shifting Landscape* (Yale University Press, 2001) and *Deccan Traverses: The Making of Bangalore's Terrain* (Rupa & Co., 2006) with Anuradha Mathur.

William Dalrymple, writer and historian, won the Duff Cooper Prize for History and Biography 2007 for *The Last Mughal: The Eclipse of a Dynasty, Delhi, 1857*. Born in Scotland, he has the following award-winning books to his credit: *In Xanadu, City of Djinns, From the Holy Mountain, The Age of Kali* and *White Mughals*. He is a Fellow of the Royal Society of Literature and of the Royal Asiatic Society. He was awarded the Mungo Park Medal by the Royal Scottish Geographical Society in 2002 for his 'outstanding contribution to travel literature'. He divides his time between London and Delhi.

Mahesh Dattani won the Sahitya Akademi Award in 1998 for his book *Final Solutions and Other Plays*. India's best-known English language playwright, he is a director, writer and dancer, equally at home in theatre, radio and films. Moored in living social contexts, his plays address questions of sexual identity, religious faith, family ties and gender, issues of significance in contemporary urban India. He lives in Mumbai and Bangalore.

Shashi Deshpande, who writes in English, has eight short story collections, nine novels, a collection of essays and four children's books to her credit, many of which have been translated into different languages. Her novel *That Long Silence* won the Sahitya Akademi Award in 1990. She was chairperson of the jury for the Commonwealth Writers' Prize, 2000.

Somathanahalli Diwakar has published more than fifteen books of Kannada short fiction, poetry, essays, translations and literary criticism. He has served as reporter, assistant editor and editor in newspapers and journals like *Samyukta Karnataka*, *Mallige*, *Sudha* and *Prajavani*. Till recently he was a Karnataka specialist at the American Consulate General in Chennai. He is currently assistant editor at *Prajavani* in Bangalore.

Geeta Doctor is a Chennai-based writer and critic. She spent part of her early life in Bangalore, with a feisty grandmother in a large and sprawling family house, with the traditional monkey tops and a garden full of the most splendid flower beds and fruit trees.

Paul Fernandes was born in Bangalore in 1958, studied at the local St Joseph's Boys School, then went to the Faculty of Fine Arts, M.S. University, Baroda. He lives and works in Bangalore as an illustrator/cartoonist.

Thomas L. Friedman is the foreign affairs columnist for *The New York Times*. A three-time Pulitzer Prize winner, he has reported on the Middle East conflict, the end of the Cold War, US domestic politics and foreign policy, international economics, and the worldwide impact of the terrorist threat. He is the author of award-winning books:

From Beirut to Jerusalem (1989), *The Lexus and the Olive Tree* (1999), *Longitudes and Attitudes: Exploring the World After September 11* (2002) and *The World is Flat* (2005).

Rajmohan Gandhi is the author of several books including *Mohandas: A True Story of a Man, His People and an Empire* (2007), *Ghaffar Khan: Non-violent Badshah of the Pakhtuns* (2004), *Rajaji: A Life* (2003), *Understanding the Muslim Mind* (2003), and *Revenge and Reconciliation: Understanding South Asian History* (2000). He currently teaches at the University of Illinois at Urbana-Champaign, USA.

Deepa Ganesh is chief sub-editor at *The Hindu*, Bangalore. She has written and translated for both English and Kannada journals and All India Radio. She adapted Mahashweta Devi's play *Rudaali* for Kannada amateur theatre.

H.L. Nage Gowda, a retired Indian Administrative Service officer, was the founder-president of the Karnataka Janapada Parishat and the Janapada Loka.

Ramachandra Guha is a fourth-generation resident of Bangalore, his great-grandfather having moved here from a village near Kumbakonam. His books include *Environmentalism: A Global History, A Corner of a Foreign Field*, which won the *Daily Telegraph*/Cricket Society Literary Award for 2003, and *India After Gandhi*.

Anjum Hasan grew up in Shillong and now lives in Bangalore. Her poems have appeared in the anthologies *Give the Sea Change and It Shall Change: 56 Indian Poets*, *Confronting Love* and *Reasons for Belonging: Fourteen Contemporary Indian Poets*. She works at the India Foundation for the Arts.

M. Fazlul Hasan, a former deputy commissioner in the Revenue Department of the Bangalore Corporation, was the honorary secretary of the Mythic Society. A former student of St Joseph's College, his interest in history was reportedly kindled by an inscription he stumbled upon in his grandfather's mango orchard in Hanumanthanagar.

Ammu Joseph is an independent journalist and author based in Bangalore. Among her books are *Whose News?: The Media and Women's Issues* (Sage, 1994 and 2006), *Women in Journalism: Making News* (Konark, 2000; Penguin India, 2005), *Terror, Counter-Terror: Women Speak Out* (Kali for Women/Zed, 2003), *Storylines: Conversations with Women Writers* and *Just Between Us: Women Speak About Their Writing* (Women's World India/Women Unlimited, 2003, 2004). She has also contributed chapters to several other books, including *Where the Rain Is Born: Writings about Kerala* (Penguin India, 2002).

Maya Kamath was a Bangalore-based political cartoonist whose career began in 1985 with *Gita*, a cartoon strip about family life for the *The Evening Herald*. Her cartoons on current affairs have appeared in the *Deccan Herald, Times of India, Illustrated Weekly of India* and *Asian Age*. After Maya's death in 2001, her work has been archived by SPARROW and compiled into a book called *The World of Maya*.

Suryanath Upendra Kamath is a historian, researcher and creative writer in Kannada. He was a lecturer and reader at Bangalore University from 1968 to 1981. He was chief editor of the state government's *Karnataka Gazetteer* from 1981 to 1995, in addition to being director of the Karnataka State Archives from 1981 to 1983. His Kannada book *Karnataka History* won him the State Sahitya Akademi first prize for humanities in 1973. He is a specialist in the medieval and modern history of Karnataka.

Ram Ganesh Kamatham is a writer/director and theatre professional. He has collaborated with the Royal Court Theatre and the BBC World Service in some international productions. He has created work for stage, film and radio, as well as video games, and is one of Bangalore's most prolific young playwrights.

P. Lankesh was one of the literary giants of Karnataka. A multi-faceted personality, he was a leading writer, popular journalist and creative film-maker. Known as the angry young man of Kannada literature in his youth, Lankesh went on to win the Sahitya Akademi Award for his short story collection, *Kallu Karaguva Samaya*. He won a national award for his debut film *Pallavi*.

Kevin Maney is a contributing editor at *Conde Nast Portfolio* and a blogger for Portfolio.com. He is the author of the critically acclaimed *The Maverick and His Machine: Thomas Watson Sr. and the Making of IBM*, published in 2003 by John Wiley & Sons. Maney also wrote the 1995 BusinessWeek bestseller *Megamedia Shakeout*. Earlier, during a stint at *USA Today* from 1985 to 2007, he wrote a significant technology column and covered the economic changes in the old East Bloc. He is also a songwriter, singer and guitarist in the band Kevin Maney and his Briefs. Earlier he made music with NotDeadYet.

Anuradha Mathur is an architect and landscape architect. She is associate professor, School of Design, University of Pennsylvania. With Dilip da Cunha, she is the co-author of *Mississippi Floods: Designing a Shifting Landscape* (Yale University Press, 2001) and *Deccan Traverses: The Making of Bangalore's Terrain* (Rupa & Co., 2006).

C.K. Meena is a columnist, freelance journalist and journalism teacher. Although she has written a novel, *Black Lentil Doughnuts*, she is somewhat squeamish about the 'writer' tag and prefers 'old hack'.

Pankaj Mishra is the author of three books of non-fiction: *Butter Chicken in Ludhiana: Travels in Small Town India, An End to Suffering: The Buddha in the World* and *Temptations of the West: How to be Modern in India, Pakistan, and Beyond*, and a novel, *The Romantics*.

Anita Nair is the author of the best-selling novels *The Better Man*, *Ladies Coupé*, and *Mistress*, and a short story collection, *Satyr of the Subway*. Visit her at www.anitanair.net.

Janaki Nair is professor of history at the Centre for the Study of Social Sciences, Kolkata. She is the author of *The Promise of the Metropolis: Bangalore's Twentieth Century* (Oxford University Press, 2005).

Prathibha Nandakumar is a Bangalore-based poet, short story writer, columnist, journalist and director of the Kriya Foundation for

Culture. She has received the Karnataka State Sahitya Akademi Award, the Mahadevi Verma Kavya Samman, Pu Ti Na Kavya Prashasti, Dr Shivaram Karanth Prashasti and Gourish Kaikini Prashasti, among others. She has presented her work at the Gothenberg International Book Fair (1997), the Asian Writers' Conference at Helsinki (1998) and the SAARC Writers' Conference at Kathmandu (2002).

Shobhana Narasimhan, a Bangalore-born theoretical physicist, works at the city's Jawaharlal Nehru Centre for Advanced Scientific Research at Jakkur. Her Ph.D. thesis at Harvard University was related to the Raman effect in silicon. She has also worked at the Brookhaven National Laboratory and the Fritz-Haber-Institut in Berlin, and held visiting positions at the Universite de Paris VII, Cambridge University and the Max-Planck-Institut in Stuttgart.

R.K. Narayan is one of India's most celebrated writers in English, the author of numerous novels, five collections of short stories, two travel books, four collections of essays, a memoir and translations of the Indian epics. His fiction was set mainly in the imaginary town of Malgudi. He was awarded the A.C. Benson Medal by the Royal Society of Literature in 1980. He was an honorary member of the American Academy and Institute of Arts and Letters. In 1989, he was made a member of the Rajya Sabha. He received the Sahitya Akademi award for his novel *The Guide* in 1958.

Nemichandra, an engineer by profession, has authored twenty books in Kannada. She is chief manager, design, at Hindustan Aeronautics Limited, Bangalore. Her short stories have been compiled as *Stories of Nemichandra*. Her biographies of women scientists and her travelogue titled *In the Sacred Valley of Peru* have won her critical acclaim and Sahitya Akademi awards.

Tejaswini Niranjana is senior fellow at the Centre for the Study of Culture and Society, Bangalore. Her publications include *Siting Translation: History, Post-structuralism and the Colonial Context* (University of California Press, 1992) and *Mobilizing India: Women, Music and Migration between India and Trinidad* (Duke University Press, 2006). Her current research interests include linguistic nationalism, music and gender in translation.

Zac O'Yeah is a Swedish writer of books ranging from crime novels to travelogues. He has also written plays and collaborated with Rangayana Theatre in Mysore. He lives in Bangalore.

Achal Prabhala lives in Bangalore. He writes, researches intellectual property and is an activist for access to medicines and to knowledge.

S.S. Prasad, born in 1980, works as a microchip design engineer in Bangalore. His poems have appeared in *Fulcrum, Semicerchio, Orbis, The Journal of Indian Writing in English, New Quest* and *Talking Poetry*. In 2006, he won the Toto Award for Creative Writing.

Pushpamala N., who studied at M.S. University, Baroda, has won many awards for her sculptures. In the recent past, she has worked mainly in photo performance and video, exhibiting widely all over India and internationally. She uses women's stories and women's material as a device to explore history, memory and contemporary society. She lives and works in Bangalore.

K.N. Raghavendra Rao has been a noted photojournalist since the 1960s. He worked for *Indian Express* and *India Today*, and is currently with *The Hindu BusinessLine* as a consultant. Known for his lyrical visual essays, he rarely recalls either scoops or exclusives, but chooses to dwell on those who have left unforgettable vibrations behind. These unusual human beings, in his living essays, include masters from the world of music, dance and art.

S.R. Ramakrishna has worked for *Deccan Herald*, Bangalore, and as assistant professor, Asian College of Journalism. He is the founder-editor of *The Music Magazine* (www.themusicmagazine.com), and composes music for theatre, television and film.

Paul William Roberts is an Oxford-educated British writer who lived in India for five years. Currently based in Toronto, he is the award-winning author of eight books and several screenplays. His personal account of the 1991 Iraq War for *Saturday Night* won a Canadian National Magazine award. His non-fiction works include *River in the Desert: Modern Travels in Ancient Egypt, The Journey of the Magi, The Demonic Comedy: Some Detours in the Baghdad of Saddam Hussein* and *A War Against Truth: Behind the Lines in the Invasion of Iraq*. He is considered one of Canada's top experts on the Middle East.

Jeremy Seabrook is a writer who has contributed to *The Statesman*, Kolkata, *New Internationalist* and *The Guardian*, among others. His most recent book, *Consuming Cultures, Globalisation and Local Lives*, was published by New Internationalist.

Siddalingaiah is one of India's foremost Dalit writers. The author of four poetry collections, two plays, essays and a study of folk deities, he was dean, Faculty of Arts, Bangalore University. He was nominated to the Karnataka Upper House in 1988, and was an independent legislator for two six-year terms. In 2006, he was nominated chairman of the Kannada Development Authority. Along with Devanur Mahadeva, he is credited with shaping the contemporary Dalit literary consciousness in Karnataka. He has been at the forefront of movements protesting caste injustice and affirming Dalit self-respect.

Sherry Simon teaches in the French Department at Concordia University in Montreal. Her most recent book is *Translating Montreal: Episodes in the Life of a Divided City*.

C.V. Shivashankar is a well-known Kannada lyricist, with over five hundred songs to his credit. He has directed over fifteen Kannada films and is the recipient of a Karnataka state award for service to the industry, besides the Kempe Gowda Award.

Chiranjiv Singh, a retired civil servant, is a respected Kannada scholar. He was India's ambassador and permanent representative to UNESCO from 1997 to 2000.

Smriti Srinivas is currently associate professor, Department of

Anthropology, University of California-Davis. Her recent publications include a book on Bangalore, *Landscapes of Urban Memory: The Sacred and the Civic in India's High-Tech City* (University of Minnesota Press, 2001, Orient Longman, 2004). She is completing a book on the transnational Sai Baba movement. Her research interests are in the areas of religion, cities and urban cultures, the social and cultural construction of memory, and cultures of the body and performance.

Nisha Susan, born in 1979, spent most of her life in Bangalore before moving to New Delhi. She has also lived in Africa and the Middle East. In 2006, she won a national contest for young writers funded by Toto Funds the Arts. Her poetry has been published in the *Journal of the Poetry Society of India* and in *New Quest*.

Sahana Udupa was a research associate for the National Institute of Advanced Studies, Bangalore study on IT and ITES professionals in Bangalore from December 2003 to March 2006. She has worked as a news reporter for over five years.

A.R. Vasavi is a social anthropologist with the National Institute of Advanced Studies, Bangalore. Her interests are in the field of sociology of India, educational issues and agrarian studies.

Kerooru Vasudevacharya began his career as a lawyer, then became a full-time Kannada writer. He passed away in 1921.

Copyright Acknowledgements

Grateful acknowledgement is made to the following for permission to reprint copyright material:

Indira Balakrishna, daughter of the late H.L. Nage Gowda, retired IAS officer and founder-president of the Karnataka Janapada Parishat and the Janapada Loka, for 'The Ballad of Kempe Gowda' from his book *Helavaru Mathu Avara Kavyagalu*.

Suryanath Kamath for 'A City Yet Unborn'.

Bhuvaneshwari Srinivasamurthy and Indian Thought Publications for the excerpt from R.K. Narayan's *The Emerald Route*.

Anuradha Mathur and Dilip de Cunha for 'From Garden City to Tota?'

C.V. Shivashankar for the lyrics of his 1966 Kannada film song *'Beledide noda Bengaluru nagara'*.

Clare Arni for the six turn of the twentieth century postcards from her private collection.

Chiranjiv Singh for 'New Shoots and Old Roots: The Cultural Backdrop of Bangalore'.

Prathibha Nandakumar for 'Directions' from *Coffee House*, a book of poems, soon to be published in Kannada.

U.R. Ananthamurthy for 'Ooru and the World', originally published in Kannada in *Udayavani* in 2006.

Pankaj Mishra for the excerpt from *Butter Chicken in Ludhiana: Travels in Small Town India*, Penguin Books India, 1995.

Sherry Simon for 'Bangalore: A Short Story' from *Translating Desire: The Politics of Gender and Culture in India*, edited by Brinda Bose, Katha, 2002.

Gauri Lankesh for 'Geleya Mani' by her father P. Lankesh, originally published in Kannada in *Lankesh Patrike*.

Tejaswini Niranjana for 'Reworking Masculinities: Rajkumar and the Kannada Public Sphere'. An extended version of this essay originally appeared in *Economic and Political Weekly* in December 2000.

Shashi Deshpande for 'Mapping Bangalore'.

The *Taj Magazine* for 'Romance of the Cantonment' by Geeta Doctor. Courtesy Taj Hotels, Resorts and Palaces.

Excerpt from *My Early Days* reproduced with permission of Curtis Brown Ltd, London, on behalf of The Estate of Winston Churchill. Copyright © Winston S. Churchill.

Anita Nair for 'A Rose Petal Life', originally published in *Saturday Times, Times of India*, Bangalore, 1995.

S. Diwakar for 'Oh, Come to Gandhibazar!' from his award-winning collection, *Naapatteyaada Gramaaphonu* (The gramophone which has disappeared), Akshara Prakashana, Heggodu, 2005.

Ramachandra Guha for 'Turning Crimson at Premier's'.

Smriti Srinivas for 'The Karaga Festival: A Performative Archive of an Alternative Urban Ecology'.

Sahitya Akademi, New Delhi, for 'Gopalaswamy Iyer Hostel' from Siddalingaiah's autobiography *Ooru Keri* published in 2003.

Janaki Nair for 'Corners and Other Childhood Spaces'.

Zac O'Yeah for 'Majestic: The Place of Constant Return'.

Maya Kamath Private Papers, Sparrow Collections, Sound & Picture Archives for Research on Women, Mumbai and Maya Kamath's family for permission to use her cartoons.

Anjum Hasan for 'Meditation on Postal Colony'.

Rajmohan Gandhi for 'Through the Mahatma's Eyes'.

Shobhana Narasimhan for 'The Wholly Raman Empire: Bangalore's Emergence as a Centre of Science'.

Nemichandra for 'In Search of the Star of David'.

Jeremy Seabrook for the excerpt from *Notes from Another India*, Pluto Press, London, 1995.

Mahesh Dattani for the excerpt from 'Do the Needful' from *Collected Plays*, Penguin Books India, 2000.

Pushpamala N. for the excerpt from the catalogue *Sthala Puranagalu*, 1999.

Paul William Roberts for the excerpt from *Empire of the Soul: Some Journeys in India*, HarperCollins Publishers, India, 1999.

C.K. Meena for 'The Sound of Two Hands Clapping'.

Achal Prabhala for 'Temples of Food'. A version of this essay was published in *Outlook Traveller* in February 2002.

Nisha Susan for 'On the Street, Everybody Watches'.

K.N. Raghavendra Rao for 'Veena Tapaswi Doreswamy Iyengar'.

William Dalrymple for the excerpt from *The Age of Kali: Travels and Encounters in India*, Penguin Books India, 2002.

Ammu Joseph for 'Back to the Future'.

Paul Fernandes for his six drawings for 'The morphing of Bangalore'.

S.S. Prasad for 'nanolore'.

A.R. Vasavi for 'Brand Bangalore: Emblem of Globalizing India'.

Thomas L. Friedman for the excerpt from *The World Is Flat: The Globalised World in the 21st Century*, Penguin Books Ltd, 2005.

Ram Ganesh Kamatham for the excerpt from his original play 'Dancing on Glass'.

Sahana Udupa for 'Call Centre Calls On'.

Kevin Maney for the lyrics of his original song, '*I Dream of Bangalore*'.

Sham Banerji for 'Bit by Byte'.

Anita Bora for the excerpt from her blog *Just A Little Something* (http://www.anitabora.com/blog).